Coping with Post-Traumatic Stress Disorder

SECOND EDITION

WITHDRAWN

McFarland Health Topics Series

Coping with Post-Traumatic Stress Disorder

A Guide for Families

SECOND EDITION

Cheryl A. Roberts

MᴄFᴀʀʟᴀɴᴅ Hᴇᴀʟᴛʜ Tᴏᴘɪᴄs Sᴇʀɪᴇs

McFarland & Company, Inc., Publishers

Jefferson, North Carolina, and London

LIBRARY OF CONGRESS CATALOGUING-IN-PUBLICATION DATA

Roberts, Cheryl A.
    Coping with post-traumatic stress disorder : a guide for
families / Cheryl A. Roberts — 2nd ed.
        p.   cm.
    Includes bibliographical references and index.

    ISBN 978-0-7864-4974-3
    softcover : 50# alkaline paper ♾

    1. Post-traumatic stress disorder.   2. Post-traumatic stress
disorder — Treatment.   3. Post-traumatic stress disorder —
Patients — Family relationships.   I. Title.
RC552.P67R63   2011
616.85'21— dc22   2011002128

BRITISH LIBRARY CATALOGUING DATA ARE AVAILABLE

Front cover images © 2011 Shutterstock

Manufactured in the United States of America

McFarland & Company, Inc., Publishers
    Box 611, Jefferson, North Carolina 28640
    www.mcfarlandpub.com

Table of Contents

Preface

Significant Armed Conflicts, 2000–Present

Turkey, 1999, Kurds
Afghanistan, 2001, Operation Enduring Freedom
Iraq, 2003, Operation Iraqi Freedom/Operation New Dawn
Sudan, 2003, guerrilla war

Ongoing Conflicts

Israel & Palestine
India, Pakistan, Kashmir
India, internal insurgents
Indonesia, separatists
Philippines, separatists
Algeria, Islamic groups
Somalia, rival clans
Sudan, Sudanese guerrillas
Uganda, internal rebels
Russia, Chechnya
Colombia, guerrilla groups
      Numbers dead, wounded, displaced: Unknown thousands

Disasters, Natural and of Human Origin 2000–Present (Selected Sample)

France, 2000: Air France Concorde jet en route to New York crashed; all 109 aboard and four on the ground were killed.

Barents Sea, 2000: Russian nuclear submarine *Kursk* sank following an explosion; 118 dead.

Thailand, Cambodia, and Vietnam, 2000: Mekong River flood waters destroyed crops and livestock; left at least 235 people dead, 4.5 million homeless.

Yemen, 2000: U.S. Navy destroyer USS *Cole* attacked by small boat loaded with explosives; 17 killed.

Western United States, 2000s: Destructive forest fires in multiple states burned 7.2 million acres.

United States, 2001: 2 commercial jets were flown into the World Trade Center in NYC; 2 more hijacked U.S. planes crashed into the Pentagon and a field in Pennsylvania. Total dead and missing numbered 2,992; 266 people aboard the planes killed including the 19 hijackers.

United States, 2003: *Columbia* Space Shuttle breaks up as it reentered Earth's atmosphere over Texas. All 7 crew members dead.

World, 2003: Severe acute respiratory syndrome (SARS) spreads across the world.

U.S. and Canada, 2003: The largest power blackout in history left 50 million without electricity for 24 hours and longer.

Madrid, Spain, 2004: Terrorists exploded ten bombs on morning commuter trains; 191 killed, 1,500 injured.

Indonesia, 2004: 9.0 magnitude earthquake caused tsunami that hit 12 countries. Death toll over 225,000.

Iran, 2005: Magnitude 6.4 earthquake, at least 612 dead, over 1,400 injured.

Angola, 2005: Outbreak of Marburg, a hemorrhagic fever similar to Ebola, over 280 dead. No effective treatment.

Japan, 2005: Commuter train derails, hits apartment building. Over 100 killed, 460 wounded.

Niger, 2005: Famine caused by drought and locusts leave over 3.6 million people facing starvation.

United States, 2005: Hurricane Katrina devastates Louisiana and Mississippi coasts, leaving thousands homeless, millions without electricity, damage to oil rigs, destruction of roads and houses.

United States, 2005: Hurricane Rita hits Texas, Louisiana coasts, over 3 million evacuated, major property damage.

Indonesia, 2006: 6.3 magnitude earthquake, over 5,700 killed, 135,000 homes destroyed.

Russia, 2007: Methane explosion in coal mine kills 110 miners.

United States, 2007: Virginia Tech student kills 32 fellow students and then himself.

United States, 2007: Eight-lane interstate bridge packed with cars breaks into sections and collapses into Mississippi River. Nine dead, 60 injured.

Peru, 2007: 8.0-magnitude earthquake, 337 dead, hundreds injured.

United States, 2008: Explosion at sugar refinery near Georgia kills 14 people and injures many more.

Myanmar (Burma), 2008: Cyclone Nargis and accompanying storm surge kill 78,000.

China, 2008: 7.9 magnitude earthquake, nearly 70,000 confirmed dead.

United States, 2008: Hurricane Ike causes 50 deaths in Texas and causes significant property damage.

Germany, 2009: 15 people shot and killed at Albertville Technical High School in Germany by 17-year-old boy.

United States, 2009: 13 people killed at immigration center in NY by Vietnamese immigrant gunman reportedly upset over unemployment and perceived police persecution.

Italy, 2009: 6.3 magnitude earthquake kills over 200 and injures 1,000.

Brazil, 2009: Air France Airbus A330 disappears off coast.
of Brazil with 228 passengers on board, en route from Rio de Janeiro to Paris. No mayday signals were sent before crashing; no survivors.

Taiwan, 2009: Typhoon Morakot causes mudslide that buries schools, homes, and at least 600 people.

Samoa & American Samoa, 2009: 8.0 magnitude underwater earthquake causes tsunami, over 115 dead.

Indonesia, 2009: 7.6 magnitude earthquake, over 1,000 killed, thousands trapped.

Haiti, 2010: 7.0 magnitude earthquake kills over 100,000, devastates capital, leaves many more homeless.

Chile, 2010: 8.8 magnitude earthquake, 750 killed, up to 1.5 million displaced.

Afghanistan, 2010: NATO airstrike kills 27 civilians.

Russia, 2010: Female suicide bombers blow up two Moscow subway stations, at least 39 dead, many wounded.

Violent Crimes, U.S.A.

14,831 murder victims (2007)
466.9 violent crimes per 100,000 people (2007)
3,263.5 property crimes per 100,000 people (2007)
2,245,189 inmates of state, federal, local prisons (2006)
    (*Infoplease*, Crime).

United Nations High Commission for Refugees

Est. 200 million people live outside of place born.
Est.14.2 million refugees in the world.
Est. 24.5 million internally displaced persons.
    (*UNHCR Statistical Yearbook* 2008).

Amnesty International's 2008 Report

81 countries in which torture is found; billions suffer from insecurity, injustice, and indignity, made much worse by world recession; additional millions suffering from poverty, greater repression, and displacement; vulnerable and marginalized peoples suffer most; torture continues to be widespread across the world; political repression, extrajudicial executions, and executions in general continue to rise.

    (Amnesty International)

I used to vote with my hands. I did it today with my toe— Sierra Leone voter mutilated in civil war, 2002.

The things he saw in Iraq ate at him. He was just drifting. And little by little, bits of hope dropped away"— Father of Coleman Bean, army veteran who committed suicide in 2008.

Do I still have a future?— Liberian refugee, 2002 (*Refugees* 2002, p. 31).

For us, time stopped that day—Escapee of massacre at Srebrenica, Bosnia, 2001 (*Refugees*, 2001, p. 31).

I just assumed my parents were dead. There was nothing I could do about it. I had to move on— Survivor of EF5 tornado, Parkersburg, Iowa, 2008.

The phobias and fears, the depression and the guilt, all seemed to build on each other— Shoshana Johnson (*I'm Still Standing*, 2010, p. 266).

Some might say that those who died are the lucky ones, while the survivors have to make sense of changed worlds: worlds with missing friends and relatives; worlds with too little food, warmth, and education; worlds that are suddenly unsafe; worlds in which the externals may not have changed but the individual's interpretation of the world is fundamentally different.

To compare the victim of a mugging in New York City with the survivor of a massacre in Rwanda may seem absurd. One walks away with an empty wallet, while the other may have lost family, friends, home, job, and possessions. But for the individuals who experience trauma, who survive a traumatic event or series of events, the filter through which they see the world has shifted and changed dramatically.

A life with stability, routine, familiar places and events has disappeared. Hopes and plans for the future vanish. The mind replays the trauma endlessly, keeping the mind's attention focused on the pain and anguish, the second guessing, the effort to understand. Survivors may feel joy immediately after a traumatic experience, and then feel horrible guilt and shame for that feeling, mistaking relief at their own at survival for happiness that others did not survive. Moss, in Stanley Kramer's film *Home of the Brave* (1949), believes he was happy that Finch was wounded and then feels terrible shame for feeling so. His Army psychiatrist attempts to convince him that being happy at his own survival is not at all the same as being happy that another did not survive. Likewise, Jesse Rodriguez, in *Nothing Like the Holidays*, suffers from survivor guilt: "I was so happy to be alive." That moment of happiness or relief does not last long, but the guilt over having survived, and having been happy to have survived, can haunt an individual forever.

Victims and survivors: certainly there are many and it is certain that there will be more. How can those who have not experienced trauma understand those who have?

Young (1995) notes that "traumatic" was first cited in the *Oxford English Dictionary* in 1656, and is related to physical wounds. In the 1800s, physicians broadened the concept to include mental stresses as well. For a time, it was believed that emotional manifestations of stress had underlying physical roots (as indeed some specialists have more recently come to believe again, though in a more complex way). In the 19th century, traumatic stress came to be related to memories of traumatic events.

Traumatic stress, however, is not a British or American invention. Indeed, Jonathan Shay (1994; 2002), a Veteran's Administration psychiatrist, has worked with combat veterans with traumatic stress for some years. In his published works, he notes parallels between Achilles and Odysseus, classic Greek heroes whose epic stories reveal the awareness of traumatic stress, even though they are described differently than they might be today. Achilles' "Now pierced by memory" (cited in Shay, 1994, p. 50) shows how traumatic events remain alive in the survivor in some way. Memory is depicted almost as a weapon that strikes against one.

British physicians during World War I identified shell shock as one of four war neuroses (Young, 1995). Soldiers could be diagnosed as pretending amnesia or other symptoms of traumatic stress in an effort to avoid combat, or they could be diagnosed as bona fide cases of shell shock. Perhaps having to demonstrate shell shock added to the trauma.

During World War II, war neuroses were seen as manifestations of severe anxiety (Young, 1995). Treatment was given close to the front in order to return soldiers to combat if possible. If treatment was ineffective, soldiers were sent to base areas. As illustrated in *Home of the Brave*, treatment included rest, narcotics, and a sort of talk therapy, which walked the patient through the trauma, forcing it to consciousness and hence allowing pent-up feelings to be freely experienced. His father encourages Rodriguez to talk about his experiences, but he finds it difficult to do so. In *Home of the Brave*, where most of the characters illustrate symptoms of PTSD, group therapy in which experiences are shared with other Iraq War veterans is shown as a first step toward dealing with PTSD.

Yet the outcomes of group therapy are not always entirely successful, as many combat soldiers have returned home yet found it difficult to readjust. Stoicism might translate into difficulty connecting emotionally with family and friends. Alcohol might become a crutch. PTSD might accompany a variety of physical difficulties; veterans from the Vietnam, Iraq, and Afghanistan wars have higher rates of amputation and other physical injuries than in previous wars (in part due to improved equipment and better and faster medical attention). Traumatic Brain Injury (TBI) is much more common with today's wars, and results in both physical and emotional difficulties, such as memory loss and depression. PTSD is never a simple problem by itself; when compounded with other problems, it can be highly challenging to treat.

Historically, the war most closely associated with traumatic stress is Vietnam, a war that is controversial on nearly every side. Soldiers of the Vietnam War were children of idolized World War II soldiers, members of the large Baby Boom generation, the first generation to grow up with television. Films and television programs extolled the glories of war, showing valiant cowboys making the world right and superheroes embodying courage and virtue. Some 2.7 million soldiers rotated in and out of Vietnam between 1945 and 1975, but numbers alone don't explain why traumatic stress is associated so strongly with that war.

Perhaps the social climate was influential. The 1960s exploded with the Civil Rights movement, the Women's Liberation movement, and the rise of youth culture, rebellious and outspoken. The assassinations of John F. Kennedy, Martin Luther King, Jr., and Robert F. Kennedy reveal the turmoil of the times.

Perhaps issues related to the war were most important, including the perception that only poor and minority boys went to Vietnam. Young men were drafted at 18, but could request deferments for higher education. Draftees, asking whether the war was just, whether the draft was fair to everyone, joined others in burning draft cards. Many protesters demanded and finally got the right to vote. (The 26th Amendment, giving 18-year-olds the right to vote, was ratified in 1971.)

Draftees and enlistees both went to Vietnam, some or many believing in serving their country; many changed their views once there. Excessive bureaucracy, an elusive enemy, civilian casualties, and a lack of front lines made some feel the war itself was wrong, and their participation in it immoral. Many describe their experiences as long stretches of utter boredom punctuated by moments of sheer terror.

As soldiers rotated home or were sent home wounded, difficulties became apparent. While many came home and resumed their lives, some brought home drug dependencies and emotional problems, including explosive anger, distrust of others and vigilance beyond what was considered normal. The problems came to the attention of the Veterans Administration medical system, and over time doctors and psychiatrists began to elaborate on the concept of traumatic stress and post-traumatic stress disorder, which culminated in an official definition in the Diagnostic and Statistical Manual of Mental Disorders III, published in 1980. Though early conceptions of Post-Traumatic Stress Disorder (PTSD) arose from male combat soldiers, women, who played a larger role in the Vietnam War than in previous wars, also sufferered from PTSD.

The more recent combat operations in Iraq and Afghanistan, however, also show high numbers of PTSD sufferers. Since the war in Afghanistan began in 2001, and the war in Iraq in 2003, one and a half to two million troops have served in one or both countries as part of Operation Enduring Freedom in Afghanistan or Operation Iraqi Freedom in Iraq. Current troop level statistics are difficult to pin down, but some 112,000 troops are currently serving in Iraq, and 68,000 in Afghanistan. Two-thirds of these troops are regular active duty; a third are reserve or guard; and a third have served multiple deployments.

Using data from the Vietnam War, the Department of Defense estimates that 15 percent of returning soldiers may show signs of post traumatic stress. In truth, the percentage is likely closer to 30 percent. More alarming, a 2010 report by the Department of Defense states that 160 active duty soldiers committed suicide in 2009, an increase from 140 in 2008. The Chairman of the Joint Chiefs of Staff says that the levels of suicide are similar across branches and include female soldiers as well as male. Suicides among veterans are higher: the Department of Veterans Affairs (VA) reports that suicide rates are up 26 percent for veterans 18–20 years old (Littlepage, 2010). This does not include cases where a veteran deliberately crashes his car into a tree, or a veteran confronted police and was shot as a result. An addict dying of an overdose or an alcoholic drinking him or herself to death might too be a form of suicide. Whatever the real numbers are, it is clearly a crisis.

The social climate at the time of the Vietnam War and the Middle East wars is certainly different. We now have a volunteer army rather than a draft; social upheaval has shifted from civil rights to economic disparities, and we all live under a cloud of international and domestic terrorism threats. The wars themselves, however, have some striking similarities: no clear front lines; difficulty distinguishing between civilian and military targets; uncertainty over who is the enemy; ambushes and IEDs (Improvised Explosive Devices); and a sense that the folks back home are not fully in support of the war.

Post-Traumatic Stress Disorder, then, is a well-established diagnosis for combat veterans. But over time it has became evident that non-combat traumas could result in PTSD as well. Personal experiences, such as rape or physical attack, could be traumatic. Auto, plane, or train accidents could trigger PTSD. Natural disasters, such as earthquakes or floods or wildfires, could be traumatic. And around the world, torture, being held prisoner of war, being forcibly ejected from one's home and land, genocide and guerrilla wars could all produce survivors who met the definitional criteria for PTSD.

Today, though the understanding of causes and symptoms of PTSD is more sophisticated, treatments are still evolving. Talk therapy remains one of the mainstays of treatment, helping survivors articulate and face the trauma as a way of gaining control. Two drugs are currently identified as effective for PTSD: Zoloft and Paxil, both antidepressants. Other drugs are used, particularly for various constellations of symptoms (for example, sleep difficulties might be treated with sedatives, anxiety with tranquilizers). Other drugs are likely to be approved for PTSD in the coming years. As mental disabilities are increasingly tied to physical changes in the brain and body, medications will continue to be used, though at this time counseling is still considered an important part of treatment.

The narrow Western view of trauma, traumatic stress, and treatment options is still predominant. Not enough work has been done to identify cultural influences, and answer questions about how different cultures articulate the concept of PTSD as well as appropriate treatments, if any. We begin to see how events all over the world might be considered traumatic, but we don't know how different cultures interpret such events, nor how individuals in those cultures understand their experiences in a social context.

There is also much work to be done in the current U.S. environment, where social critics discuss a growing tendency for all kinds of people to view themselves as victims. An implication is that we are all victims of something or other, and, therefore, none of us are victims at all. Yet those who have survived traumatic events truly are different, as though an exceedingly bright light has illuminated and changed them from the inside out. They are neither malingerers nor groupies joining the latest trends. Dismissing them as simply claiming victim status is unjust.

Equally, we live in a climate of unfocused anxiety about wars, terrorist events, and unpredictable disasters, which does not constitute PTSD. While it can feel traumatic to live in uncertainty, it is not equivalent to surviving a cataclysmic event that changes a person at some deep level, for years to come. Generally, everyday anxiety is somewhat amenable to rational thought, while PTSD strikes so deeply at one's emotional self that it may be beyond rational resolution.

My own interest in Post-Traumatic Stress Disorder is the outcome of a variety of personal interests and experiences. I have always wondered how people think and feel. What makes them behave the way they do? Why do some suffer from mental illnesses and others don't? Where do mental illnesses come from — genetics, upbringing, and in what combination? How do people cope with or treat mental illnesses? And why does Western culture view mental illness suspiciously but physical illness with sympathy?

My educational and professional experience has been in the field of applied linguistics and teaching, in part because of a lifelong love of language. Additionally, though, I have long been interested in other cultures and societies, and through my training as an English language teacher and teacher trainer, I had opportunities to live and work in different cultures. From such a vantage point, I could see my own culture more clearly. Language, of course, is a major part of any culture, and it intrigues me to see language as a mirror for how people interpret their environments and lives. In particular, the words we use in some way condition us to believe and behave in certain ways. So when people use a lot of passive sentences — "It was broken" rather than "I broke it" — they avoid taking blame. When people use "should," they are expressing moral imperatives. Often we are unaware of how our language conditions our thinking, and that by changing our language, we can often also change the way we think.

My marriage to a Vietnam War veteran has also led me to investigate PTSD, first by exploring the war itself, and then by seeing the effects of the war, now some 40 years in the past, on veterans and their families today. The number of Vietnam War veterans who have been married multiple times, have had difficulty keeping a job, have raised second or third families, or have been estranged from their own children or other family members seemed to me to be beyond mere coincidence. Observing my own husband's interactions with his first set of children, his ex-wives, and our family assured me that although the war is long over, his battles, and hence mine, are not. Meeting other wives and children of Vietnam War veterans confirmed my observations.

Yet as complex and difficult as that war was, I also saw that people surviving floods or plane crashes, torture or rape had similar difficulties readjusting to life after such traumas. Sadly, there is no shortage of traumatic events. As I was writing this book, the Twin Towers of the World Trade Center were destroyed, the *Columbia* space shuttle broke up upon reentry, and a young girl was kidnapped and held prisoner for some nine months before being discovered and reunited with her family. Since the first edition of this book, the war in Iraq has been ongoing, the war in Afghanistan has become more important, and many of the soldiers facing combat, both men and women, are young and have little previous combat or life experience. Some American troops are being held as POWs. Terrorist attacks have been staged in virtually every part of the world, including Pakistan, Russia, Indonesia, Spain, and the U.S. Major earthquakes, flooding, and droughts have afflicted countries both rich and poor.

I am convinced that a significant percentage of the survivors of these and other such events will develop PTSD. As a result of my research, I believe there may be promise in identifying those most at risk for developing PTSD; I believe immediate intervention may help deflect it in some of those survivors, and I believe that treatments can help those whose acute stress reactions become chronic. I do not believe that PTSD can be "cured," because the traumatic event that occurred in the past cannot be removed or erased. And I believe that if PTSD goes untreated, not only will families suffer, but children may well mirror the symptoms of PTSD that they see modeled in their families. PTSD may, in a sense, be passed down from generation to generation.

I am a typical representative of my culture and my generation in believing that individuals can be helped and can help themselves. But I also believe that individuals exist in the context of their families, friends, communities, and larger world. When one member of the community suffers, all members suffer. Thus I would like to see society recognize PTSD and respect it as a legitimate disorder, one that merits empathy and treatment.

Traumatic stress and PTSD are not new ideas, and even as the concepts evolve and grow, their existence has been with us for centuries and beyond, and likely will be with us for centuries into the future. Understanding and empathy are tools with which we should approach victims of trauma, whether these survivors are family members, friends, or ourselves. As we mature into greater understanding of the disorder and its treatment, perhaps we can begin to both eliminate the causes and facilitate the recovery of survivors of traumatic stress.

Introduction

My husband slit his wrists in the shower, with one of the knives from Vietnam that he had sometimes used on me. I almost left him after he used me for target practice one night. But I blame Vietnam for this, not him (Matsakis, 1996, p. 14).

His was what passed for a happy story in Rwanda. Still, I had the impression ... that as he told it he was seeing the events he described afresh; that as he stared into the past the outcome was not yet obvious, and that when he looked at me, with his clear eyes a touch hazy, he was still seeing the scenes he described, perhaps even hoping to understand them (Gourevitch, 1998, p. 122).

In my mind I see chunks of concrete falling from the building but I know it was really people that I saw falling ... jumping." As she spoke, I could not help myself from forming my own images of falling debris coalescing into anatomical features. (Gentry, 2002, p. 38).

Sending someone to combat is a life sentence (Glaser, 2001).

What is Post-Traumatic Stress Disorder (PTSD)? It is an ongoing, life-affecting disorder resulting from experiencing a traumatic event. An individual who survives a traumatic experience may be irrevocably changed, reoriented to life in a distinctly different way, and may be somewhat or severely disabled. Traumatic stresses may be caused by natural disasters such as floods, earthquakes, tornadoes, hurricanes, or fires, or they may be caused by human actions, such as war, torture, child abuse, rape, or auto or plane accidents. A young infantryman in Vietnam under fire from an unseen enemy, a woman trapped on the roof of her home as floodwaters rise, a child who is raped by a visiting relative, or a retired businessman held hostage by a bank robber: these victims may survive these events only to go on to develop PTSD. In the face of life-threatening danger, a person acts to ensure survival. The infantryman may fire aggressively at anything that moves, including harmless farm animals. The trapped woman might resort to prayer and hallucinate rescuers. The child might distance herself mentally from her attacker, and blame herself for "causing" the rape. The businessman might become childlike in order to please the hostage takers and save his life. In ensuring the individual's survival of the traumatic event, these strategies are quite functional. But when the trauma ends, such adaptive responses might be dysfunctional.

The child, for example, may experience emotional numbness and be unable to feel close to others. The businessman may become fearful of others whom he perceives to be stronger than he is. The flood survivor might move to a home on higher ground and refuse to leave home in case something might happen. The infantryman might react to everything in his environment as if it were a potentially deadly threat. Fearing his own loss of control under stress, he might "bunker in" to his home and refuse to leave it or to interact with others who might trigger his reactions.

It has been estimated that about 30 percent of those who experience a traumatic event will go on to develop PTSD. Nearly everyone will experience some level of disruption immediately after a highly stressful event. Survivors of trauma initially suffer from what is known as Acute Stress Disorder. It is only when symptoms such as anxiety, difficulty sleeping, and emotional numbness persist that the diagnosis is changed to PTSD. Unfortunately, it is not possible to predict who will go on to develop PTSD after a traumatic event. There is some evidence that having the support of family and friends, being resilient, and getting professional counseling early can help prevent PTSD. But there is still much we do not know about the human reaction to stressful events, and the general public may not have much understanding of PTSD. One World War II veteran's wife cannot understand why her husband came home and led a "normal" life while her son, a Vietnam War veteran, has had difficulty holding a job and has been married multiple times. (The husband, in fact, spent many nights pacing the living room with the television on for background noise, but he went to work each day and so was considered to be fine.) A lack of understanding on the part of others exacerbates the difficulties of living with PTSD. Vietnam veterans sometimes point to the lack of a "welcome home" as a factor for their feelings of isolation. Extended family members and the larger society seem to suspect that PTSD survivors are malingerers and that they should stop feeling sorry for themselves. Even the survivors might adopt the same attitude, and wonder why they have trouble leaving the traumatic events behind.

It is not only those who directly experience the trauma who may develop PTSD. A Congressional hearing in 2007 regarding civilian workers in Iraq found that many diplomats, intelligence analysts, contract administrators, and so on also showed symptoms of PTSD. Though presumably safe in the Green Zone of Baghdad, the periodic rocket fire and general sense of insecurity were perceived as potentially life threatening (Congress).

Furthermore, secondary traumatic stress disorder, or "vicarious traumatization" (McCann & Perlman, 1990) or "compassion fatigue" (Figley, 1995) affects those working with survivors of traumatic events, and indeed, those living with survivors.

Why should PTSD be of interest or importance to the general public? Aside from feeling compassion for those who suffer, or supporting intervention for victims of natural or man-made disasters, why should we as individuals care? First, given the number of stressful events that characterize society and indeed the world, it is likely that each of us will personally know someone who suffers from PTSD. The National Institute for Mental Health (NIMH) estimates that "about 3.6 percent of U.S. adults ages 18 to 54 (5.2 million people) have PTSD during the course of a given year," and further estimates that 30 percent of those who have served in combat zones will have PTSD. A million Vietnam War veterans are diagnosed with PTSD (perhaps an undercount; not all those with PTSD have clinical diagnoses or go to the VA for assistance) and as many as 8 percent of Gulf War veterans develop PTSD (*Facts about Post-Traumatic Stress Disorder*, 2001). Some 1.5 to 2 million troops have served in Iraq, Afghanistan, or both, and many have served multiple tours. The Department of Defense estimates that 15 percent have been or will be diagnosed with PTSD, though the numbers are likely higher. Suicide rates from the current conflicts continue to rise (301 suicides in 2009, up from 140 in 2008) and affect all branches, male and female soldiers both (UPI, 2010). Survivors of the September 22, 2001 attacks on the World Trade Center and Pentagon and NYC residents developed PTSD at a rate of 16 percent, with higher figures for those involved in rescue efforts.

Second, people really do not live as individuals. John Donne's famous observation in *Devotions* that "No man is an island, entire of itself: every man is a piece of the continent" rings true. Symptoms and reactions become an issue for the family, and as the family attempts to adjust to its changed circumstances, it too can become skewed. The family's coping strategies, in reaction to the trauma survivor's symptoms, tend to be dysfunctional because they are short-term responses to a deep-seated change. Families might seek to protect the survivor by shielding him or her from the outside world, thus becoming isolated as a family. Survivors who self-medicate with alcohol or drugs (legal or illegal) may be propped up with enabling behavior by their spouses or children ("Get daddy a beer, honey"). Employment difficulties may lead to financial problems, or to role reversal with the wife becoming the wage earner. Such a reversal may exacerbate the PTSD husband's sense that he is "less than a man." The wife, too, might feel resentment for having to be responsible for the family income. Sometimes one of the children will become the scapegoat of the family, attracting negative attention to protect the survivor from the consequences of his or her behavior. Spouses and children might experience secondary trauma as they care for the PTSD survivor.

Finally, children do tend to pass on what they have learned in their families, repeating patterns that may not be healthy, but are familiar. It is of value to everyone to break the cycle. Fortunately, families dealing with PTSD do have strengths; surviving and coping with PTSD is evidence that there is much strength that can be drawn on to help a family function in a way that is healthy for all its members.

The purpose of the present work is to describe PTSD — what it is, who might suffer from it, what causes it, how it affects families, and how individuals and families can be helped to cope with it. The term "survivor" is used intentionally, indicating that individuals with PTSD are survivors of trauma, not merely passive victims or current sufferers. Survivors have succeeded in living through the trauma, and it is important to remember that success rather than to focus on continuing difficulties.

The first chapter defines PTSD and related disorders, describing characteristics and symptoms and how these are manifested in daily life. Causes are described, and secondary PTSD is defined, primarily as it affects couples and families; a discussion of its effect on professional caregivers is provided in a later chapter. Traumatic brain injury (TBI) is a growing problem for

Iraq and Afghanistan combat troops; the U.S. military often groups PTSD and TBI together due to similar symptoms and so TBI will also be defined and described in this chapter.

Chapter 2 discusses how PTSD is diagnosed, how symptoms are assessed and evaluated, and who conducts such assessments. Chapter 3 addresses what is known of risk factors for PTSD and efforts to prevent PTSD in populations known to be at risk, in particular, combat troops.

Chapter 4 provides cross-cultural perspectives on PTSD, and describes the effects of cultural differences on the diagnosis and treatment of PTSD.

Chapter 5 goes into more depth about how PTSD affects an individual's life, from emotional to mental to physical difficulties. Disorders that may occur comorbidly (jointly) with PTSD and the possible physical disabilities resulting from the trauma are also described. Since the constellation of possible problems and symptoms is quite complex, illustrative rather than definitive answers are the goal. Finally, the strengths that may result from PTSD are recognized and described.

Chapter 6 considers the PTSD individual in his or her family system. How do the individual's specific problems affect the couple? The family? The extended family? And how do members of the family react to the individual's problems?

Chapter 7 continues the family discussion by looking at families from a systems perspective, and by comparing the characteristics of healthy families with those of PTSD families. How do families handle normal developmental tasks, such as children beginning school, becoming teenagers, moving away from home? As with the discussion of PTSD survivors, this chapter also looks at the strengths of PTSD families. Such strengths may be the foundation for growth toward more functional living.

Chapter 8 describes mental health approaches to treating PTSD, including individual counseling, rap group or support group counseling, help with substance abuse and related problems, and combined therapies. Techniques such as exposure therapy, Eye Movement Desensitization and Reprocessing (EMDR), and Traumatic Incident Reduction are discussed. In addition, couples and family counseling are also covered.

Chapter 9 describes drug treatments for PTSD, including anti-anxiety and anti-depressant medications, which are perhaps the most popular but by no means the only choices available. Other drugs that are used either singly or in combination are also discussed.

Chapter 10 reviews some alternative approaches to treating PTSD, including biofeedback, relaxation techniques, herbal medications, and others. Combination therapies, including counseling, medications, and newer approaches may be effective, and suggestions for finding the most appropriate combination are presented.

Chapter 11 summarizes and synthesizes earlier chapters, reviewing how PTSD affects individuals and families and suggesting healthy and effective strategies for living with PTSD. While there is no "cure," there are a variety of ways to learn to live with PTSD.

Chapter 12 looks ahead to newer trends in PTSD research and treatments. There is a tremendous amount of research being conducted, particularly in the military, and the findings promise better and more effective ways to understand PTSD.

The conclusion draws together what is known about PTSD, what isn't known, and posits directions for future research.

Appendices at the end of the book include the definitional criteria for PTSD from the Diagnostic and Statistical Manual of the American Psychiatric Association, fourth edition (DSM IV), a list of resources for PTSD survivors and their families, and information about veterans' benefits for those who served in the armed forces. An annotated list of recommended books and a short filmography are also provided, with suggestions on different PTSD topics and suggestions for readers and viewers of different ages.

It is hoped that the information and ideas in this book will help us all become more aware of and sensitive to the needs of PTSD survivors in our midst.

CHAPTER 1

What Is Post-Traumatic Stress Disorder?

My father left his emotions in a foxhole on Iwo Jima (DW, personal communication, 2001).

I had terrible feelings of guilt about those other children [at the orphanage].... I thought about the ones I had known personally — the little girl in the trash can, the little boy without hands — and I couldn't imagine why I was worth saving and they weren't (Kim, 2000, p. 77).

I feel safe at home, it is my fortress and I have my weapons locked and loaded ("Snoopy," personal communication, 2001).

Even though time and years have passed, those things are always inside my mind. It doesn't matter how many years are ahead of me. Those things will always be inside my heart, and I can always look back to it and say, "Gee, what kind of life I went through" (Hmong refugee in Faderman, 1998, p. 76).

Survivors of trauma, whether resulting from natural or man-made disasters, may find that even though they survived the original trauma, their troubles are not over. Ongoing feelings of fear, difficulties in sleeping, avoidance of others, and painful memories may interfere with their ability to rejoin life, and to experience joy in living. Not all survivors of traumatic events will suffer from the symptoms of Post-Traumatic Stress Disorder, or PTSD, but a significant number do. Unfortunately, there is no way to definitively predict who will or will not develop PTSD as a result of a stressful event, though estimates suggest the range is between 10 and 30 percent. One 1992 study of Holocaust survivors found that 46 percent of study participants had symptoms diagnosable as PTSD (Kuch & Cox, 1992).

PTSD was first codified by the American Psychiatric Association in its 1980 *Diagnostic and Statistical Manual of Mental Disorders*, Third Edition (DSM III). But PTSD is not a new disorder; it was known as shell shock in World War I, battle fatigue in World War II, operational exhaustion in the Korean War, and combat fatigue in the Vietnam War (Clark, 1990). Rundell and Ursano (1996) report that symptoms in post–World War I and World War II soldiers were called "nostalgia," "shell shock," or "war neurosis" (Sargent & Slater, 1940; War Office, 1922; both cited in Rundell & Ursano, 1996). Civilians, too, are exposed to war: "90 percent of casualties during the war in the republics of the former Yugoslavia were civilians" (Rundell & Ursano, 1996). And attacks on civilian populations, including but not limited to rape, tend not to be highly publicized yet inflict trauma on individuals, families, and communities alike.

Combat soldiers and civilian survivors of war are not the only ones to suffer from PTSD; others include Holocaust victims; prisoners of war; displaced persons and refugees; survivors of natural disasters such as tornadoes, earthquakes, floods, hurricanes, and so on; and victims of rape, assault, serious auto accidents, and plane crashes. Children may be just as affected as adults, or perhaps more so, and may regress in behavior, cling to caretakers, become irritable and whiny, or aggressively compete for adult attention (FEMA, *Coping with Stress*, n.d.).

Survivors of terrorist attacks are at risk. In a survey conducted in November 2001, researchers found that 44 percent of a nationally representative sample of adults in the U.S. (560 participants) reported at least one significant stress symptom (feeling upset by reminders of 9/11, having difficulty sleeping or concentrating, irritability, recurring dreams or memories). A remarkable 90 percent reported lower levels of stress symptoms. Thirty-five percent of the children sampled (170 children aged 5 to 18) also exhibited at least one significant stress symptom (Schuster et al., 2001). These stress symptoms do not fully meet the criteria for PTSD (which is not diagnosed until at least a month after the traumatic event). In addition, the survey participants were vicariously experiencing the trauma. For such a large number of individuals who merely observed the traumatic event to be affected is certainly cause for attention.

Finally, disaster workers, emergency personnel, mental health counselors, and close family and friends of trauma survivors may show symptoms of PTSD. In fact, officials who regularly inform family members of a death may accumulate many small stresses that can lead to PTSD. Given the number and range of potential sufferers, awareness and recognition are key to understanding this disorder.

Definition and Characteristics

Post-Traumatic Stress Disorder (PTSD) might be simply defined as difficulty in coping with everyday life after experiencing or witnessing a significant, life-threatening event. According to the American Psychiatric Association's *Diagnostic and Statistical Manual of Mental Disorders*, 4th Edition (hereafter referred to as *DSM* IV) the individual must experience a real or perceived threat to his or her life, or witness an event that threatens the life of another. In addition, the person's response "must involve intense fear, helplessness, or horror" (*DSM* IV, p. 424). Soldiers who survive ambushes or see a friend killed by a booby trap, or who spend hours at night on guard against an unseen enemy, are at risk. Rescue workers who see victims of terrorist bombings, Holocaust or genocide victims who see others marched to a gas chamber or a killing field, and prisoners of war (declared or undeclared, by an insurgent group or their own government) who hear the screams of others being tortured are all at risk.

During and immediately after the experience, the individual is consumed by the need to cope, and might function effectively or even heroically. During a firefight, the soldier fires back, and may even charge the enemy. The medic exposes himself/herself to danger to help a wounded comrade. Firefighters in New York on September 11, 2001, rushed into burning and collapsing buildings to help others. Concentration camp inmates focus all of their resources on simply staying alive, and helping others do the same.

At times of severe stress, our bodies generate adrenaline, a powerful hormone that stimulates us to respond to a threat or perceived threat: our heart rates go up, breathing becomes more shallow, and blood pressure rises. A second stress hormone, cortisol, increases blood sugars and dampens nonessential systems, such as digestion, in order to divert energy to muscles and so on. Typically, when the threat is over, the hormones decrease and bodily systems return to a more natural state. However, in combat, this heightened response might occur repeatedly, accustoming a person to live at a high level of readiness. Some Vietnam veterans are jokingly called "adrenaline junkies"; upon their return to the U.S., they missed the "high" of being flooded with adrenaline, and engaged in behaviors to stimulate those feelings again. One Special Forces veteran took up sky-diving because the "rush" of jumping out of an airplane made him feel "alive" again. Vietnam War nurses came home and chose to work in emergency rooms rather than in less exciting parts of hospitals. Medics work as emergency medical technicians. In the movie *Fearless*, Jeff Bridges' character, having survived a plane crash, believes himself to be invulnerable as a result and intentionally puts himself in life-threatening situations to prove it.

The human body becomes habituated to living under extreme stress; biologically the heart and other organs can be damaged due to the higher hormone levels and psychologically, the mechanisms that carry us through a crisis may be hard to leave behind when the crisis has passed.

Having experienced real physical, emotional, and psychological adaptations to crisis, an individual cannot simply go back to a pre-crisis way of being and functioning. The body has changed, physically, and thus emotionally and psychologically as well. The effects can be permanent.

One way to look at PTSD is a response to a traumatic event that collapses time; the PTSD individual reexperiences the trauma through flashbacks or nightmares, experiences anxiety and stress at reminders of the original trauma, and seeks to avoid triggers that remind him/her of the trauma. The avoidance can be cognitive, as when the individual tries not to think about the event; emotional, as when the individual numbs the painful feelings that accompany reminders of the event; or behavioral, when the individual stays away from activities that might remind him/her of the trauma. PTSD sufferers might avoid war or violent movies, might avoid making close friends, or might abandon a previous hobby such as hunting, as does Robert DeNiro's character in *The Deer Hunter*. By limiting exposure to potential or real triggers, an individual might also eliminate pleasurable thoughts, emotions and activities.

While it is not possible to predict which combination of symptoms an individual with PTSD might express, the DSM IV cites the common symptoms that are used to diagnose the disorder. These include symptoms in three categories; the first is *reexperiencing* the trauma.

(1) Recurrent and intrusive distressing recollections of the event, including images, thoughts, or perceptions.

(2) Recurrent distressing dreams of the event.

(3) Acting or feeling as if the traumatic event were recurring (includes a sense of reliving the experience, illusions, hallucinations, and dissociative flashback episodes, including those that occur on awaken ing or when intoxicated).

(4) Intense psychological distress at exposure to internal or external cues that symbolize or resemble an aspect of the traumatic event.

(5) Physiological reactivity on exposure to internal or external cues that symbolize or resemble an aspect of the traumatic event (p. 426).

To be diagnosed with PTSD, the individual has to exhibit one or more of the reexperiencing symptoms. The second category is *avoidance*, and diagnosis requires three or more of the following:

(1) Efforts to avoid thoughts, feelings, or conversations associated with the trauma.

(2) Efforts to avoid activities, places, or people that arouse recollections of the trauma.

(3) Inability to recall an important aspect of the trauma.

(4) Markedly diminished interest or participation in significant activities.

(5) Feeling of detachment or estrangement from others.

(6) Restricted range of affect (e.g., unable to have loving feelings).

(7) Sense of a foreshortened future (e.g., does not expect to have a career, marriage, children, or a normal life span) (p. 428).

As stated previously, avoidance can be cognitive, emotional, and/or behavioral. The third category is increased *arousal*, or a higher state of alert than most people are accustomed to. Two or more of the following are required for diagnosis:

(1) Difficulty falling or staying asleep.

(2) Irritability or outbursts of anger.

(3) Difficulty concentrating.

(4) Hypervigilance.

(5) Exaggerated startle response (p. 428).

The DSM IV additionally notes that these symptoms last longer than one month and significantly impair the individual's functioning (see Appendix A for a complete list of the DSM IV criteria). Looking at several specific examples will help illustrate the range and severity of symptoms.

A medic in Vietnam who rushed to help the young soldier who tripped a booby-trapped sign thought only of saving a life. Years later, when he is back in the United States, his inability to save that soldier returns to haunt him. Although there was nothing he could do, he continues to feel sorrow over that loss of life. He feels guilty that he survived while others around him died, and he wonders why. Survivor guilt is common among trauma survivors, and prevents them from enjoying the lives they have. "Why him? Why not me?" The medic exhibits distressing memories (reexperiencing), cannot recall certain details of the soldier's death and tries to avoid thinking about it (avoidance), and has difficulty concentrating and sleeping (arousal). All three categories of symptoms are present.

A woman who as a child was repeatedly abused by a family member lives alone, works in a law office, and rarely goes out at night or on weekends. She has not communicated with her family for years, has few hobbies or interests and feels close to no one (avoidance). She becomes upset when she receives a letter or a phone call from her sister (reexperiencing) and jumps when the doorbell or phone rings (arousal). Her life seems very limited, but it feels safe to her, and she prefers the safety of isolation to the possible pleasures — and risks — of personal relationships.

A World War II veteran returned home and couldn't tolerate noise, so his wife and daughter cowered in the living room with earphones to hear the television (DW, personal communication, 2001). Other World War II veterans sought refuge in alcohol. An infantryman during the Vietnam War recalls a Korean War veteran shaking his hand goodbye and saying, "I don't write dead men." He had learned not to get close to other people. The infantryman goes on to say that he feels permanently numb. "If I read in the paper about a number of people dying in some tragedy, [I] am left unfeeling" ("Snoopy," personal communication, 2001). He avoids cues that might remind him of the loss he witnessed during the war, and he feels detached from others.

One Holocaust survivor describes the loneliness of living with PTSD, in a poem entitled "Life Without Liberty":

> The struggle goes on and on
> Until one day we depart,
> With regret, with fright.
> Darkness and solitude
> Is our price.
> Such a high price
>   to give
> For a hard life
>   to live [Herzberger, 1975, p.88].

She survived the Holocaust, but found that the trauma persisted. The sense of isolation and struggle is palpable in her poetry.

A National Guard soldier deployed in Iraq tried to save a fellow soldier who was blown out of a truck that ran over an IED; "I think about it every night when I go to bed. It's on my mind." He still keeps a part of the axle of the truck, thus ensuring he will remember (reexperience) the trauma, and the difficulty sleeping that accompanies the memories (arousal) (Sennott, 2010).

Refugees from war may exhibit signs of PTSD as well. The Hmong who fled from Laos after the Vietnam War left agricultural lives and villages, survived weeks, months, or even years in the jungle trying to reach refugee camps, then experienced horrors in refugee camps before being repatriated to safer countries. While physically safer, many of these refugees experienced deep feelings of loss for their homes, country, ancestors, language, and customs. In resettling, they found the children acculturating and becoming the de facto heads of the families. For many their lives were truly shattered. Similarly, in the 1970s, city-dwelling Cambodians were forced by the Khmer Rouge to work in rice paddies and suffered disease, starvation, and murder. In Rwanda in the 1990s, mass genocide took place as the Hutus massacred Tutsis. Many Tutsis fled to refugee camps in neighboring countries, but these camps became places of horror as well.

The human cost of natural disasters along with the overwhelming number of examples of humans' cruelty to one another means that PTSD is likely to continue to affect human populations. A closer look at the symptoms characterizing PTSD may provide further insight into the varied patterns of response shown by survivors.

Symptoms

The first category in the DSM IV diagnostic criteria is reexperiencing. Often, with PTSD, the individual relives and reexperiences the original trauma through nightmares or flashbacks. Of course these memories are painful; they also interfere with daily living. In a very direct way, they take the person out of the present and back into the traumatic situation. The flashbacks might be triggered by sounds, such as a helicopter overhead; by sights, such as a child with a bleeding cut; by smells, such as barbecuing or diesel exhaust fumes; or by cues not directly related to the trauma itself. For example, one Vietnam veteran overreacted to his three-year-old son's stubbornness — a natural developmental stage for a three year old, but a trigger to his father, who might have felt that disobeying an order could lead to death in a combat situation. These reactions are hard for others to understand; we may only see an exaggerated response to a mild provocation, not realizing that the PTSD individual is also responding to the post trauma.

In an effort to shield themselves from flashbacks, some survivors attempt to avoid anything that might trigger one. Since the possible triggers are so many and so prevalent in the environment, one solution is to stay home. A veteran of the war in Iraq refused to leave home during daylight hours for months after his return. Sealing themselves off from the outside world and normal adult interaction, sufferers may become more intensively fearful of the world and even more isolated. A not uncommon example are people suffering from agoraphobia (not all agoraphobics have PTSD, nor do all PTSD sufferers have agoraphobia); these individuals are fearful of leaving home, and of being in public places. They may be unable to work as a result of their fear. An extreme example from the Vietnam War are the so-called "trip-wire vets," who, upon returning from Vietnam, found it impossible to live in ordinary society and retreated to areas of wilderness, setting up camps and living lives isolated from the rest of society. More common is the ongoing habit of simply avoiding crowds, which might rule out movie theatres, shopping malls, parades or fairs, even family get-togethers.

Sometimes flashbacks occur in the form of nightmares, visiting the survivor at night, perhaps when his/her normal defenses are relaxed. Not only are these highly distressing to the individual, they are physically disabling as well. Extreme examples include combat veterans who attack their spouses during a nighttime flashback and fearful individuals who sleep with guns or knives under their pillows. One veteran of the war in Iraq experienced "extreme fear of being captured by the enemy. He would take his clothes off, camouflage himself and hide somewhere" (Holmes, 2010). But an extreme reaction is not necessary to make these nightmares debilitating. Nightmares disrupt sleep; disturbed sleep patterns lead to a host of problems, ranging from daytime hallucinations to sleeping during the day to compensate. Sleep deprived people are irritable, have trouble concentrating, and may become depressed. They also tend to disrupt the sleep of those around them, so the spouse may become sleep deprived as well. Being unable to sleep well, with or without compensating by sleeping during the day, makes it difficult or impossible to hold a job. Employment difficulties bring financial difficulties, and self-esteem difficulties; essentially, sleep problems ripple out to affect every area of a person's life.

Avoidance is the second DSM IV diagnostic category. Having experienced loss through the original trauma, PTSD survivors might employ emotional numbing or isolation to avoid feelings of loss in the present. In Vietnam, when a new soldier joined the unit, the "old-timers" might avoid even learning his name. Since he might die at any time, it was simply foolish to get close to him. Many Vietnam veterans do not know the names of the men in their units. For self-protection, nicknames were used. Years later, a veteran can describe in vivid detail how his friend "Tex" died, but cannot remember his name in order to visit a grave or write to the family. Today, that veteran avoids making new friends. Another veteran recalls the constant stress of eight months of combat in Iraq: "It definitely was always intense. Eventually, we became numb to everything" (Mueller, 2010).

Sometimes a survivor of childhood abuse or incest also seeks escape in emotional numbing. She (or he) might pretend to be elsewhere, or simply shut down so as not to feel the horror and shame. As an adult, this person may avoid having close friends, or any friends at all. The sense of isolation and loneliness experienced during the abuse is recreated, endlessly, if an adult cannot make emotional connections with others.

Emotional numbing affects disaster and crisis workers, too. In order to survive their repeated exposure to death and dying, disaster workers may need to emotionally deaden themselves in order to carry on. This protective reaction indeed helps them get through a crisis; after the bombing of the Murrah Building in Oklahoma City, rescue workers carried out the bodies of children. Without steeling themselves to the horror of the scene, they wouldn't have been able to continue their rescue work. Later, however, they might find that the numbing has become habitual, and they are unable to experience feelings of love and intimacy.

Arousal is the third category in the DSM IV criteria. Hypervigilance develops when exposure to a traumatic event creates a profound sense of vulnerability. Vietnam combat veterans, for example, served in a war without front lines, in which the enemy was difficult to distinguish from the civilian population. As a result some spend much of the night prowling their homes, checking "the perimeter," making sure doors and windows are locked. In one case, a veteran does not like lights to be on at night in his home; he fears that such lights make him an easy-to-see target. The terrorist attacks on the World Trade Center have left many people feeling that danger is potentially everywhere and difficult to guard against. Needing to exert some feeling of control over an essentially uncontrollable situation, we insist that our children stay close to home, we avoid taking long trips, and we obsessively watch news programs, hoping to find answers that are slow to come. Knowledge, however, is not necessarily comforting. Law enforcement and emergency workers may be even more anxious as a result of hearing more details or knowing more about how investigations are proceeding.

While not a symptom of PTSD, clinical depression is found in many survivors of trauma. Like PTSD, depression is characterized by difficulty sleeping or by sleeping too much, lack of pleasure in everyday activities, sad mood, significant weight gain or loss, fatigue, feeling worthless or guilty, difficulty concentrating, irritability, and possibly thoughts of suicide. Depression is more than having a bad day occasionally; it is persistent and affects most or all areas of life. Depression typically results in difficulty in functioning in daily life, so difficulties with family members, employment, and so on are part of depression. When depression accompanies PTSD, the dysfunction is magnified. The sense of despair accompanying depression may make it difficult for the PTSD sufferer to seek help, since there is little expectation that anything can be done to help. Fortunately, there are well-established treatments, both drug and counseling, for depression, and at least one drug originally developed to treat depression has been approved to treat PTSD as well. But an individual in such depths of pain might not pursue treatment, and if the person is also isolated, he or she might not have close family or friends who can encourage them to seek treatment.

Sufferers of PTSD are also at risk for becoming alcoholics or drug abusers; perhaps this is an effort to "self-medicate," a way to escape memories and painful feelings, an effort to find relaxation and pleasure. These efforts only add a new layer of difficulties to the sufferer; short term relief becomes a chronic disease on top of the original PTSD.

Given the potentially devastating effects of PTSD, could it be avoided if we better understood the causes? Could we limit or eliminate the causes? Could we prevent PTSD if we could prevent the causes of PTSD?

Children and PTSD

Children are a somewhat different population when it comes to PTSD. They may also suffer through traumatic events, either first hand or as members of a family facing PTSD in one of its members. Because children are still developing physically, emotionally, and cognitively, they may be at higher risk. Children have been found to show different symptoms than adults, and thus should be assessed with instruments and personnel trained to work with children. For example, children may have physical symptoms such as headaches, stomachaches, or sleep difficulties. They may have behavioral symptoms, such as acting out, clinging to adults, or developing irrational fears. Emotional symptoms include withdrawal, preoccupation, or a belief that their lives may be cut short. Finally, children may regress to an earlier developmental stage and begin wetting their beds, rocking, or even not speaking (Porterfield, 1996). Because children may not be able to understand or explain what they are experiencing, it is important to watch for these symptoms and seek assistance for the child.

The Diagnostic and Statistical Manual of the American Psychiatric Association is working on expanding and revised the definition and criteria for PTSD to include specific information related to children. The DSM V is expected to be published in May, 2013.

What Causes PTSD and Who Suffers from It?

In 1992, nearly fifty years after World War II, two doctors found that 58 percent of Holocaust survivors reported symptoms of PTSD. Survivors of the Holocaust, for example, may feel isolated as a result of being told to forget about the trauma and go on with their lives. Worse, they may be told they should feel "lucky." They might feel undeserving, and have difficulty finding meaning in their lives. Unable to move on psychologically, they become stuck in unhealthy patterns of coping.

American veterans of World War II also exhibited symptoms of PTSD in the postwar years. In the film *The Best Years of Our Lives,* one of the veterans drinks alcohol as a means of avoiding his family, of avoiding intimacy. Another character experiences a flashback triggered by visiting an aircraft graveyard in the desert. Prisoner-of-war studies (World War II and Korea) suggest that PTSD, initially affecting as many as two-thirds of survivors, may decline over time, with about 20 percent still experiencing symptoms several decades later (Port et al., 2001). In an effort to deter combat-related psychological problems, the U.S. military in Vietnam devised a program of treating such problems immediately, in hopes of heading off long-term consequences. In fact, some soldiers were treated and immediately returned to their combat assignments. While the intent was good, the result might have been exposure to additional traumatic events: Multiple experiences are a predictor of the later development of PTSD.

A study conducted in 1997 compared Persian Gulf War veterans with military personnel who were on active duty during the war, but not posted to the Persian Gulf. Self-report data indicated that PTSD was twice as high for those who served in the Gulf. Their symptoms included alcohol abuse, depression, and anxiety (Iowa Persian Gulf Study Group, 1997). Another study measured symptoms and severity at one month after return, and again at six months. Self-report data reveal that hyperarousal was more severe than other symptoms (reexperiencing and avoidance) and further, that the symptoms did not abate appreciably in the intervening months of the study (Southwick et al., 1993). Finally, a 1996 study examined symptoms of PTSD in Persian Gulf veterans at five days and 18 to 20 months after their return home. Expecting to find the overall rate of PTSD lower compared to Vietnam War veterans because of a shorter time in combat and less intense fighting, the researchers instead found that not only were significant symptoms of distress present within five days, but that at the 18 to 20-month time, levels of distress had approximately doubled (Wolfe et al., 1996). The authors suggest that exposure to stressful events may result in traumatic stress symptoms even if time spent in actual combat is limited.

Natural disasters are likely to result in high levels of PTSD as well. Tornadoes, earthquakes, floods, hurricanes, wildfires, and others may produce the sorts of traumatic stressors, such as loss of life, that result in PTSD. Studies cite a 59 percent rate of PTSD in tornado victims, and up to 67 percent among victims of earthquakes in Armenia. Firefighters in the 1983 Australian bush fires showed a rate of 30 percent. After the 1980 Mount St. Helens eruption, 39 percent of responders experienced PTSD symptoms one year after the disaster, and 23 percent 26 months later.

Other stressors for PTSD include the so-called man-made disasters. Coffey (1998) cites a U.S. Department of Justice statistic stating that rapes, robberies, and armed assaults occur 850,000 times each year; Brewin et al. reported in 1999 that some 20 percent of crime victims suffered from PTSD. In that case we could estimate that some 170,000 individuals might develop PTSD. Feelings of fear and helplessness, and the feeling that one should be able to fight off an attack, contribute to a higher potential for development of PTSD. The September 11, 2001, attacks on the World Trade Center and the Pentagon, and United Airlines Flight 93 which crashed in Pennsylvania, can be considered man-made disasters as well. The loss of over 3,000 lives, combined with the incessant television pictures, may contribute to PTSD even in those not close to the event. The threats of anthrax-contaminated mail following September 11 might bring a sense of danger closer to home as well.

It is important to include disaster workers in the category of those who might develop symptoms of PTSD. Ursano et al. (1999) note that emergency services personnel, body handlers, and military graves registration workers are all likely to have increased rates of PTSD. In the post–September 11 world, we can expect the thousands of disaster workers to be at risk and in need of assistance.

It is important to remember that physical problems may contribute to and interact with PTSD. The traumatic event may include physical as well as psychological wounding. Combat veterans return home paralyzed, or with limbs amputated. Some carry shrapnel the rest of their lives. Others, for example in Vietnam, contracted malaria, which can recur later in life. Assault or auto-accident victims may be injured; rape victims may have been wounded physically. These visible wounds can remind trauma sufferers of their psychological wounds; they may feel less than complete, "less of a person," marked in some way as being different from others. Physical wounds may lead to isolation from others, either of necessity (paraplegics unable to get out as much) or by choice (one veteran with scars from severe burns was embarrassed to be seen in public). On the other hand, a physical and visible disability is often perceived by others as preferable to a mental disability; somehow we can accept the physical problems, but assume that mental ones are under the control of the individual. More than one PTSD sufferer has experienced people, including family and loved ones, telling him/her to "just get over it." Even survivors of the Holocaust find that few seem to want to hear their stories. After all, they survived when so many didn't; they should be grateful and get on with living. That, of course, is precisely what PTSD sufferers have difficulty doing.

Physical issues also arise from the coping mechanisms that some survivors employ. For example, those who seek danger in order to feel alive do indeed experience a rush of heightened awareness. Unfortunately, repeatedly flooding the body with adrenaline has been found to have physical effects. The constant stress on the heart muscle, in particular, can lead to irreparable damage. Perhaps this is one reason that so many Vietnam veterans seem to die relatively young, in their 50s. An informal check of obituaries in one small city in Iowa revealed some thirty deaths of Vietnam War veterans over three years in the late 1990s. The sense of having a shortened life is yet another symptom of PTSD.

The range of possible symptoms can be hard to pin down; what are some of the disorders that are distinct from PTSD?

Subtypes and Related Disorders

There are actually several types of PTSD. Psychiatrists distinguish between acute PTSD (symptoms last less than three months), chronic (symptoms last three months or longer), and/or delayed (symptoms begin six months or more after the original stressful event) (DSM IV, 1994, p. 425). Virtually everyone who experiences a hurricane, earthquake, tornado, or other natural disaster, whose homes and belongings and lives could potentially be lost, will show acute symptoms immediately following the disaster. Those who experience "man-made" disasters, such as the 9/11 attacks, the Oklahoma City bombings, rape, abuse, and violent assault, will also show acute symptoms. They will likely have trouble sleeping, will have recurrent and intrusive memories of the event, and may become hypervigilant, living fearfully in anticipation of another trauma.

While acute symptoms may occur in a high percentage of survivors, the number going on to develop chronic symptoms will be lower, yet still potentially considerable. That is, after some period of time many survivors will find their way back to something like life before the trauma, but a significant number will not. Interestingly, those surviving a "natural" disaster seem to develop chronic PTSD at a lower rate than those living through a "man-made" disaster, like war or assault. Natural disasters, as "acts of God," are perceived as being less under the influence of the individual, thus relieving the individual of some of the responsibility for somehow causing the traumatic event. Unfortunately, there is yet no effective way to predict who will go on to develop life-disabling PTSD and who will not. Resilience is often cited as protective against developing PTSD, and is defined by Hinshaw as including intelligence, flexibility, faith, interpersonal skill, a strong work ethic, and optimism (Hinshaw, 2002). Still, resilience is often an explanation after the fact, rather than a predictive factor, since until one is tested, one may not know what one is capable of handling.

Delayed PTSD seems to be especially associated with the Vietnam War, though World War II vets and others who "got to work" right away, and developed symptoms later, have also been found to have chronic symptoms. In cases of rape and childhood abuse, some survivors find that hypervigilance, distance from others, and self-isolation date from the time of the abuse. The controversial category of recovered memories has become a potential source of explanation for some individuals' difficulties with daily living, but many question whether these are authentic memories that are recovered, or are memories in some way constructed in the present to explain past mysteries.

Several disorders considered distinct from PTSD are described in the DSM IV. One of these is Acute Stress Disorder. This diagnosis is called for when symptoms occur within four weeks of the trauma and are resolved within that time period. The acute subtype of PTSD specifies symptoms resulting within three months. Many of those directly involved in the September 11 attacks might be considered to suffer from Acute Stress Disorder, with symptoms such as emotional numbing, feeling of detachment, and anxiety. If these symptoms persist for more than four weeks, the diagnosis can be changed to PTSD.

Similarly, a diagnosis of Adjustment Disorder is appropriate if the individual's response does not meet the established criteria for PTSD or in situations in which the "symptom pattern of PTSD occurs in response to a stressor that is not extreme (e.g., spouse leaving, being fired)" (DMS IV, p. 427). Again, PTSD requires that the stressful event be perceived as life threatening. An individual experiencing symptoms such as numbing, flashbacks, or sleep disturbances in response to non–life-threatening stressful events is considered to suffer from Adjustment Disorder rather than PTSD.

In Adjustment Disorder, emotional and behavioral symptoms develop within three months, and must be significantly beyond what would be expected. It is unclear whose expectations are used as a benchmark, however. Generally, problems in social or occupational functioning are indicative of an adjustment disorder. Typically, these disorders are expected to resolve in six months unless the stress is ongoing, as with a chronic illness. The DSM IV lists several subtypes of adjustment disorders, and notes that stressors may include business crises, living in high-crime neighborhoods, or natural disasters; it also notes that such a stressor might occur at times of normal developmental events, such as leaving the parental home, getting married, having children, retiring from a job, and so on. Such events in and of themselves would not normally provoke an adjustment disorder, which specifies the individual's response to the event. So stage-of-life changes are not considered Adjustment Disorder unless the individual's response to the change is significantly more severe than would be expected.

Often, Adjustment Disorder is diagnosed only if no other disorder is diagnosable, though it can be diagnosed along with another disorder, particularly if the symptoms are not accounted for by the primary diagnosis. That is, an individual might be diagnosed as suffering from major depression; if he or she is also easily startled or fearful (symptoms not typical of depression), adjustment disorder might be diagnosed in addition to depression. Adjustment disorders may be seen in adolescents navigating their way through their teenage years. In the absence of a major psychiatric disorder, problems getting along with parents or resolving peer disputes fall into the category of adjustment disorders. These are generally expected to resolve as the individual grows and matures (and rarely indicate an underlying problem). Some young people go though these adjustments on their own and some need guidance from a counselor or therapist. Adjustment Disorder may then be a rather vague category for what are expected to be short-term difficulties in life (Staker, 2002).

The DSM IV identifies bereavement as a separate classification, neither Adjustment Disorder nor PTSD. It is, in fact, classified as one of other "conditions that may be a focus of clinical attention" (p. 683). For many years, expectations in American culture of those who lost a close family member were that after a socially defined "appropriate" time of grieving, the individuals "get on with their lives." Earlier this century a year was considered appropriate; then just three months or so were considered enough time. With the publication of Elizabeth Kubler-Ross's influential book *On Death and Dying* in the early 1970s, we came to realize that grief is a process, and that it is unrealistic to expect people to go back to living as though there were no lasting effects. Indeed, it is considered normal to be depressed after the death of someone close, and it is recognized that "normal" durations of grief vary among individuals and cultures. If, however, the individual seems to have strong guilt feelings, thoughts of suicide, preoccupation with feeling worthless, or hallucinatory experiences related to the deceased person, an additional diagnosis might be appropriate; these are considered atypical (and dysfunctional) responses to bereavement. If such symptoms occur with bereavement, an additional diagnosis can be made.

Depression is often considered to be comorbid with PTSD; while it may accompany and result from PTSD, PTSD does not result from depression. Statistics on depression show that more women than men suffer from it, and that middle age is a vulnerable time of life. However, depression in and of itself is not necessarily tied to a traumatic event. Depression may occur seemingly suddenly, but often develops over the course of days or weeks, and may coincide with bereavement or poor physical health.

Some of the symptoms of PTSD and depression overlap, such as loss of interest or pleasure in daily activities, difficulty sleeping, irritability, difficulty concentrating, and suicidal feelings; but depression is classified as a mood disorder, while PTSD is an anxiety disorder. Depression is generally considered according to the individual's affect, and the effects of depressed mood on social or occupational functioning. In contrast, PTSD focuses on a traumatic event or recurrent traumatic events as the source of impaired functioning.

It is not difficult to see how depression might result from PTSD. The characteristic PTSD symptoms of emotional numbing, flashbacks, intense anger, and so on, can certainly cause an individual to feel sad, worthless, and lacking in energy. Still, those with PTSD do not always develop depression, and those with depression will not develop PTSD unless they also suffer a traumatic event.

So how do we specify PTSD as a disorder distinct from depression, bereavement, or adjustment disorders when the symptoms can be similar and the consequences (of impaired social and occupational functioning) nearly identical? Assessment issues are discussed more fully in Chapter Two, but Young (1995) notes that the existence of the traumatic memory particularizes PTSD as distinct from other disorders.

What Is Secondary PTSD?

Secondary PTSD or *vicarious traumatization* (Rosenheck & Nathan, 1985, p. 538) are terms applied to those who do not directly experience a traumatic event, but are exposed on an ongoing basis to those who have. Sometimes the terms are used interchangeably, although Pearlman and Saakvitne (1995) differentiate between the two terms, saying that vicarious traumatization typically applies to trauma workers who empathize with their clients, and whose own personal history might be included (p. 151), while secondary traumatic stress focuses more on symptoms and less on context. A broader term, burnout, is also sometimes used to describe how counselors and disaster workers might feel traumatized themselves as a result of their work.

Families of those with PTSD are certainly not unaffected by its presence. One child recalls the attack on Pearl Harbor and how adults were so frightened; the child concluded that if the adults were afraid, how could the child ever feel safe again? (Tuttle, 1993). In some ways, the fears of that time were mirrored in the children — the parents' anxiety was contagious. Not only that, but society as a whole, with the air raids, safety drills, and blackouts, added to children's uncertainty and resulted in nightmares, difficulty sleeping, and so on. Later, as adults, some of these children still feared airplanes (Tuttle, 1993).

Family members may experience trauma at a distance, as when a father/husband is in a combat situation. It is difficult for a family to manage both the fear of loss and keeping the family focused on its appropriate tasks. At other times, the family member who has suffered a trauma becomes the central focus of the family, and members might feel so sympathetic and attached that they begin to take on the PTSD characteristics themselves, including being hypervigilant, irritable, emotionally numb, or having sleep disturbances. Or family members, in their efforts to cope with the individual's PTSD symptoms, may develop coping strategies that result in impaired functioning, such as codependence or avoidance of the individual, or isolating themselves from the larger family and/or community. It is not uncommon for families of those with PTSD to have limited outside contacts, no supportive friends or family, and a lack of pleasurable activities within the home. Families are a system of interlocking members, and when one member is suffering, their families, both immediate and extended, are, too. This "secondary traumatization" has the potential to affect following generations. This is discussed in greater detail beginning in Chapter Three.

Finally, caregivers, whether in the family or outside, may identify so closely with the survivor that they see themselves as fellow victims (Valent, 1995). Spouses of veterans battling the Veteran's Administration for benefits and/or insurance may well feel victimized by the system. Social workers or counselors may begin to feel overwhelmed by the survivor's needs and difficulties, and may become irritable, have trouble sleeping, and so on. Those who work with PTSD individuals may need some attention as well.

PTSD has become more widely understood, but has not yet achieved the same public recognition that grief or depression have as mental health issues. Descriptions of syndromes that sound much like PTSD can be found in the Greek classics and indeed, in literature throughout time. As our understanding has matured, our diagnostic tools and cross-cultural understanding have improved as well. The next chapter discusses diagnosis of PTSD and related issues.

Traumatic Brain Injury

Traumatic brain injury (TBI) is an injury to the brain that results from a fall, an auto accident, a combat explosion, a blow to the head, or the entry of an object into the brain. TBI is not new; mild TBIs are often called concussions and result from bicycle accidents, sports injuries, and so on. However, the wars in Iraq and Afghanistan (particulary Iraq, where IEDs have been widespread), have led to greater public awareness of TBI. An IED blast can cause the head to snap forward or back; the brain itself doesn't move but as a result of the head's movement, the brain may hit the skull and become damaged.

The U.S. Department of Defense has tracked TBIs and finds that the numbers of diagnosed cases has steadily risen since the year 2000. In that year, 10,963 cases were diagnosed. In 2009, some 27,862 cases were reported (DVBIC.org, 2010).

TBI injuries are classified as mild, moderate, or severe. Mild TBI symptoms include disorientation for less than 24 hours, a loss of consciousness for 30 minutes or less, and memory loss up to 24 hours. Most individuals seem to recover without permanent damage or specialized treatments. Moderate TBI symptoms include disorientation for more than 24 hours, loss of consciousness longer than 30 minutes but less than 24 hours, and memory loss from 24 hours to seven days in length.

In 2009, severe TBI was diagnosed in fewer than 300 cases, with moderate being diagnosed in over 3,000, meaning the great majority of cases were diagnosed as mild TBI (DVBIC.org, 2010). Severe TBI is diagnosed when disorientation and loss of consciousness last more than 24 hours, and when memory loss lasts more than 7 days. In diagnosing TBI and its level of severity, physicians look at eye movement and opening in response to stimuli (such as speech or pain); verbal responses that can range from confused to nonexistent; and physical responses including no response, an abnormal reflex, and withdrawal from pain (DVBIC.org, 2010).

Symptoms immediately after the injury include some degree of amnesia, confusion, and possible loss of consciousness. However, additional or other symptoms may appear later, and these should be watched for. Physical symptoms include headaches (the more severe, the worse the injury), pain, tiredness, difficulty sleeping, and possible difficulties with seeing or focusing. Emotional and cognitive difficulties may also develop, including irritability, difficulty concentrating, physical aggression, impulsive behavior, personality change, and depression (MIRECC, Department of Veterans Affairs, 2010). In part, it is the emotional and cognitive symptoms, along with possible depression and difficulty sleeping, that have led the military to group PTSD and TBI in a similar category for the purposes of treatment.

Treatment protocols for TBI in a combat situation involve stabilizing the individual, particularly the neck and spine to prevent further injury, and working to make sure the blood supply and flow to the brain and other parts of the body is adequate. Additional testing may be done, including x-rays or computerized imaging, to identify fractures or cracks and so on (NIH.gov, 2010) Sometimes swelling results from a TBI and in that event, fluids must be drained from around the brain.

Depending on the severity of the TBI, there may be a need for physical therapy, occupational therapy, speech therapy, counseling or psychiatric assistance, and disability services. While most individuals who suffer from mild TBI with recover with no difficulty, those with moderate or severe TBI may need ongoing care and support which may change over the course of time. Recovery from TBIs is difficult to predict, and each individual may need a different set of tools.

TBI is also conflated with PTSD because brains that have been injured may continue to release stress hormones beyond what is continued normal (which is that these hormones are released in response to a crisis, and then decrease, returning the body's blood pressure and blood flow to normal levels). These hormones are implicated in the development of PTSD and later physical ailments. At Fort Campbell in Kentucky, PTSD and TBIs were seen as directly correlated to an alarming increase in suicides on base in early 2009 (Thompson, *Time*, 2010). Both medical and psychiatric resources have been severely stressed by the high levels of PTSD and TBI, at this base and many others, and so treatment may be inadequate or lacking for the sufferers. Worse, the lack of trained medical professionals may mean that the problem is being underdiagnosed and therefore untreated (Tanielian and Jaycox, eds., 2008).

For potential suffers of PTSD the issue of diagnosis is critical, and a variety and combination of instruments are used to properly diagnose the disorder. These are described in the next chapter.

CHAPTER 2

How Is PTSD Diagnosed, and by Whom?

History ... is a nightmare from which I am trying to awake (James Joyce, *Ulysses*, 1914).

All you can think is, "If I can survive this moment, then that is the greatest gift I could have" (Hmong refugee, Faderman, 1998, p. 48).

I couldn't ride in an elevator, because when those doors closed I was inside a cage again. So much of my life was tailored to keeping me out of situations that would trigger that terror. And I also despised myself for that weakness (Kim, 2000, p. 193).

The past is never dead. It's not even past (William Faulkner, 1948).

The diagnosis of PTSD is more complex than appears on the surface. PTSD is typically diagnosed with reference to the DSM IV's diagnostic criteria (see Appendix A). Those criteria first require that an individual "has been exposed to a traumatic event" (p.427), that the event was life-threatening to either the individual or to other persons, and that the individual responded to the event with "intense fear, helplessness, or horror" (p. 428). The event, the threat, and the response to the threat are key parts of the diagnosis.

The September 11 attacks on the World Trade Center and Pentagon are without doubt traumatic events. Individuals immediately involved must have felt that their personal safety or the safety of others was threatened; furthermore, their reactions to the events included great horror or helplessness. All three elements are confirmed for those immediately impacted. But what about those who watched the attacks on television, at a distance? We were not truly physically threatened, and yet may have felt equally fearful and unsafe. Were we exposed to a traumatic event? Did we feel that our lives or the lives of others were threatened? And did we react with fear and helplessness? The answer to all three is yes, for many of us. But because of our physical distance from the stressor event, we would not likely be diagnosed with PTSD; perhaps we would be given a lesser diagnosis of a stress syndrome. Yet there are surely many who watched in horror and fascination the repeated tapes of the planes slamming into the towers, and who to some extent have flashbacks or relive the moments of that day. How do we evaluate an individual's subjective response?

In diagnosing PTSD, the first task to be accomplished is confirming the existence of a traumatic event. This seems to be a concrete and verifiable step, yet it is known that traumatic events can result in temporary or permanent amnesia of the event. Confirmation may be available, for example, for those who have been in war, where a psychiatrist might request military records as evidence of trauma, in additional to the survivor's personal testimony. The military keeps records of events, casualties, lessons learned, and medals awarded, all of which may be evidence of traumatic events. In addition, others who served with the individual may be able to attest to particular events.

For survivors of torture, there may be physical scars that attest to the violence. Survivors of incest or rape may, however, have more difficulty providing physical evidence of the trauma. Then the survivor's memory, and perhaps the memories and/or confessions of others, are relied on. Some survivors find their testimony questioned, as in the case of "recovered memory." There are some who doubt that memories recovered years after the abuse are authentic, in part because memory is subjective and influenced by later events, people, and thoughts. Those survivors may have a more difficult time providing proof of an original stressor. But it may not be necessary to "prove" the traumatic event; if an individual is seeking treatment, such proof may not be necessary. If, however, an official diagnosis is necessary for insurance or disability benefits, evidence might be required.

In all cases, a qualified psychiatrist is the individual charged with determining a diagnosis. However, a variety of instruments may be employed to assist in the diagnosis. These are described below according to the type of instrument used.

Surveys are self-report instruments that are commonly used, easy to administer, and fairly inexpensive. The Traumatic Stress Schedule (TSS) asks clients if they have experienced robbery, physical assault, sexual assault, loss of a loved one, personal injury, serious property loss, evacuation in response to a dangerous event, motor vehicle accident with injury, or some other "terrifying" experience (Friedman, 2001, p. 79). Other self-report instruments include the Potential Stressful Experiences Inventory (PSEI), which seeks to assess lifetime exposure to traumas; the Traumatic Events Questionnaire (TEQ), which evaluates the severity of the threat associated with the trauma; and the Evaluation of Lifetime Stressors (ELS), which begins with a self-report survey and is followed by an interview with the diagnostician (Friedman, 2001, p. 80).

Adults may also be asked to complete the Trauma Assessment for Adults — Sept-report (TAA), which is a 17 item scale that uses yes/no questions related to a number of possible stressors, including combat, assault, car accident, and so on. The Trauma History Questionnaire (THQ) similarly uses yes/no questions but adds frequency and age at time of event. The Trauma Screening Questionnaire (TSQ) uses yes/no questions but asks about symptoms which are directly related to the DSM-IV criteria, such as anxiety when reminded of the event and so on. The PTSD Checklist (PCL) is used for screening, diagnosing, and assessing change of symptoms over time. There are three versions, one directed at military audiences, one civilian, and one focused on a particular event. There are other surveys as well; the National Center for PTSD (www.ptsd.va.gov) has descriptions and examples of these.

While most surveys are designed for adults, a few are directed at children, particularly older children. The Child PTSD Symptom Scale (CPSS) is one example. It is a 26-item measure including events, symptoms, and impairments with answers on a scale ranging from "not at all" or "absent" to "multiple times per week" or "present." The scale produces a score that indicates severity of symptoms and impairments (National Center for PTSD).

Another category of diagnostic tool is scales, used and administered by a trained individual, and including instruments that ask the individual to report experiences that might be considered stressful events, such as childhood abuse, domestic violence, torture, or combat exposure. In each case, the purpose is to attempt to use instruments that show some degree of reliability and validity across a population of survivors. The Clinician

Administered PTSD Scale (CAPS) measures severity by assessing both the intensity and frequency of PTSD symptoms (Friedman, 2001). Other instruments narrow the focus to the specific symptoms of PTSD. Among them are the PTSD Symptom scale (PSS), the Keane PTSD Scale (PK) derived from the Minnesota Multiphasic Personality Inventory (MMPI) (Foa, Keane, and Friedman, 2000), the Impact of Event Scale-Revised (IES-R), the Mississippi Scale for Combat-Related PTSD (M-PTSD), the Trauma Symptom Checklist–40 (TSC-40) and the Trauma Symptom Inventory (TSI). These may be selected by the diagnostician according to the nature of the original traumatic event; for example, the Mississippi Scale for combat veterans, the Trauma Symptom Checklist for adults who were sexually abused as children, and the PTSD Symptom Scale for rape victims (Friedman, 2001).

A valuable screening tool for a primary care physician is a simple four-item measure, used by a general practitioner, to identify individuals who should be referred for PTSD diagnosis. The questions are yes/no and relate to the PTSD symptoms of avoidance, vigilance, emotional numbing, and reexperiencing (flashbacks or intrusive memories). This simple measure is a valuable tool for identifying those who may not realize they are suffering from a diagnosable and treatable condition (National Center for PTSD).

Paper and pen measures, whether doctor administered or self-reported, are useful because they can be used to gather data from a larger population, can be used pre- and post-events, and can be assessed for reliability (consistency) and validity. They have shortcomings, however, as they may miss important information by not asking the right questions, or they may be inaccurate, as when an individual chooses not to self-report honestly. In any event, for a diagnosis of PTSD to be made, an interview by a trained professional is required. Interviews are more time-consuming but richer in the data they provide the clinician. It can be harder to judge reliability and validity in interviews, which are often subjective in nature. However, there are several instruments that seek to overcome subjectivity. The PTSD Module of the Structured Clinical Interview for DSM-IV (SCID), developed by the National Center for PTSD (Friedman, 2001). Having a structured interview instrument provides some consistency in diagnosis while also allowing for individualized responses. Its comprehensiveness permits identifying comorbid (co-occurring) disorders (AXIS 1) but it does not evaluate severity of the trauma. It also requires trained clinicians, as do most if not all of the diagnostic instruments. In a 1999 study investigating diagnoses of long-term numbing and avoidance symptoms among Buffalo Creek (W.Va.) flood survivors, Honig et al. (1999) found that the SCID failed to capture some of the symptoms of PTSD, in particular missing avoidance and numbing symptoms. The authors used a less structured clinical interview and assert that, by doing so, they were better able to recognize resistance during the interview and uncover more signs of avoidance and numbing (Honig et al., 1999). Again, such an interview requires a trained interviewer with some experience with PTSD.

The Structured Interview for PTSD (SI-PTSD) is another example which focuses on symptoms, frequency, and severity; the 17 PTSD items relate to the diagnostic criteria in the DSM-IV. There are instruments designed for children as well; the Children's PTSD Inventory (CPTSDI) and the Childhood PTSD Interview. The inventory asks a broader set of questions while the interview allows for more in-depth probing (National Center for PTSD).

Other measures may be used which are not directly focused on PTSD. One widely used tool is the Minnesota Multiphasic Personality Index (MMPI), which consists of a set of ten scales designed to measure personality types and mental disorders (Young, 1995). With 399 yes/no questions, the MMPI is supposed to be difficult to "cheat" on, making it a reliable measurement tool, and a well-regarded starting point. Results may then be used to determine which more specific tools would be most useful.

The task of the diagnostician, then, is to administer the appropriate measurement tools, conduct at least one interview with the client, and draw some conclusions about whether the individual can be diagnosed with PTSD, and if so, what the symptoms and their severities are. PTSD individuals can vary widely in the specific symptoms they present, and a trained and experienced diagnostician is best able to comprehensively assess PTSD. At the Veteran's Administration, clinicians also want to confirm that the PTSD results from a service-connected trauma, and must determine the degree of disability for compensation purposes. The VA's diagnosis process might include multiple interviews with the survivor, perhaps group meetings with other psychiatrists, and physical checkups as well. When a veteran files a claim for PTSD, family members and friends are asked to write letters describing the individual's daily functioning, how that individual changed after the traumatic event, and descriptions of interpersonal relationships. All of this evidence becomes part of the diagnostic procedure.

While the assessment of PTSD may seem to be relatively straightforward, given the existing instruments, structured interviews, and trained clinicians, areas of contention still exist. Some of the ongoing issues in PTSD diagnosis are discussed next.

Diagnosis of Traumatic Brain Injury

Traumatic brain injury (TBI) may be easily assessed by medical personnel on the scene; an obvious physical injury to the head should certainly be followed by efforts to measure short term and/or long term damage. Beyond obvious physical damage, however, TBI should be confirmed and specified, preferably by brain imaging technology (CAT scan, MRI, PET scan), physical, occupational and speech therapists to measure specific impairments, and assessment by a trained neurologist to evaluate cognitive functioning and possible deficits. A commonly used scale, the Glasgow Coma Scale, measures motor response, verbal response, and eye response in order to categorize TBI as mild, moderate, or severe (Traumaticbraininjury.com). Typically, the more severe the injury, the poorer outlook for treatment and progress. However, it is always important to remember that brain injuries are highly specific to the individual, and factors beyond the physical may have an impact on recovery (motivation, support systems, and so on).

Issues in Diagnosis

The diagnosis of PTSD depends on exposure to some traumatic event, and in many cases, traumatic events are easy to establish. Survivors of combat, terrorist attacks, personal assault, or natural disasters might be assumed to have experienced a traumatic event. Yet such a survivor might find it difficult to talk about the event, or might have buried it deeply in memory because it is so painful. To take a combat veteran back to events which he or she clearly finds distressing may be difficult to do, particularly early in an interview, before a relationship has been achieved between the counselor or psychiatrist and the client. Some clinicians might diagnose PTSD in the absence of any remembered traumatic event, based on symptoms the individual is showing. As Young (1995) points out, one of the symptoms of PTSD is difficulty recalling details of the traumatic event (p. 289). In other words, if the individual exhibits PTSD symptoms, but cannot recall an original stressor, then the lack of recall may confirm the diagnosis of PTSD. But if PTSD can only be diagnosed with reference to an original stressor, and that memory is hard to recover, how can PTSD be definitively established?

Even upon establishing the traumatic event, PTSD cannot be diagnosed with certainty. The DSM IV criteria further state that the individual's response must have included great fear or helpless feelings. Not all who are exposed to traumatic events go on to develop PTSD; thus the diagnostician also has to evaluate the survivor's reaction to the trauma. Perhaps the survivor responded to the trauma with great courage and competence, and the feelings of fear and helplessness develop later. Perhaps emergency workers expect to be exposed to trauma and therefore do not respond with fear or helplessness. Perhaps some who are exposed do not realize how close they might have been to death or severe injury and thus they too might not respond with strong feelings of fear. Finally, for those whose symptoms developed many years after the event, as with delayed-onset PTSD, fearful or helpless responses can be difficult to gauge.

Young (1995) points out that the DSM III-R (1987, "revised") included the description of the event as being "outside the range of usual human experience and that would be markedly distressing to almost anyone" (p. 124). That is, the stressor is abnormal but the individual is normal in his/her reaction to the trauma. Young then points out that many diagnosticians would consider it sufficient to establish that the traumatic event was distressing to the particular client being assessed, regardless of whether the event would be distressing to anyone else. He further notes that some of the events considered traumatic for Vietnam War veterans, for example, were not experienced as traumatic at the time. It has been speculated that the killing of hundreds of civilians at My Lai may have been psychologically stress relieving at the time, as soldiers avenged their comrades killed on previous occasions. He also points out that "outside the range of usual human experience" should be interpreted in its sociocultural context, taking note of community standards and expectations. In some parts of the world, violence is more a part of daily life. The author recalls that in Colombia in the early 1980s, violent street crime and guerrilla and narcotics activities made violence almost predictable. Avoiding dangerous areas and trying to avoid stray bullets was simply part of the day's activities, and not considered particularly stressful.

The American Psychiatric Association, in the DSM IV, revised the diagnostic criteria for PTSD, omitting "outside the range of usual human experience and that would be markedly distressing to almost anyone," with the result that a wider range of events might meet the criteria. Young (1995) notes that by specifying that the event must be perceived as life-threatening to the individual, it is now necessary to consider that some events which might be regarded as benign to one person could be perceived as highly threatening to another. The individual's *perception* of his/her experience is thus critical to the diagnosis. The diagnostician needs a high level of skill and repeated meetings to be able to accurately assess an individual's perception of events, and to determine how stressful the event is to the individual being diagnosed. Proposed revisions to the diagnostic criteria in the DMS V downplay the individual's perception and use the wording "actual or threatened serious injury...." Perception is implied, to some extent, but the assessment of threat may also be inferred by the diagnostician (APA).

In short, though a number of instruments exist, and though there are established criteria for diagnosing PTSD, it is simply not possible to superficially conclude that anyone exposed to an event that elicits sympathy from most of us must be suffering from PTSD. The growing public awareness has been helpful in lessening the stigma of the disorder, but has also resulted in individuals claiming to have PTSD who have not experienced a traumatic event. Or perhaps it is that traumatic events are now a much broader category. One young woman who had a near-wreck on a dark road is now afraid to drive on that road at night; she claims to suffer from PTSD (yet looks blankly at her combat-veteran father who questions her self-diagnosis). Nevertheless, the fact that some might be frivolous in their understanding and use of the term does not detract from the very real experiences of many whose symptoms are severely disabling.

CHAPTER 3

Who Is at Risk for PTSD?
Can PTSD be Prevented?

Everything can be taken from a man but one thing: the last of the human freedoms — to choose one's attitude in any given set of circumstances, to choose one's own way" (Viktor Frankl, 1959, p. 86).

He was the life of every party.... He came back somber, dark, morose, depressed and occasionally angry (Father of Iraq War combat soldier, April 2, 2010).

Can PTSD Be Predicted?

Who is at risk for PTSD? Is everyone equally likely to develop PTSD after a traumatic experience? We know that not everyone who is exposed to a trauma will develop PTSD; in fact, the range is from 15 to 30 percent, depending on the severity of the event and other factors. If not everyone will develop PTSD, can we identify those who will? Are there risk factors and can we identify them? Is PTSD predictable?

If we could predict who would develop PTSD following a trauma, we could screen those most at risk and guide them away from occupations or activities that might lead them encounter traumatic events (combat, firefighting, paramedic or emergency room training). We could perhaps provide some kind of training and/or preparation such that at-risk individuals would be less likely to develop PTSD. We could potentially plan for immediate intervention and treatments that might prevent the development of PTSD. What does research tell us about who is most likely to develop PTSD?

49

Investigating risk factors for PTSD is not a new idea; indeed, such research began in tandem with the inclusion of PTSD in the DSM as an official diagnosis. Early studies tended to focus on the nature of the traumatic event, and found that the severity of the event and the frequency of exposure to traumatic events were clear risk factors for PTSD. These are still considered strong predictors, but again, not everyone exposed to the same severe trauma or to the same frequency of trauma will go on to develop PTSD. Therefore, there has been increased interest in potential individual factors. Several reviews of existing research have attempted to consolidate what we know about individual risk factors, which can be grouped into three categories: emotional/cognitive factors, biological/physical factors, and social/contextual factors.

Risk Factors for PTSD

In the Department of Defense's Strategic Plan for fiscal years 2010–12, Goal 4 is to "ensure superior care and support for the Total Force and their families." Subgoal 4.4 specifically focuses on suicide prevention, resilience programs, and early intervention. The military uses screening measures to try to identify "psychological distress" and then refer soldiers for additional evaluation.

The DoD's efforts to prevent PTSD are worth noting; at this time it is not possible to predict who may develop PTSD, though some factors are known to increase risk, such as a weak social support system, severity of trauma, and multiple deployments. The military has implemented various surveys that soldiers fill out before, during, and after deployment, and are also using brain scans, DNA, and other physical measures to identify those who may be at risk. Such research has yet to yield definitive results. It may be helpful to look at risk factors in several categories: emotional, biological, and contextual.

Emotional/cognitive factors: Personality characteristics that may be predictive of PTSD include having an avoidant or antisocial personality (Breslau, 1998; cited in Halligan & Yehuda, 2000). Such individuals are less likely to have or to avail themselves of the social support that we know is important for healthy functioning. Psychological difficulties preceding the traumatic event are also a risk factor (Mayo Clinic, NIMH, 2009); it seems that the specific difficulty (depression, anxiety) is less important than the exact nature of the difficulty. Macklin et al. (1998; cited in Halligan and Yehuda, 2000) also found that a lower IQ was somewhat predictive of developing PTSD, though it is possible that a lower IQ may lead to more exposure to trauma. While these factors are suggestive, it is premature to say they are predictive. In virtually every case, there are interaction effects (avoidant personality with little social support, anxiety heightening the sense of trauma). Much more research will be needed to tease apart the contributing factors.

Biological/physical factors: Several studies have looked at families for clues to the development of PTSD. Having a parent or close relative with PTSD or depression has been found to increase risk (Mayo Clinic, NIMH, 2009). Children of Holocaust survivors, for example, are at high risk. However, is this a biological/genetic factor? Or is it due to the influences of family patterns of beliefs and behaviors? True et al. (1993; cited in Halligan & Yehuda, 2000) conducted a study of twins to find out if there were a genetic contribution. They found that up to 30 percent of symptoms could be attributed to a shared genetic background, which is an intriguing finding that needs to be replicated in more focused research studies. Finally, lower cortisol levels (a stress hormone in the body) seemed to be related to later PTSD (Halligan & Yehuda, 2000). This is a fascinating area of research; Slater et al. (2009) looked at biochemistry to identify risk factors for suicide. They found that levels of neurotransmitters in the brain (such as dopamine and serotonin) were different in individuals with suicidal ideation. A physical test could be used in conjunction with professional medical evaluations to determine who might be at risk of considering and/or attempting suicide.

Social/contextual factors: Again, as noted above, previous traumatization and severity of the traumatic event continue to be identified as risk factors for developing PTSD. In addition, family instability, lower educational level, divorce or death of a partner, lower socioeconomic status, and possibly gender were all found to be possible risk factors for PTSD (Halligan & Yehuda, 2000). However, it is difficult to ascertain whether these are factors in and of themselves, or factors which lead to a greater liklihood of experiencing trauma. Women, for example, may be at greater risk for assault, such as rape or domestic violence, and it is the assault which is the predictive factor. Factors such as having family and social support have been found to be protective factors against developing PTSD (Mayo Clinic; NIMH, 2009).

The military has been researching the area of predictability as well, with the goal of identifying and perhaps preventing PTSD in its troops. In reports regarding the military or presented by the Department of Defense, taking a life puts a soldier at greater risk of developing PTSD. Multiple deployments, not merely because they provide the opportunity for exposure, but because they entail a great deal of stress themselves, are also risk factors for developing PTSD. Longer deployments also increase the risk of developing PTSD (Real Warriors Campaign, Department of Defense).

Finally, a landmark study by Brewin et al. (2000) analyzed a number of studies in order to try to isolate and identify risk factors. The studies were varied in many ways: number of subjects, areas of focus, methodology of studies, etc, and this made it a challenge to isolate the factors that were truly significant. The authors conducted a meta-analysis on 14 separate risk factors, including gender, age, socioeconomic status, education, psychiatric history, previous trauma, family psychiatric history, trauma severity, lack of social support, and others. Their findings revealed that gender, for example, contributes relatively little when military and civilian populations are considered as a whole (women tend to be more at risk from rape, men from combat). More importantly, trauma intensity and post-trauma factors such as family support were more predictive of developing PTSD than pretrauma factors, such as previous psychological difficulties or previous traumatic experiences. The authors suggest that perhaps the reaction to a previous experience is more important than the event itself; if an individual coped well with a previous traumatic experience, that individual might be less likely to develop PTSD following another traumatic event. Given the number of confounding factors, the analysis suggests areas for further focused research.

Can PTSD Be Prevented?

Given that PTSD is difficult to predict for any one individual, but fairly easy to predict for a population exposed to trauma (combat soldiers, survivors of natural disasters), research has been conducted in an effort to find and implement ways to prevent PTSD from developing in an at-risk population.

Early intervention is held to be effective; one study discovered that intervention with medical treatment can be helpful. A study investigating the role of morphine, for example, found that soldiers receiving morphine directly after injury were less likely to develop PTSD than those who did not receive morphine (the authors speculate that other opiates would have similar results). Perhaps the morphine, in alleviating pain and anxiety, prevents the development or consolidation of traumatic memories (Wilson, 2010). Certainly it would not be difficult to implement this as a standard of care; nevertheless, not all who develop PTSD have experienced a physical injury.

In addition, the military also seeks to prevent stress disorders by providing predeployment resiliency training. Essentially a cognitive behavioral approach, the training asks participants to challenge assumptions and learn new ways of perceiving situations. For example, catastrophizing is when we assume the worst though there is no evidence to support it. A family member mentions having a cold and the soldier imagines a life threatening illness which is being kept from him/her. Becoming enraged at a perceived unfair assignment may be avoided by seeing the assignment as evidence of strength and reliability. In essence, resiliency training seeks to provide better emotional coping skills. Will it work? The culture of the military typically downgrades the importance of emotion, but the military hopes that adding resiliency training to physical training will be accepted and will prove to help prevent stress disorders. Plans to evaluate the success of such recently implemented programs are included in the programs.

Identifying severe stress levels during combat is a second area of attention. There are several aspects of this area. First, medics and corpsmen receive special training to recognize the signs of severe stress and respond. One program, titled Battlemind Warrior Resiliency Training, uses what is called the TAIL light effect:

Tell the soldier you are concerned;
All soldiers are affected by war and should watch out for each other;
Insist that the soldier see someone, such as a chaplain or higher level medical professional;
Look for ways to help — accompany them, make a phone call, and so on.

Medics are also asked to share their training with others in order to increase awareness. And medics are also susceptible to severe stress and thus are told to watch for symptoms within themselves.

Another educational initiative has been a program called ACE, which involves distributing cards with an ace of hearts to military personnel encouraging them to *Ask, Care, Escort* fellow soldiers who may be under stress. Symptoms such as drug or alcohol abuse, dangerous personal behaviors, and dramatic changes in behavior are all given as signs that require attention.

There are several U.S.–based programs that focus on retaining soldiers in the military by addressing stress difficulties. One of these is the Montana National Guard's Yellow Ribbon program, prompted by guard member who committed suicide after serving in Iraq. The program provides soldiers and their families a weekend together in a non-military setting and offers them information on programs available to assist them, including educational benefits and counseling. During deployment, the families are contacted at least once a month, and upon arriving home, both soldiers and their families are given debriefings, informed about signs of PTSD, and encouraged to maintain bonds both with their combat colleagues and their families. As a follow-up, the Montana National Guard also assesses the mental health of each guard member every 6 months for two years. The program is being considered for use nationally.

A couple of other programs are the Warrior Combat Stress Reset Program at Ft. Hood, Texas, which provides three weeks of structured activities that include group and individual counseling, behavioral training such as coping skills and biofeedback, and alternative therapies such as yoga, acupuncture, and massage. A similar program at Ft. Bliss, Texas, is called the Restoration and Resilience Center. It focuses on soldiers diagnosed with PTSD who want to remain in the military. This is a six month residential treatment with three months of follow up care. It too includes alternative therapies such as a meditation room, acupuncture, and yoga, along with cognitive behavioral therapy, and counseling.

By far, the largest initiative undertaken by the military to address both suicide and PTSD in troops is the Real Warriors Campaign, a product of the Defense Centers of Excellence for Psychological Health. This is a wide reaching program that tries to fight the stigma attached to seeking help for psychological problems.

Real Warriors Campaign

Real Warriors is essentially a campaign that first, seeks to demonstrate that there is no shame in seeking help. Accordingly, it uses print materials, media outlets, and social networking that highlight stories of "real warriors" who sought and received help, and as a result are succeeding in their military or civilian lives. Real Warriors has a page on Facebook that sends multiple notifications daily. It also uses youtube videos, twitter, and other similar media. The campaign partners with a variety of other units, such as the VA, local public health partners, private practice clinicians, and so on; part of the campaign is to inform those interested of resources that they may not be aware of.

The initiative also has six different centers. The Center for Deployment Psychology trains mental health professionals. The Center for the Study of Traumatic Stress focuses on education and outreach for best practices in mental health treatment. The Deployment Health Clinical Center helps with assessment for post-deloyment stress for military and families.

The Defense and Veterans Brain Injury Center focuses on medical care and initiatives for those with TBI, traumatic brain injury, which according to military professionals has much in common with PTSD (memory issues in particular). The National Center for Telehealth and Technology, as might be guessed, uses technology to reach those whose access might be limited due to mobility issues or a rural environoment. And the National Intrepid Center of Excellence investigates and tests new approaches and innovative techniques in the diagnosis and treatment of PTSD and TBI.

Two other aspects of Real Warriors are important. First, there is a resource called "Army One Source" which seeks to gather in one place all the programs, referrals, services, and so on so that soldiers and families can go to one site for multiple needs rather than try to sort through what might be available in a variety of places. Second, the Real Warriors Campaign, though it does use the term PTSD, also uses the term "battlemind." Battlemind is defined as "the Soldier's inner strength to face fear and adversity with courage." The problem of course is that "battlemind" is vital in combat but problematic in civilian life. There are several documents related to battlemind on the Army's Behavioral Health page, including advice on how to transition from combat to home. Battlemind is actually an acronym, but it is so long that it is probably not very helpful. It stands for Buddies, Accountability, Targeted aggression, Tactical awareness, Lethally armed, Emotional control, Mission operational security, Individual responsibility, Non-defensive (combat) driving, Discipline and ordering.

These campaigns, programs, and approaches are real initiatives with funding, staffing, and organization. How successful are they likely to be in lowering suicide and stress disorders in active duty military?

The Bliss program and others may have an impact. They work with individuals, in a group setting which is in a military environment. If they also involve the family, there is greater opportunity for success. IF the participants do not feel stigmatized or intimidated, they may well be able to work through their traumas with others who understand and accept. Enlisted men and women are more likely to participate, as the officer corps still likely considers mental health assistance to be a detriment to their careers. The key to these programs is to note what aspects are successful and apply them more widely, while still allowing flexibility for local conditions.

Efforts to instruct medics in recognizing severe stress symptoms, and encouraging "battle buddies" may also be successful. These efforts take advantage of the soldiers' commitment to one another. As in Vietnam, many may say they are fighting for and with each other, not with a particular larger political goal in mind. This bond among soldiers on the ground may lead them to care for each other not only for physical wounds but for psychological ones as well. Again, it is more likely to succeed with enlisted soldiers rather than officers.

Women deserve a special mention here; although they are not technically in combat positions, they are certainly serving in combat operations and support. Women in the military feel they must prove their strength and so would be less willing to admit to mental distress. Opportunities for women to talk with other women are essential.

The multifaceted Real Warriors campaign is an interesting initiative. It seeks to do no less than change the culture of the military. How successful will it be? We have seen cultural changes resulting from massive advertising, education and propaganda efforts. Antismoking, antidrug, and anti–drunk driving campaigns can all point to some measure of success. However, these campaigns do have target audiences, such as elementary school children or high school students. The Real Warriors Campaign is aimed at a military audience. That audience is not a general population; enlistment is voluntary and therefore may attract individuals with greater interest in the military or in combat; i.e., those with a larger dose of "warrior" thinking in the first place. They may be harder to convince. We should also not assume that all 19 to 25-year-olds spend great amounts of time on Facebook or Twitter or even the internet in general. They may, but it isn't likely to be across the board. The message of Real Warriors is delivered in a number of ways, but it is heavily biased toward technology. It shouldn't be difficult, actually, for the military to track how often its pages are visited; if it does so, it will be better able to assess the success of its message and methodology.

It is true that while those in combat operations are enlisted personnel, a large number may never have expected to be deployed in actual combat. National Guard units in particular may be more representative of the general population. It is essential that the military analyze its approach and results to achieve success.

It is fortunate that PTSD has become less stigmatized and more public in recent years. Raising awareness of the issue, illustrating that PTSD is not a form of personal weakness, and devoting greater resources to prediction, prevention, and treatment of PTSD are all positive signs of progress, both in the military and in civilian spheres.

CHAPTER 4

Cross-Cultural Perspectives: Is PTSD a Universal Disorder?

An old woman whose only son dies asks a holy man for help in making him live again. The holy man sends her to find a mustard seed from a home that has not known sadness and grief. Each home she visits has had tragedies, and she stays to help as she herself understands what loss is. In the process, she heals herself (and of course never finds a family, rich or poor, that hasn't suffered) (Chinese folktale in Kusher, 1989, p. 110–111).

"Where was God in Auschwitz?" ... it was not God who caused it. It was caused by human beings choosing to be cruel to their fellow man (Kusher, 1989, p. 81).

While the United States may be thought of as a fairly cohesive society with shared values, we do have subcultures with distinct experiences and values. Immigrant communities bring their cultures with them, and may interpret events according to their original cultures. Italians, Poles, Chinese — all who come in sufficient numbers to form communities in the U.S. — may maintain some or many of their former values. Marrying young or entering into an arranged marriage might be expected and accepted in an Indian community and hence not stressful. Becoming a second or third wife might be accepted cultural practice to some, while to a young American girl it might be an alarming prospect.

Refugees who resettle in the U.S. might have been traumatized by having to flee their homes and country. Southeast Asian refugees, who faced harrowing boat rides with fears of attack, rape and robbery by pirates, surely experienced traumatic events. And refugees, unlike immigrants, have fled a country rather than having chosen a new home. Thus the "reward" for surviving their journey may merely be the absence of continued repression rather than the presence of opportunity. That is not to say that refugees are unwilling resettlers — they may choose where they resettle; for example, Vietnamese "boat people" have resettled in Australia, France, Northern Europe, Canada and the U.S. But the immigrant experience may be distinguished from the refugee experience by the greater sense of control over one's fate, which helps deter the development of PTSD. How prevalent is PTSD in American subcultures?

The Hispanic population in the U.S. is growing rapidly, and in some areas of the country Hispanics constitute a majority of the population. According to Canive and Castillo (1997), Hispanics were the second largest American minority in the Vietnam War, and more than 19 percent were either wounded or killed. In addition, 29 percent of Hispanics who served in Vietnam were diagnosable with PTSD (National Vietnam Veterans Readjustment Study), compared to 20 percent of European Americans (p. 1). For this population, the diagnosis of PTSD is problematical in part because diagnostic instruments tend to be developed with reference to the European-American perspective, which doesn't necessarily take into account variables that are important to Hispanic Americans, such as religion, family, expectations of direct advice, and tendencies, especially among males, to equate needing help with being weak (Canive & Castillo, 1997). Similarly, PTSD treatments developed for Americans of European background might not be successful with Hispanic Americans.

Marsella et al. (1990) also point out that both Hispanics and African Americans who served in Vietnam have higher rates of PTSD than Anglo Americans; in part, they say, this may be attributed to their different experiences in battle. Minorities might have been stereotyped or experienced racial discrimination, they may have felt that they were fighting on behalf of rights that they felt were not theirs at home, and they may have found the traditional military structure incompatible with their own cultural upbringing. In the diagnosis of PTSD, Marsella et al. (1990) point out that "individuals from non–Western cultural traditions often fail to present classical symptoms of these disorders and are misdiagnosed as suffering from somatic disorders" (p. 2). Further, they note that standard treatments may fail with these populations, as their perceptions of illness and health, treatment and support, may be different from those developed by the larger European-American culture.

Native Americans also suffer from PTSD at higher rates than does the general population (Robin et al., 1997). In a study of almost 600 members of a southwestern American Indian community, researchers found a lifetime rate of about 22 percent. Combat experience was a predictor for males, and a history of physical assault was predictive for females. The researchers attempted to limit bias in diagnostic instruments by following up with in-depth interviews. And again, treatment that seems reasonable to Anglo Americans — taking a pill, talk therapy — may be completely rejected by Native Americans, who have a more holistic view of health and healing, and who stress spirituality and harmony with nature.

Refugees have come to the United States in fairly large numbers from Bosnia and Southeast Asia, and in smaller numbers from Ethiopia, the Sudan, Haiti, the Dominican Republic, and Somalia. These groups may provide further insight into the cross-cultural dimensions of PTSD.

During the 1990s, the war in what used to be Yugoslavia created a great deal of displacement. Bosnian refugees to the U.S. who experienced "ethnic cleansing" were found to have rates of PTSD as high as 65 percent (Weine et al., 1995, p. 1). These refugees lived through a genocidal war, lost family members and friends, fled homes and hid from mortar shells. Their properties were seized or looted, wives were separated from husbands, daughters were raped in front of their parents. Some individuals were forced to work or were beaten and tortured. There was little food, little shelter, and little hope. The survivors may both forget aspects of their traumatic experiences and relive them in dreams or nightmares. Many (35 percent in Weine's study) suffered from depression as well as PTSD.

In a study by Kinzie et al. that investigated PTSD among 322 Southeast Asian refugees in the U.S., researchers found that an astounding 70 percent met the diagnostic criteria (Kinzie et al., 1990, p. 1). After the reunification of Vietnam in 1975, the new government punished those who had fought on the losing side by taking away employment opportunities, educational opportunities, and so on. One survivor, Tran Tri Vu, was in a reeducation camp for some years after the end of the war. He describes the impossibility of forgetting fellow camp inmates, such as ex-pilot Tuong, and tormenters like "the cruel, conceited Dr. Cung ... assigning heavy work to members of his group whose bodies were wracked with hunger and their hearts torn by desperation" (1988, p. xiii). Laos and Cambodia, too, experienced warfare: the film *The Killing Fields* describes the deaths of many thousands in Cambodia. The pro-western government in Laos also fell. Further, in all of Southeast Asia, there are minority groups — the Hmong, the Tai Dam, the Montagnards (the last a catchall for Vietnamese ethnic minorities). Many refugees left Southeast Asia, hoping to find a better life elsewhere. Yet in fleeing, many families and communities were broken up and refugees arrived at resettlement camps alone, some waiting for years before being able to finally resettle and begin new lives. They brought with them few material possessions but many memories of trauma and loss. For example, Vang Xiong, a Laotian Hmong refugee, fled Laos and resettled in Chicago in 1980 with his wife and child, leaving behind war but also family members (Sue & Sue, 1999). Shortly after resettling, he began to have difficulty sleeping and was experiencing nightmares. Indeed, his distress was so great that he was afraid to sleep for fear that he would never wake up. Typical Western responses might include discussing traumatic events of recent years and perhaps prescribing sleep-aids and antidepressants. However, mental health professionals also recognized that many Southeast Asian men, especially Hmong, were dying within the first two years of resettlement from something called "Sudden Death Syndrome" (Sue & Sue, p. 188). There seemed to be no physical cause of death, yet death occurred nonetheless. Because there was a sizeable Hmong community in the area, it was possible to see explanations and treatments within the cultural context. A shaman was called in who listened attentively to Vang Xiong's description of spirit visits in the night. She interpreted these as belonging to previous apartment tenants, and performed ritual tasks to send the spirits away. The healing ritual was effective and Vang Xiong was able to sleep without nightmares again.

Western medicine might well have diagnosed the Hmong man with severe and possibly permanent mental disorders. The treatment deemed appropriate might well have included powerful medications and even hospitalization. It would not have included family participation and support, or any level of community involvement. However, the community shaman conducting familiar rituals in the apartment with family members was successful, in part because the shaman shared Hmong cultural values and beliefs with the individual and family, and in part because the family believed in the healing power of the shaman's rituals.

Mary Pipher, in *The Middle of Everywhere*, writes about refugees in her community of Lincoln, Nebraska. She notes that some 40 percent have been tortured, while many more have seen members of their families killed, been forced to torture or murder others, or lived in camps and felt totally helpless about controlling their own destinies. When they first arrive in the U.S., they are relieved and happy to be somewhere safe. Yet as they attempt to negotiate the demands of their new environments (jobs, school, a new language, transportation and food), they may become overwhelmed with how much they have to learn (Pipher, 2002). Memories and regrets may well weigh them down. Symptoms of depression and PTSD may emerge.

These may be made worse by family upheaval: children typically acculturate more quickly than adults, particularly adults who are busy earning a living. Children may become the translators of the family. They may acquire American values. Parents feel disrespected, their language and culture forgotten. Physical disabilities may compound their problems. But they often do not seek out or accept mental health aid. Language cannot be understated as a problem. Refugee and immigrant parents might well have poor English language skills (and counseling relies to some extent upon nuances of conversation). Further, as Jamaica Kincaid points out in *A Small Place* (2000), English may not express the horror experienced by the individual. While she is speaking of racism, it is also true of PTSD. A second language, particularly if poorly spoken, cannot always express the magnitude of feelings that one has.

The concept of personal counseling may be foreign to many refugees or immigrants. Perhaps it is considered shameful to discuss problems outside the family. Perhaps in the home culture problems are considered gifts of God and cared for rather than eliminated. Often language can be a barrier, as well as transportation, finances, and even the luxury of time spent in a therapist's office. Other cultures might feel that medicine men or priests or elders are the appropriate individuals to take one's problems to. And often, mental health problems are manifested in physical problems (stomachaches or headaches), since mental health problems might be considered shameful. In addition, many mental health counselors may be unfamiliar with other cultural backgrounds, and may unknowingly offend their clients. Perhaps an entire family will come with the individual client, to help out, but the therapist shoos them all out of the room. Sexism, racism, or ethnocentrism, even if unintentional, may inhibit cultural minorities from seeking help.

Treatment for PTSD often assumes that it is healthy to face the trauma, talk about it or work through it. Other cultures, however, might believe that it is better to leave the pain behind, and perhaps seek joy in nature or play. The therapist who insists on revisiting the traumatic experiences will have little success without understanding this cultural difference.

In an excellent book titled *The Spirit Catches You and You Fall Down*, Anne Fadiman describes how epilepsy, perceived by American society as a disease to be treated, is perceived by the Hmong as a special gift from God. These conflicting views led to an epileptic child being removed from her home for a time because the parents refused to give her the prescribed medicine. Suspicions and mistrust of mainstream medical authorities may prevent both settled Americans and refugees and immigrants from seeking assistance with mental health problems. The DSM–IV-TR (*Diagnostic and Statistical Manual*, 4th ed., Text Revision, 2000) includes guidelines for taking into account varied ethnic and cultural backgrounds (Appendix I, p. 897). In addition to directing diagnosticians to consider cultural identity, cultural interpretations of illnesses, and cultural aspects that might influence the client-clinician relationship, the DSM-IV-TR describes twenty-five of the better-known, culturally specific illnesses of people of different cultural backgrounds.

One syndrome is "amok," found by various names in Malaysia, Laos, the Philippines, Polynesia, and Puerto Rico. Angry silence erupts into anger and violent behavior, and the individual might claim that others are persecuting him (it appears to afflict males). Following the outburst, the individual may be exhausted and unaware of the outburst.

Native Americans may experience "ghost sickness," with symptoms such as nightmares, dizziness, anxiety, hallucinations, weakness, and a feeling of suffocation. Sufferers are preoccupied with death and the dead.

"Susto" (literally "fright"), is found in Central and South America, Mexico, and among immigrants from these countries in the United States. As a result of a terrifying event, the individual's soul becomes ill or absent and the person has bad dreams, pain in the body, loss of appetite, and so on. Susto can even result in death. Tovar Klinger (2001), in his investigation in Southern Colombia, notes that this illness, known there as "espanto," particularly affects children and can result in death. Less severe forms are treated by not bathing the victim for three days and giving herbal medicines for nine days.

The DSM-IV-TR (2000) describes other illnesses for Latin Americans, Native Americans, and immigrants from West Africa and Haiti, as well as those of Chinese, Korean, and Japanese cultures, Eskimo communities, and North African and Middle Eastern societies. The listing of these syndromes is not meant to be exhaustive, but to suggest a range of beliefs and symptoms that may not fit with typical Western medical perspectives.

The U.S. context, then, can be seen as more complex than it may first appear. And the U.S. is not the only country with refugees, immigrants, and subcultures. The World Refugee Survey of 2001 (Pipher, 2002) estimates some 14.5 million refugees and asylum seekers, with more than 20 million internally displaced persons, all over the world. The movement of peoples is unprecedented in human history, and the traumatic events that force them to move are unprecedented as well. Wars, famine, genocide, competition for resources and land, natural disasters, the gap between rich and poor, all lead to increased possibilities of traumatic experiences for large numbers of the world's population. To what extent are traumatic experiences universal? Do individuals react in similar ways all over the world? Do stressful events for some of us become "normal"?

The author lived in Colombia, South America, for three years. In the first six months or so, the experience of living in a large city (over 2 million people) with high levels of street violence, occasional guerrilla activity, and the increasing cocaine trade, resulted in stress and fear that was palpable. After the first six months, however, the same events became part of normal everyday life. Precautions became second nature (avoid certain parts of town, vary the route to work every day) and previously stressful events became familiar, and were no longer perceived as life threatening. A bomb set off at the language institute provoked sleepless nights for some time, but a later attack at the same school did not have the same effect. The author had changed her perception to fit a different reality.

Many critics contend that PTSD is a western construct, and indeed, the diagnostic tools and descriptions reflect western culture. Assessment devices, both paper-and-pen and physician led, may be inappropriate if used in other cultures. They may result in over or underdiagnosis of PTSD or worse, may miss entirely the culturally distinct manifestations of stress responses and disabilities.

Some research in international contexts has looked at the results of natural disasters. For example, De la Fuente (1990; cited in Marsella et al, 1992) reviewed the aftermath of the 1985 earthquakes in Mexico City and found that 32 percent of the survivors suffered from PTSD. Another study of Israeli soldiers who participated in the 1982 war with Lebanon found that soldiers who suffered from combat stress reactions were more likely to develop PTSD. However, these and similar studies involve populations that are arguably western in their cultural patterns and beliefs.

To continue the examination of cross-cultural aspects of PTSD, it is possible to look at two major aspects of cultures. First, cultures may be community oriented or individual oriented. Second, religions play a large role in many cultures. These will be discussed in the following sections.

Collectivistic vs. Individualistic Cultures

In looking at cultures throughout the world, some researchers have categorized cultures as collectivistic or individualistic. Collectivistic cultures are those in which the group's goals are more important than the individual's (Rogers & Steinfatt, 1999). Japanese culture, for example, is considered collectivistic; the individual subordinates his/her own goals to those of the group. Individualistic cultures, such as the U.S., value individual goals and choices over the well-being of the group. Of course, in all societies there will be consideration of both the group and the individual, but cultures tend primarily to one or the other.

An individual with PTSD might well be viewed differently by these two types of cultures. In a collectivistic culture, getting along with others and maintaining social harmony is more important, and so the individual's difficulties might be given less importance. In an individualistic culture, in contrast, a person with PTSD might be seen as someone whose needs and problems demand attention.

More importantly, the concept of PTSD has been delineated in the context of an individualistic culture. Concern for a single person with PTSD might be uninterpretable in a collectivistic culture. Western medicine also focuses on precise definitions, symptoms, and treatments rather than more holistic considerations of the individual in his/her total context, including the person's physical, mental, emotional and spiritual self embedded in a social context. In other words, the etiology of PTSD fits into the western individualistic context, but might make no sense at all in a collectivistic society. Hence treatments seen as appropriate in the mainstream U.S. might have no place in other societies.

Besides the broad brushstrokes of collectivistic vs. individualistic cultures, religion plays a major role in our attitudes and beliefs. How do world religions view suffering and our human response to trauma?

Religious Perspectives

In Christianity, particularly Protestantism, both individuals and communities are important. Individuals are believed to have a personal and direct relationship to God, and to have free will. Because a person has free will to act, he or she may consider a trauma to be his/her own fault. Believing that we have control over our lives means we also have to take responsibility for events that occur. Maslow's Hierarchy of Needs, for example, places self-fulfillment and individual growth at the pinnacle of the pyramid (Woodcock, 2001, p. 164). It is difficult to believe that one's personal growth is of paramount importance and also feel that events are not under our control. A Protestant believer suffering from PTSD may believe it is his/her responsibility to overcome the trauma alone, or with the support of prayer and other believers.

Roman Catholicism tends to have a more fatalistic view of life: sometimes events happen that are not under our control. Events may be predestined. In that case, we may not see a traumatic event as resulting from our own actions, though we may still ask why such a tragedy happens to us. Does God cause natural disasters? Is God testing us or giving us trials in order to make us better people?

Many Christians believe that disasters happen as a natural result of humankind's original sin and separation from God. If suffering is a part of life, then it should be accepted. Christians "tend to emphasize the need for endurance in the face of suffering" (Woodcock, 2001, p. 177). Still, individuals are to work to overcome such suffering and problems. We may seek support from the community and from God, but ultimately it is up to the individual to persevere.

Judaism, which shares the Old Testament with Christianity and thus has many of the same historical connections, is more focused on the community than on the individual. Original sin and separation from God are part of Jewish beliefs as well. In his bestseller *When Bad Things Happen to Good People* (1989), Rabbi Kusher seeks to answer the question of human suffering, and discusses views of God as punishing people, or allowing tragedies to occur capriciously. He notes that insurance companies refer to natural disasters as Acts of God, and states, "I don't believe that an earthquake that kills thousands of innocent victims without reason is an act of God. It is an act of nature" (p. 59). Thus he suggests that tragedy is a natural part of life, not sent in retaliation or, indeed, in any sort of personal way at all. Thus individuals need not feel that they have caused trauma to occur. An individual with PTSD may be able to view the trauma as resulting from events outside his/her control. Not blaming oneself can lessen the severity of PTSD.

Kusher further discusses the Book of Job, the story of a man who apparently led an honorable life and yet was afflicted with many tragedies. Job, he states, "needed sympathy more than he needed advice.... He needed compassion.... He needed friends who would permit him to be angry, to cry and to scream, much more than he needed friends who would urge him to be an example of patience and piety to others" (pp. 89–90). The Book of Job, then, is not an effort to explain *why* humans suffer, but instead to suggest how to behave in suffering, that is by accepting that sometimes tragedies occur for no particular reason, and that rather than blame ourselves or God, we should stay connected to God in our search for comfort.

Islam is another major religion with roots similar to Judaism and Christianity. In all three religions, Abraham is the father of the Semitic peoples. Muslims believe in one God (monotheism), as do Jews and Christians, and agree with Jews that Jesus was a wise teacher, though not the Messiah. In addition, Muslims believe that Mohammed is a prophet of God, and his works are detailed in the Koran. According to Islam, suffering occurs for complex reasons; more important is that adherents should continue to believe in God, and to associate with other believers for support and community (Woodcock, 2001). Tragic events may in fact be testing our faith, but we are also to look to God for help and mercy. Thus the individual suffering from PTSD should be humble and accepting, and seek support in a community of believers and remain faithful to God.

Another major world religion is Hinduism, which holds that, "In a sense, suffering is the essence of the universe" (Bowker, 1970, p. 200). Hindus see tragedies as resulting from the gods or from our own karma. Perhaps we have failed to propitiate the gods appropriately, or perhaps in past lives we have acted badly or failed to act positively. While in either case the believer bears the brunt of responsibility, Hinduism also suggests that suffering is universal, that individuals are not singled out, we all experience suffering of some sort. By enduring suffering, we become better people, thus lessening the amount of suffering we might have to experience in a future life.

Hinduism also stresses dualities, in particular the duality of good and evil. Duality is said to be a source of suffering as well, and as we begin to recognize the unity of the universe, our suffering decreases (Bowker, 1970). PTSD individuals in this context may seek to live better lives in order to atone for previous failures. However, if an individual suffering from PTSD believes that he/she caused the traumatic event to occur, and further believes that she/he deserves to suffer, it is unlikely that that individual will believe that he/she is suffering from a diagnosable medical disorder or will seek assistance from medical professionals. Furthermore, the disabling symptoms will influence the lives of family and friends, and perhaps be reflected in the behaviors of the children.

Buddhism, like Hinduism, recognizes the ubiquity of suffering. However, in Buddhism suffering is said to result from our desires. When we stop desiring, and no longer feel envy or covet material goods, we will no longer suffer (Woodcock, 2001). Loosening and then losing our attachments to worldly goods will lead us to become more enlightened, though the process is understood to require vigilance and perseverance. One application to a PTSD survivor or family is that we should stop desiring life to be different, even though we are angry at the trauma and the survivor, we wish she or he would be different, we wish we didn't have to deal with this disability. Buddhism suggests that our first task is to stop wanting our lives to be different, and to stop seeking to change the past. Thus, acceptance of the situation is the beginning of being able to deal with it.

The suffering of a PTSD individual, which results from experiencing a traumatic event, cannot be categorized as simply resulting from worldly desires. But accepting that the trauma has occurred, and that the individual has changed because of it, changes our focus from wishful thinking to more realistic strategies for addressing the situation.

Christianity, Judaism, Islam, Hinduism, and Buddhism are the best known world religions, each with many millions of believers, but there are as many other religions and religious belief systems as there are cultures and societies. While it is impossible to discuss all of these, many cultures share similar traditions — ancestor worship and/or animism, for example. Ancestor worship is the belief that our deceased ancestors continue to exert an influence on us in this life. Perhaps they are ghostly guardians, promoting fertility and harvest, long life and good health. In order to ensure their continued support, their graves should be cared for and a variety of rituals are to be performed. There may be an altar in the home for the ancestors. Traumatic events that befall an individual (or individuals in a family) might be due to a failure to properly worship the ancestors, and the remedies involve various sorts of rituals to reestablish a good relationship.

During the Vietnam War, U.S. military planners decided on a strategy to resolve the difficulty of distinguishing guerrilla fighters from the civilian population. They created large camp-like areas, gathered up the "friendlies" from small villages, and resettled them in the new camps. Thus, the civilian population would all be within the camp and everyone outside could be considered the enemy. Unfortunately, families began to leave the camps to return home, because that is where the graves of their ancestors were. They needed to be near those graves in order to care for their ancestors. Because the military planners did not understand the people's attachments to their homes, they created a great deal of distress.

The same problem occurred when Southeast Asian refugees fled their homes and countries, and resettled in Australia, the U.S., Sweden, or other countries. In addition to the traumas of war that they had experienced, they also had to leave their ancestors' graves behind, untended. In a sense, they felt they had left behind their connections to their pasts, and perhaps felt that the spirits of their ancestors had stayed as well, and had not accompanied them to their new homes as protective and loving spirits. Refugees suffering from PTSD were thus also cut off from a potential source of healing.

Animism, the belief that all things have a sprit, is another very widely accepted spiritual belief. Rocks, trees, the sun and planets, rivers and the earth itself all have sprits that can be helpful or malevolent. At the very least, each should be treated with respect and some appreciation of their spirits. Tragedies can happen because of a malevolent spirit, or because an individual or community has offended the spirits. Rituals are conducted to remain on good terms with the spirits, and shamans or traditional healers may be called on to restore balance. Native Americans, for example, believe in the power of animals as totems or spirit guides, and different animals represent different qualities or characteristics. Skunks are a sign of evil to some groups; robins are associated with health and happiness. The wolf is a pathfinder, while turtles are protectors (www.jfblittlefeather.om/animal_omens.htm). In this belief system, individuals may bring tragedy upon themselves as a result of their own bad behavior or their failure to perform particular rituals. A PTSD survivor may thus blame him or herself for the traumatic event. Yet there is also some hope for the PTSD survivor, as spirits, rituals, or a shaman may all be resources that can be tapped for assistance.

The importance of beliefs in dealing with PTSD cannot be stated too strongly. As in the placebo effect, where we think a medicine will help even if it is a sugar pill, our beliefs have great power to influence our healing. Any diagnostician, therapist, or medical doctor must take into account the worldview and religious or spiritual beliefs of the individual in seeking to understand both how the individual might view the diagnosis, and how PTSD might be best treated for that individual.

Bracken & Petty (1998) point out that our western views of trauma simply do not take into account the larger picture of cultural values and behaviors. They note that between 1960 and 1987, sixteen African countries experienced conflict and violence, and refugees in Africa have increased from 1.4 million in 1960 to over 18 million in 1992. And most of the warfare in these countries has been interethnic or ethnic groups against their governments, thus including issues of social identity, loyalty, nationality, and so on, factors that are largely ignored in western medical diagnoses, not to mention treatments. Because the problems are seen as larger than individuals, treatments should go beyond traditional one-on-one counseling and perhaps involve group counseling and community outreach and support efforts.

For example, would it be helpful to offer one-on-one talk therapy for a Japanese POW of World War II? Or to offer an antidepressant medication to a Rwandan survivor of that country's genocide? At best, such treatments might be useless — perceived as of little value and therefore not taken seriously. At worst, the treatment might mark the individual as putting his/her own goals first, resulting in being stigmatized by his/her own social group. Isolating an individual from societal support cannot help and is likely to cause further harm.

The clinician who diagnoses PTSD, then, must be cross-culturally aware and sensitive. Having some knowledge, experience, and empathy is a necessary first step. Of even greater value is an understanding of an ethnologic approach to other cultures. This entails attempting to view another culture from within, rather than viewing it in comparison to one's own culture. An example might be interpreting the Hmong child's epilepsy as either a problem to be solved (as it is in U.S. culture) or listening and observing to understand that epilepsy is a special gift given only to some children, one requiring appreciation rather than education.

The diagnostician who can understand the individual's own interpretation of his/her trauma will be better able to assess how it affects that individual's sense of well-being and ability to function in the life he/she has chosen. And certainly, that diagnostician will be better able to recommend treatments that do not violate the individual's values, and that have a greater probability of improving quality of life. Cross-cultural counseling is discussed in greater detail in Chapter 6, which recognizes that the very concept of mental health therapy may require modification for culturally different populations.

PTSD is complex and difficult, and much more so with different cultural traditions and values. Ultimately, though we can generalize about PTSD, each individual might have differing symptoms and degrees of impairment. The next chapter describes PTSD as it affects the individual.

CHAPTER 5

PTSD and the Individual

I'll never forgive myself ... that my men died and I didn't (Lt. Col. H.G. Moore, a character in the film *We Were Soldiers Once — and Young*).

I knew that awful things happened at night, and if I relaxed my guard, something would hurt me (Kim, 2000, p. 200).

I was so scared that I just forgot what scared is in my heart. You're just numbed by the scene in front of you. You just run and hope that it was not you that got hit (Hmong refugee quoted in Faderman, 1998, p. 53).

PTSD is not very well understood among the general population. Indeed, the reactions of many to an individual with PTSD are often, "Why can't he (or she) just get over it?" Given this reaction, it is not surprising that some Holocaust survivors or World War II veterans pretended to do just that, or buried their feelings in alcohol or work. Years later, these reactions reinforce the belief; one wife of a World War II vet believes that her husband *did* "get over it" and thus perceives her Vietnam veteran son to be choosing to suffer. The stigma attached to mental disorders in general, and PTSD specifically, may arise because blaming the sufferers relieves us of the responsibility for feeling empathy, and taking steps to help (Coffey, 1998). Many still believe that a physical disability is beyond a person's control, but mental disorders are a failure of will power.

The diagnostic criteria for PTSD include exposure to some traumatic event in which actual or threatened death or serious injury occurs, and to which the reaction of the individual is intense helplessness or fear (DSM IV, 1994, pp. 427–428). Thus, PTSD involves both a traumatic event and

72

the individual's response to it. Not all combat veterans suffer from PTSD, and among those who do, there are degrees of suffering. Those who experienced more combat, especially exposure to and/or participation in violence against noncombatants, seem to have more serious problems after the war (Young, 1991). The question of why some can experience trauma without developing PTSD remains to be answered.

As described previously, common symptoms of PTSD include reexperiencing the trauma through flashbacks, memories, hallucinations, and dreams; hypervigilance, irritability, difficulty sleeping; and avoidance of memories, activities, and people associated with the trauma, as well as general emotional numbing. These wide-ranging symptoms affect every area of an individual's life: emotional, mental, physical, and behavioral, all of which interact. This chapter describes these distinct aspects and their interactions. Certainly no single individual will express all of these characteristics.

Emotional Aspects

"I almost enjoy it when Bob explodes. At least I know he's there" (Matsakis, 1996, p.11). Here are the two extremes of emotional interaction: none at all and volatile outbursts. Some PTSD survivors are so emotionally numbed that they avoid all human interaction. Fearing hurt, and protecting themselves from future hurt, they become withdrawn. They may avoid interaction by not having a job, or choosing a job that limits human contact: factory work, night security guard, custodial work. Limiting outside interaction can include not participating in social activities, not attending religious services, staying away from parties or community events, even shopping or buying gas at off hours to avoid people.

"My husband was a loner ... he tended to lose friends easily" (Matsakis, p.13). Losing friends or failing to make new ones is not uncommon. Some Vietnam veterans have made no new friends at all since their time in the military, and friendships from before their service are not maintained. This leaves the family as the primary source of interaction.

Within the family, however, the isolation might continue. Extended family members may be shunned, and family celebrations avoided. PTSD survivors who are married and/or have children might find even that level of contact to be threatening. One vet withdraws to his bedroom with the television on to drown out the normal noises of the home. A closed door is a clear signal that he prefers to be left alone. Those who seek to interact with him may be met by the other extreme of an emotional explosion. Shoshana Johnson, who was part of the convoy ambushed and taken prisoner in Iraq in 2003, was afraid to carry a picture of her daughter because she feared that an enemy captor would find it. She showed stress symptoms upon repatriation to Ft. Bliss, which included irritability, anger, depression, and survivor guilt. In addition, the media attention and the army's scheduling of public appearances for her added to her distress (Johnson, 2010).

How does the lack of emotional connectedness affect an individual? Surely humans are social creatures, meant to live in social groups, and meant to experience varying degrees of emotional relatedness, from casual friendship to intimacy. The loss of companionship suggests a halt in human growth. The individual may be stuck at an earlier stage of development, unable or unwilling to move forward.

Indeed, the individual succeeds in avoiding loss, yet there is no possibility of gain without risk. It must be profoundly unsatisfying to trade apparent emotional safety for the rewards of personal relationships.

Even the loss of something not typically considered valuable can provoke an outburst of rage. GH, a Marine gunnery sergeant, enjoyed watching rabbits in his neighborhood. One day he discovered one that had apparently been killed by loose dogs. He confided that he was so outraged, he wanted to kill the dogs and cripple their owners. What he saw as the senseless loss of something that gave him pleasure caused a dramatic outburst. Fortunately, he did not follow through on his urge to retaliate. Other combat veterans express rage at hunters, whom they perceive to be killing for the sport of it. To them, killing is not a sport.

Some PTSD survivors may shut down completely. It may seem as though they have no emotions at all, but in reality there may be tremendous efforts to avoid feelings that seem overwhelming. Guilt and shame may be constant companions. Survivor guilt has long been recognized as common in survivors of traumatic events. An endless tape of "Why me? Why did I survive when she didn't?" plays through their minds. Humans have a natural urge to find meaning in events, and shrugging one's shoulders and ascribing survival to luck or chance is not enough. Unable to find a satisfying reason, unable to feel deserving in some way, the individual suffers profound guilt and may replay scenes with "What if I had..." or "if I had only..." The survivor may feel undeserving of having survived. In one study of Vietnam combat veterans with PTSD, the authors found that combat guilt, survivor guilt, depression, anxiety and severe PTSD were all significant predictors of suicide attempts and/or ideation (Hendin & Haas, 1991).

In the film *Jacknife*, Robert De Niro's character believes himself to be responsible for the death of a friend; in *In Country*, Bruce Willis's character imagines his dead buddies sitting together in a village, wondering where he is, and he wishes he were there with them. How can one live with such feelings of guilt and loss? In many cases, the choice is to attempt to feel nothing at all, reinforced by the belief that one does not deserve to feel happy. In both films, some release is obtained by sharing these secret stories of having survived, but shame makes it extraordinarily difficult to share, even with one's most intimate friends, and keeping such terrible secrets requires a great deal of psychological energy, leaving little for the building of relationships based on honesty and trust.

Spiritual aspects may be related to emotional effects, and particularly to feelings of guilt and anger. PTSD survivors question the existence of God and the meaning of life. They may be angry at God for allowing good people to die or permitting accidents or disasters to happen. The faith they may have grown up with is severely tested in times of trauma, and many may feel abandoned by the God they once had faith in. Unable to believe in God, or in humanity, or in the safety of the world which they now believe to be an illusion, they lose the sense of a larger purpose to life.

William Mahedy, who was a chaplain in Vietnam, notes that many veterans feel that the God who had promised to be on their side and "lead them to victory over evil" hadn't followed through. They felt betrayed, called God obscene names and questioned his existence (Mahedy, 1986, p. 5). One veteran, 30 years after the war, says God was "back in The World trying to get good Americans to stop the war, but it took several years longer than he had first hoped, because 'good' Americans are few and far between and the others are extremely hard-headed" (EFA, 2002, personal communication). Having come to believe that the war was wrong, this veteran saw God as working to end the war, not very successfully. The same veteran had entered seminary after the war, hoping to make a difference, but declined ordination as he found fellow veterans who needed him more. Medic Joseph Dwyer, who served in Iraq in 2003, returned home "a different person" (Sanchez, 2008). Formerly religious, he began drinking and abused illegal substances, eventually dying of an overdose in the summer of 2008 in spite of having a wife and child.

Emotional burdens such as these may often develop into depression, a frequent comorbid condition of PTSD, and categorized by the DSM-IV as a mood disorder. The world is bathed in a dark shadow of despair and hopelessness, it will never get any better, and there is nothing that can be done to make it better. William Styron, writing about depression, states "It is hopelessness even more than pain that crushes the soul.... One does not abandon, even briefly, one's bed of nails, but is attached to it wherever one goes. And this results in a striking experience — one which I have called, borrowing military terminology, the situation of the walking wounded" (1990, p. 62). Suffering from depression himself, Styron eloquently captured the bleakness of living with depression.

In fact, depression so often accompanies PTSD that some treatments aimed at relieving depression seem to help overall with PTSD. While there are degrees of depression, ranging from mild mood fluctuations to deeply disabling despair, milder symptoms may not call for medications but instead be treated with counseling and support. Still, the depression that many PTSD survivors experience is often disabling, preventing them from finding pleasure in activities that they previously enjoyed and causing them to withdraw from the company of others, resulting in lowered energy and a fatalistic sense that the depression defines who they are, rather than that it is something affecting them that can be changed.

Why should a trauma survivor experience such disabling depression? As newer therapies and research implicate an imbalance in brain chemicals, it might be that the flood of adrenaline, often sustained, that carries us through a trauma is also somehow responsible for changed patterns of response in the brain itself. This medical perspective is appealing to many of us in the western world, since once we identify a problem as physical in origin, we find it easier to solve, and we can also avoid blaming ourselves. A common characteristic of clinical depression is the perception that when something bad happens, it is total, permanent, and self-caused. Those not so depressed might interpret the same bad event as an isolated case of bad luck. So even if there is a strong physical component to depression, it is inextricably tied to our emotions and thought patterns.

Some point out that depression may result from unexpressed anger.

Feeling very angry about a perceived or real injustice, but being powerless to correct it, we may turn our anger inward, tying ourselves up in knots, isolating ourselves by feelings of rage, and fears that we might express them. Survivors of traumas related to natural disasters might feel angry at their god for allowing the disaster to happen, or might blame themselves for not anticipating and avoiding the disaster, though such foreknowledge is often unrealistic. Certainly if one knew for a fact that floodwaters would wash away one's home, one would have left it. Thus, logically, not evacuating means the individual did not in fact know that the waters were so dangerous. But our feelings often seem more "right" to us than rational thoughts. Indeed, in depressed individuals, the self-blaming refrain often repeats and reinforces guilt.

Survivors of other types of traumatic events, such as rape, torture, or war, may also have deep and extreme feelings of anger. They may blame themselves for allowing the rape to happen, or they may blame authorities for putting them in positions of danger.

Depression is such an insidious condition that fleeing consciousness through sleep or even death may seem the best way to deal with it. Yet sleep is often disturbed in depressed individuals, and suicide is a last resort, yet one that too many may employ who despair of ever getting better.

Another emotional effect is anxiety, a constant worry about what is happening or might happen, to the individual, his/her family, and indeed, in the world as a whole. One Vietnam War veteran videotaped the entire Gulf War, watching obsessively the 24-hour television coverage, sleeping and eating little. He lost 25 pounds over the course of that short war. When the September 11, 2001, attacks occurred, he again seemed unable to stop watching the endless loop of the planes hitting the World Trade Center. In addition to videotaping, he collected newspaper and magazines devoted to the events. He was attempting to control his anxiety over these events by immersing himself in them.

Severe anxiety can result in anxiety or panic attacks. Some common anxiety symptoms include "sweating, shaking, hyperventilation, chest pains, dizziness, throwing up" and more (Mason, 1998, p. 252). Panic attacks may be even more frightening, with the sufferer experiencing extreme dread and fear of dying. Efforts to reassure the individual might be unsuccessful, as such attacks seem beyond the reach of rational thought.

Emotional difficulties accompany and interact with mental or cognitive symptoms. Thoughts represent our efforts to make sense of the world; while our beliefs may seem irrational to others, we deeply believe them to be true. And perhaps at the time of the trauma, they were true. For example, an incest survivor may believe that allowing others to mistreat her is the only way to survive. A young child may not feel powerful enough to resist. Yet years later, being taken advantage of by others at work is not something she must acquiesce to in order to survive. But that deep belief that her survival depends on not confronting others still controls her life and her reaction to others.

Mental or Cognitive Aspects

To a PTSD survivor, the world is truly different. We all have unique perspectives and outlooks on our world, influenced by our upbringing, our experience, our knowledge. For trauma survivors, the world has literally changed. They do not see the same world that others may see.

As children we often invoke "magical thinking," believing that we can influence the world by not stepping on cracks, or by closing our eyes to make ourselves invisible. Magical thinking gives us a feeling of control over our environment. Most people outgrow magical thinking (though some of us still believe that washing a car brings on a rainstorm!) but traumatic events can arrest emotional and cognitive development, keeping us thinking like children. We may also resort to magical thinking in the absence of any better explanation for the cause of the trauma. And if, indeed, we do have such control over the world, then if we only do "x" or never do "y," we should be safe.

Hypervigilance can be a result of such thought processes. The combat veteran who won't allow his family to turn lights on at night, or who refuses to put up Christmas lights, is responding to an old reality, in which lights did indeed cause one to be visible to the enemy. That enemy is no longer present, yet the belief persists and results in actions that no longer make sense. Sleeping with a gun or knife under the pillow similarly protects against a danger that is no longer realistic. Refusing to leave home because strangers may attack is not a rational response to a potential but by no means assured danger.

The belief that one can control everything is itself irrational. PTSD survivors seek to control their environments, with locks or physical barriers, and to control other people by limiting social interaction with them. They may seek control over their own emotions by avoiding intimate relationships and withdrawing emotionally. As unsatisfying as this may be ultimately, it does give the survivor a sense of control.

Another cognitive effect is difficulty concentrating, a sense that one is unable to focus clearly or persist until a task is done. Chores that are relatively automatic (especially if they precede the trauma), such as driving a car, might be unimpaired while more complex or new tasks, such as setting up a VCR or assembling a child's toy, might feel impossible. Shoshana Johnson (2010) states:

> I now have a difficult time remembering things. I have to set my cell phone alarm to remind me to take medications and to remind me about appointments. There are alarms and bells all over my life now that have to be set or I'll forget that I have something on the stove or clothes in the wash, bills to pay, or even forget that I'm in the middle of a task that I'll wander away from [p. 263].

Perfectionism is an effect not uncommon in PTSD survivors, who feel that they must get it exactly right or something terrible will happen. Tasks begun may not be completed. A letter to a friend never gets finished. The books never get organized. The dripping faucet is never repaired. Other tasks may never even be started. A small simple task becomes large and complex — before the books can be organized, shelves must be built. Before shelves can be built, wood must be bought. Before wood can be bought, the truck must be cleaned out. Before... It may seem like procrastination, but perhaps it is perfectionism at work. After all, minor mistakes can cost lives, therefore it is imperative not to make any mistakes, however small. The best way to avoid a mistake is to do nothing.

Flashbacks and intrusive memories associated with PTSD are also cognitive effects and may be impossible to control. In extreme cases, hallucinations can feel terrifyingly real. More commonly, ordinary events can "trigger" a flashback. Fireworks on the 4th of July, for example, may sound like gunfire to a war veteran. A hug from a friend might trigger memories of rape to a rape survivor. The smell of diesel fuel triggers one vet's memories of being in an armored personnel carrier, which to him is a comforting rather than threatening memory.

During a flashback the individual feels that he/she is reexperiencing the traumatic event and the emotions felt at that time flood into the survivor's mind and emotions. She or he might physically react — diving behind the greenery at the mall, or running from a perceived aggressor. The experience feels so real that the individual cannot interrupt the reaction. Later, however, the reaction is seen as absurd, uncalled for, and the survivor experiences shame or embarrassment.

Avoiding such flashbacks and their triggers may then become a survival strategy. Limiting exposure to any potential trigger might again result in near-total withdrawal from virtually all encounters, even to programs on television (including or especially news programs). Or, an individual might endlessly expose himself/herself to triggers in order to rob them of their power. Indeed, some therapies for PTSD are founded on repeated exposure to memories of the original trauma, in order to rob them of their potency. In either case, the survivor is reacting to what was, rather than what is, and the reaction is likely to seem inappropriate to others.

Flashbacks may also occur in the form of nightmares, leading some to fear sleep or others to drink alcohol in order to sleep too soundly to be aroused. Both result in unnatural and unsatisfying sleep patterns, which in turn affect all aspects of life and living.

Physical Aspects

Difficulty sleeping, in fact, is one of the common symptoms of PTSD (and of depression, as well). Difficulty falling asleep and staying asleep are part of category D, increased arousal. Many PTSD veterans report being unable to sleep more than three or four hours at a time, and sleeping during the day in an effort to catch up. One vet sleeps during the day because he still feels the need to be on guard during the night. An incest survivor keeps all the lights on in her apartment so she'll be able to see if danger approaches, but has difficulty sleeping with all the bright lights.

Sleep deprivation has been related to a large number and wide variety of impairments. Sleep-deprived people have trouble concentrating, are irritable, nod off at inappropriate times, cannot sustain attention, and feel tired. They have more automobile accidents. Work performance suffers. Personal relationships also suffer. Given the global effects of sleep deprivation, it becomes a priority in treating PTSD survivors.

Besides the emotional, cognitive, and physical effects of PTSD, other physical issues may affect an individual. There may be wounds associated with the traumatic events. Fire victims may have permanent scarring. Auto or other accidents can result in amputation or paralysis. Rape or incest can leave permanent physical damage. And combat, of course, may result in physical disabilities.

During World War I, many wounded soldiers died because there were as yet no antibiotics and transporting the wounded to medical facilities was much more difficult. Antibiotics were developed during World War II, resulting in more saved lives. Medical intervention was further advanced during the Vietnam War, as a series of field hospitals were set up and helicopters were used to transport the wounded quickly. In addition, medics were attached to field units and offered on-the-spot treatment until medical evacuation could take place. As a result, there are many more surviving wounded soldiers from the Vietnam War, and many more amputees and paralyzed veterans. These veterans have physical disabilities and needs that complicate the picture if they also have PTSD. As might be expected, medical care has continued to improve, and veterans of the wars in Iraq and Afghanistan have the highest survival rates to date. One dramatic development has been the number of soldiers who suffer Traumatic Brain Injury (TBI) as a result of concussion or wounds from improvised explosive devices (IEDs). TBIs share some symptoms and characteristics with PTSD and so treatments for both may be similar, depending on the symptom.

In addition, veterans of the Vietnam War may suffer illnesses associated with exposure to Agent Orange, a potent herbicide used to defoliate the jungles. At the time of its use, the U.S. government stated that there were no known health risks to humans (though subsequent investigation challenges that assertion). Since then, however, a number of conditions have been identified as Agent Orange–connected, including several types of cancer, and adult-onset diabetes. Certain birth defects among children of veterans have been identified as well, and more conditions may well be identified in the future.

Other physical characteristics of PTSD survivors include a possibly weakened immune system, heart difficulties (perhaps due to increased flooding of stress hormones) and general, diffuse pain throughout the body. Survivors may also have somatic reactions to events, literally feeling a physical pain in response to an emotional or mental trigger. One survivor experiences gall bladder pain whenever he has to spend time with his mother-in-law. Another gets painful headaches. Certainly the pain is real, but the cause or source of the pain may be more emotional than physical. Finally, a rapid heartbeat — again, possibly related to adrenaline — may be a problem for some PTSD survivors.

Behavioral Aspects

PTSD can manifest itself in severe life-threatening choices. Sometimes the guilt over living is so painful that a trauma survivor chooses suicide. Unable to find a reason to live, the sufferer sees death as an attractive alternative. In one small regional group of veterans in Iowa in the early 1980s, no fewer than twelve Vietnam veterans killed themselves. Among combat veterans, guns are an attractive means, though not the only one. Imagine the veterans who are left behind: yet again they are the survivors, and their guilt over not "saving" their buddies intensifies. In fact, multiple traumas lead to greater probabilities of having PTSD.

Young (1991) states that more veterans have committed suicide since the Vietnam War than died during the war, about 60,000. Others state that the numbers are much higher. It is impossible to accurately count, because many "accidents" might be intentional or unexplained. For example, a relatively new concept in American society is "suicide by cop," in which the individual essentially provokes a police officer into killing him (or her). While it may fulfill the individual's death wish, it surely provides a stressful event to the officer.

Perhaps equally self-destructive, some survivors use alcohol or drugs as an escape. This "self-medication" may also be a way of punishing themselves. Because substance abuse is life-threatening (alcohol-related auto accidents, drug overdoses, bar fights), the survivor may be inviting death in a less direct way.

PTSD survivors may overreact to relatively minor problems. A car that won't start is treated as a major crisis, requiring immediate and total attention. A wheel broken off a toy tractor elicits rage and condemnation. A loud noise can startle a survivor, who leaps to find out what caused it. It seems sometimes that there are no intermediate reactions, little balance, as the survivor swings between apathy and excessive response. Failure of others to respond similarly may evoke rage; the spouse or family of the survivor may become equally reactionary in response, setting up a pattern of family behavior that is hard to change.

Survivors may prefer the safety of routines, and may be disturbed by changes in their environments. They often avoid unfamiliar places and activities. One PTSD survivor reluctantly agreed to go out to a new restaurant for an anniversary dinner with his wife. Upon arriving, he proceeded to examine the restaurant, indoors and out, and locate all the exits. He finally consented to sit at a corner table with his back to the wall so he could see all the activity in the restaurant. Similarly, a rape survivor finds herself highly anxious when her children's school schedule is changed, for teacher in-services, semester breaks, or bad weather. She lacks the flexibility to cope with such changes. Some survivors become agoraphobic or avoid any place that may involve large numbers of people.

The life of an individual with PTSD seems quite bleak, given the possible emotional, cognitive, and physical symptoms that may be expressed. Yet this is perhaps too dark a view. Might not the very strategies that led to survival and now seem maladaptive be sources for strength and growth in the future?

Perhaps it is wise for someone who is emotionally volatile to limit his/her interactions with others. That individual shows recognition of a particular problem, and a solution of sorts. The emotion of guilt can be a powerful motivation to change or make amends. One medic 30 years later finally wrote to the parents of a man whose life he could not save. In fact, no one could have saved Kenny's life, but the medic continued to feel responsible until the parents wrote back and thanked him for telling the story.

Depressed people who resist the idea of suicide show the power of the will to live. Life may seem a terrible burden, but in choosing life, there must as well be hope. Hypervigilance, too, can be a strength, preventing accidents or causing the sufferer to act quickly in a crisis. Effective action in a crisis can be a source of self-esteem and pride. If we view PTSD as only and ever a disabling condition, we miss the positives that can be drawn on in the journey toward healthier living.

Even in the midst of the difficulties caused by PTSD, there is reason for hope. The next chapter discusses how the individual with PTSD influences the immediate and extended family, and how the family system shifts to accommodate PTSD.

CHAPTER 6

PTSD and the Family

Even when they are "forgotten," memories can still be present and pervasive.... People continue to tell their stories whether or not they are aware of it (Karen Saakvitne, 1992; cited in Coffey, 1998, p. 31).

My father's marriages did not last more than 4 years to either his second or third wife... I don't believe my father continued to earn an income. My father spent most of his time in our home. This still continues to this day (KW, personal communication, Sept. 2002).

And it's sometimes hard for him to know how to fit in, because the family has managed fine without him for a year and a half (Matt, aged 16, in Ellis, 2008).

Somehow I picked up on the "fact," in my family, that some things are too dangerous to touch, to feel, to explore, or certainly to discuss (Hinshaw, 2002, p. 203).

The previous chapter details the myriad emotional, cognitive, behavioral and physical problems that PTSD survivors might exhibit. But rarely are one person's problems limited to the individual. People with PTSD are sons and daughters, sisters and brothers, husbands and wives, co-workers and friends. They live and work with the rest of us. How do their often-invisible wounds influence our relationships with them? In exploring this question, this chapter describes relationships within couples first, then nuclear families, extended families, and finally the community at large.

The effects of PTSD are far ranging. An individual who is isolated and seeks to isolate his/her family might cut the family off from the emotional support of others. A wife might find herself without friends. Children may grow up distrusting the world, expecting it to be dangerous.

Sometimes in a dysfunctional family, one child will become the "scape-goat," and, by misbehaving, attempt to draw attention away from the family member who is suffering from PTSD. Holidays become impossibly stressful. The family's financial status might be precarious. One seven-year-old child whose father died in the World Trade Center attacks had trouble sleeping and wanted to be with his mother full time; the mother was under a great deal of stress, which added to the child's level of stress (Webb, 2004). Children of that age often have trouble comprehending the finality of death, and certainly the exposure to repeated media images of the WTC intensifies an already traumatic memory. Of course, not all families will be so dramatically affected. In fact, as families attempt to find balance in an unstable situation, they employ coping mechanisms that reveal the strength and motivation of a family to heal itself. These mechanisms may not be the most effective, but they reveal resiliency and potential for new growth.

Couples

A couple cannot help being affected by one partner's PTSD. Intimate relationships are a crucible in which our most personal attachments are tested. Those who know us best, and whom we know best, see many sides of our personalities. It is impossible to maintain a façade within the closeness of marriage. A couple in which one partner has PTSD might have met and married before the PTSD developed, or after. In both scenarios, difficulties emerge.

Couples may first suffer from the separation and anxiety caused by a military deployment. A recent study of wives whose husbands were deployed longer and/or more frequently showed higher incidences of depression, stress, anxiety, and difficulty sleeping (Knickerbocker, 2010). Furthermore, wives expressed concern that seeking mental health assistance would negatively affect their husbands in the field; feeling uneasy about asking for help adds stress to an already stressful environment.

In marriages with combat veterans, many couples were married before the spouse saw combat. Often young, with dreams for the future, the couple is unprepared for the changes wrought by wartime experiences. The spouse may describe the veteran as coming home "a different person than before he left" (Scaturo & Hayman, 1992, pp. 275–276). How disconcerting it must be for a wife to find that her cheerful, outgoing husband has become sad and withdrawn. One veteran describes being picked up by his wife when he returned home, and finding her chatter about shopping and appointments to be uninterpretable: doesn't she realize where he has been, what he has seen and done? Of course, she cannot know that. Eager to welcome him back to "the world," she focuses on what she knows; but for him, it is inconceivable that she can "prattle on" when he has just been through life-changing events. At best, the couple merely misunderstands each other and can in time meet again on common ground. At worst, the couple cannot recover from the changes in one partner, and the relationship dies. Hardest for such a couple may be letting go of previous dreams and renegotiating, in light of changes, the dreams they may again come to share.

In the case of war, a wife might find herself learning to be competent while her husband is away. She may discover she can pay bills, raise children, and solve household problems on her own. Her husband may return home and feel there is no need or place for him, particularly if the wife has filled both parental roles. In *Coming Home*, Jane Fonda's character grows active in the antiwar movement and changes so dramatically that the couple has difficulty reconnecting. In addition, issues of fidelity (on the part of both spouses) may be contentious, as in the film.

Fantasies that sustained both spouses during separation may be wildly unrealistic. And when the soldier has been a prisoner of war, issues are magnified. Mateczun and Holmes (1996) found that open communication and agreement about roles helped such couples stay together.

Alternatively, a couple may meet and marry after the veteran returns home, or after one partner has experienced a traumatic event. If the PTSD is delayed onset, they may be much like a couple who met before the symptoms of PTSD became a problem. They believe themselves to be unaffected, "normal," and are ill-prepared for the dramatic changes that PTSD can reveal. They too will go through the marriage-threatening disruptions PTSD brings. In other cases, the couple has met and married after one partner has already shown signs of PTSD. Marriage may seem a solution to the loneliness that a PTSD sufferer feels; yet the demands of marriage may become overwhelming.

Why would a woman marry a man with PTSD? In some cases, a veteran's PTSD may actually have been what attracted his wife to him; she may believe she can help the veteran (Scaturo & Hayman, 1992). DeFazio and Pascucci note that women who marry combat veterans are often efficient, capable, and motherly, taking over the responsibilities abandoned by the veteran; such a woman typically idealizes her husband (1984, p. 85). Further, Armstrong and Rose (1997) found that partners of veterans being treated for PTSD tended to be rescuers. Later marriages (midlife) exhibit a pattern of one partner (the wife) being overadequate and the other (the veteran) inadequate (Scaturo & Hayman, 1992). Yet, while "saving" the veteran (or any survivor of PTSD) may seem attractive, partners may later express feelings of being overwhelmed by responsibilities and in a state of near-constant crisis management (Coughlan & Parkin, 1987).

Suicidal survivors may present a heavy burden for their spouses. Drinking too much, playing with guns or knives, keeping large quantities of medication in the house, having unpredictable and unreliable associates — all these can keep one partner focused on simply keeping the other partner alive. Sometimes the burden becomes too great, and the healthy spouse leaves. Loving the partner yet feeling unloved in return creates resentment, and even a feeling of being emotionally held hostage.

Some partners overidentify with the PTSD spouse and begin to see themselves as victims, too. They may vacillate between caring too much and caring too little. They may feel guilty for not doing enough, yet angry about all they are doing. They feel victimized by a disorder that seems to afflict them as much as their spouses.

Multiple marriages (serial monogamy) are not uncommon among PTSD survivors. Combat veterans may marry three or four or more times over their lifetimes, perhaps as a result of the push-pull of intimacy. Seeking closeness and then finding closeness unbearable, the pattern of being alone and being part of a couple may be repeated. Veterans who have families shortly after their wartime experience may have a second family later in life, seeking to "do it right this time." One PTSD survivor is estranged from one son from his first marriage and spends a great deal of time helping the other son, who is highly irresponsible. This takes time and energy away from his second wife and the two children he now has at home. Some PTSD survivors simply abandon the possibility of having an intimate relationship, and stay single and isolated, feeling that at least they are not inflicting their problems on others.

Whatever the marital context — early, late or multiple marriages — some problems are common with PTSD survivors. Getting and keeping a job may be first among them. Many PTSD survivors have difficulty with authority figures (Scaturo & Hayman, 1992). In Vietnam, for example, officers may have represented the "people who could get you killed" (EFA, personal communication, 2000). Employers, bosses, managers of all types may be seen as equivalent to those distrusted and disliked officers. A childhood incest survivor similarly sees that those who were in charge (fathers or mothers) failed to protect her, or actively abused her. She is suspicious and distrustful of any authority figure as a result. Survivors of human disasters may believe the authorities failed to protect them, and/or failed to help them sufficiently after the traumatic event. They too view authority figures with distrust and perhaps even hatred. These feelings for authority figures make it difficult to be employed, so some survivors will start their own businesses, or work at jobs that permit them a great deal of independence. Others may simply remain unemployed.

If unemployed, how do they survive financially? While some do live on the margins of society, others rely on their partners to provide the family income. In cases where the PTSD survivor is the wife and her husband is the breadwinner, this distribution of responsibility is acceptable both to the couple and the society. In other cases, however, where the wife becomes the breadwinner, both partners may resent the resulting role reversal. They may both feel disapproval from the wider society that expects the man to be productively employed (Matsakis, 1996). And in today's society, where both partners are often employed, the financial stress of having only one income may mean curtailment of dreams such as owning a home or having a larger family.

PTSD is a compensable disability for many combat veterans, but the Department of Veterans Affairs (VA) also represents an authority that some veterans refuse to interact with. In addition, the process of filing a claim, which is often denied and must be appealed, can be so daunting that some are discouraged from even attempting. Even those receiving a disability income may not be financially stable. A PTSD survivor who is stuck in the past may not show much emotional maturity, and may spend the income on frivolous or personal items rather than on family necessities.

A second major difficulty for couples in which one partner has PTSD is intimacy. According to Penk and others (1981, cited in Carroll et al.,

1985), PTSD veterans have difficulty expressing emotions, controlling their anger, and trusting others. Physical and verbal aggression may further weaken a couple's relationship (Rosenheck & Nathan, 1985). Adding to the stress might be the survivor's refusal to discuss the trauma. For example, a veteran's refusal to discuss the war makes the wife feel left out, cut off, and unable to be of help to her husband. One wife says "He [her husband] used to enjoy putting his arms around me and giving me hugs.... Now, sometimes, he acts as if I am poison. It seems at times he even goes out of his way to avoid touching me" (King, 2010, p. 38). Even if the wife intellectually understands why her husband avoids her, she still feels that there is something wrong with *her* that is causing the problem.

PTSD survivors of rape may have difficulty with sex, and the expectations of both partners about the role of sex in an intimate relationship may increase the difficulty. The wife might find it impossible to talk about, and the husband might well not want to hear it. Yet with such a large unspoken issue between them, they will be unable to feel intimate with each other or solve the practical issues of how to achieve sexual intimacy.

A frequent corollary of difficulties with intimacy is the PTSD survivor's withdrawal from friends and people in general, which may cause others to view him/her as unstable (Brown, 1984). While being alone might be comfortable and safe for the survivor, how does the partner feel? The loss of "couple friends" limits the partner to developing friendships on his/her own, and the PTSD survivor may well feel jealous and suspicious of those activities that are perceived as threatening the relationship. Sometimes it is the case that friends abandon the couple, or abandon the well partner because of his/her attachment to the survivor (Matsakis, 1996). Sometimes the loneliness that results from not having intimate or friendly relationships leads to compensating behavior, possibly through promiscuity or substance abuse.

Couple problems may also result from the hypervigilance, the triggers and angry outbursts, of a PTSD survivor. Wives of combat veterans call it "walking on eggshells" or "the eggshell shuffle," trying to avoid triggering a reaction from their vet husbands. It is impossible to avoid, however, since the survivor is exquisitely tuned to everything around him/her, reacting instantly to anything, and perceiving anything as threatening. PTSD survivors often do not distinguish between minor disruptions and major threats. They seem to be biologically primed to react very quickly in either fight or flight mode; when this is an overreaction, as it often is, it catches the partner off-guard and she/he is in turn bound to react to the outburst. Thus arguments quickly escalate and the spouse becomes hypervigilant as well. In time, she/he might also become equally sensitive to triggers of any sort, in efforts to anticipate and head off the PTSD survivor's instant and total reaction.

Nightmares and flashbacks keep the couple unbalanced as well. Extreme cases of wives waking to find their husbands holding knives at their throats are reported, but hopefully are not very common. Less extreme but no less debilitating is the sleep disruption for both partners, the inability of the spouse to calm the PTSD survivor's nightmares, the difficulty convincing someone deep in a flashback that the reality they are experiencing is not really there.

In a study investigating PTSD symptoms in spouses or significant others of disaster workers, Fullerton and Ursano (1997) surveyed partners of rescue personnel who helped with the United Airlines crash in Sioux City, Iowa, in 1989. They found that even though the partners were not directly involved with disaster relief, they nonetheless reported symptoms such as intrusive thoughts, distress, and avoidance; these were perhaps due to fear of loss, the demands of empathizing with and caring for their partners, the limited support received from their partners, and perhaps the memories of previous traumatic experiences in their own lives. PTSD in some ways can be "catching" to partners.

Truly, a PTSD survivor seems stuck in a past time, reliving a trauma or multiple traumas that are no longer present but seem very real to the survivor. A couple can be stuck yet beset by the turbulence of a tornado, having trouble seeing their way through and even more trouble taking steps to free themselves. And frequently, couples have children, bringing yet more players into the game. How is the nuclear family affected by one parent's PTSD?

Nuclear Families

Much evidence exists to show that family members of trauma survivors may show related symptoms. Families are a system of interlocking members, and when one member is suffering, their families, both immediate and extended, are, too. This "secondary traumatization" (Rosenheck & Nathan, 1985, p. 538) has the potential to affect following generations.

One daughter of a PTSD father describes finding her father outside the house many mornings, passed out after a night of heavy drinking. She became his parent at those times, waking him up and getting him in the house before getting herself ready for school (KW, personal communication, 2002). She claims today not to have been particularly affected by this role reversal, but she is the child of the family who shoulders responsibilities, and who also finds herself handling many responsibilities at work.

One daughter of a Vietnam combat veteran finally read her father's mental health evaluation:

> As I read the report, I felt a wave of recognition wash over me. Problems I had been grappling to understand for years seemed suddenly clear. I'd never had a language for Dad's illness, and simply seeing his diagnosis written on a piece of paper made his pain somehow manageable. I believed, as I studied the report, that Dad would finally accept that he was sick and get help [Trussoni, 2006, p. 94].

Unfortunately, despite having a diagnosis and a language to describe what was happening, the father believed he had survived the war without injury. Still, it was helpful for the daughter to have outside confirmation of her father's constellation of difficulties.

Husbands' and wives' difficulties may be mirrored in the children of the family. In one case, Alan J., the son of a Vietnam combat veteran, reacted to his father's difficulty sleeping by becoming fearful of sleep himself. He also showed anxiety and guilt for not being able to help his dad, and even treated his younger brother the way his father treated him (Rosenheck & Nathan, 1985). Because he loved his father, he became over-identified with him. This seems more common in the older children in the family, particularly children of the same sex. Similarly, one daughter describes how she learned from her father: "I had incorporated all his traits — his sharp temper, his unrealistic expectations, his self-absorption" (Trussoni, 2006, p. 234).

In *Off to War: Voices of Soldiers' Children*, Ellis comments that a 2007 study in Ontario found that children would feel a sense of panic if called to the main office of their school because they feared hearing that a parent had been killed. In the same study, other children reported hiding and pretending not to be home out of fear of officers coming to their homes

(2008). Not hearing bad news doesn't change the news, of course, but is certainly an understandable effort to avoid such a tragedy.

Several studies (cited in Jensen & Shaw, 1996) reviewed the effects of military fathers' absence (but not necessarily suffering from PTSD) on their children. Findings suggested that first-born boys had higher IQ scores, while younger boys with older siblings showed higher levels of aggression and dependency. Some positive effects could be related to developing greater strength out of necessity, suggesting that absence itself may not be detrimental; rather, how the family responds to such absence is more important. Similarly, having one parent with PTSD might spur greater growth rather than preventing it.

In a study of twelve children of five World War II veterans with PTSD, Rosenheck (1986) found that the children identified emotional intensity as high in their families. In addition, some of the children had fused with their fathers and even showed symptoms such as nightmares. Both daughters and sons might become rescuers; some daughters married men with PTSD themselves. Several children were emotionally remote from their fathers. The most balanced children tended to be the younger siblings, perhaps because they were sheltered by their older siblings or mothers. In most cases, the fathers had said little or nothing about their wartime experiences, and therapy for the family had not been a possibility. This in part reflects the different attitudes of society and veterans after World War II; those veterans were brought up not to complain, and society's attitude toward mental problems was much more negative than it is now. Ironically, World War II veterans could have talked about their war since many people in society were very supportive of it, but often chose not to.

In contrast, Vietnam veterans would have benefited from being able to debrief after their war, but found a non-supportive society that did not want to hear about it. For a time, the Vietnam War was almost a taboo topic of conversation. Interestingly, Scaturo and Hayman note that many Vietnam combat veterans are sons of World War II veterans, completing the father's "mission" or fighting the father's battles (1992, p. 283). The film *Born on the Fourth of July*, based on the life of Ron Kovic, a Marine Vietnam veteran, suggests that Ron blamed his war experiences on his father, a World War II vet, because he failed to tell Ron what war was like. Other Vietnam veterans have made similar complaints about their fathers.

In the absence of direct information, gung-ho movies and propaganda glorified war for the Vietnam War generation. Finding out that war, or at least their war, was not glamorous in the least added to the sense of betrayal felt by many.

Additionally, veterans of the wars in Iraq and Afghanistan are learning more about their fathers' or uncles' experiences in Vietnam. One Marine veteran of the battle at Khe Sanh was emotionally distant from his son; his son served in Iraq and upon his return, began exhibiting symptoms such as drinking and nightmares. His father recognized the signs and encouraged him to seek help; as a result, father and son have become closer (Sennott, 2007).

Scaturo and Hayman (1992) use the family life cycle to describe how PTSD might affect a family, beginning with the veteran's avoidance of the birth of the children, followed by the veteran's either being too detached from or too enmeshed with (overly protective) of his children. Later, the veteran feels abandoned and/or betrayed when the children leave home, and finally the veteran has difficulty dealing with memory flooding after retirement, and feels a lingering need to deal with unresolved conflicts. Normal development elicits different reactions from a PTSD parent. Haley (1984) describes a case study in which a father identified his three-year-old child's normal aggressiveness as being his fault, and overreacted in trying to control it. Garland (1993), in a study of children of concentration camp survivors, points out that a similar dynamic might occur at adolescence, with the father perceiving the child as an aggressor, and/or becoming the aggressor himself in response to perceived aggression in the adolescent.

Children may also suffer if there is role reversal in their parents' marriage. They may feel rejected by their father's emotional withdrawal and feel isolated from other families and other members of their extended families. Some reject their fathers for not working (Scaturo & Hayman 1992), and may lose respect for their mothers both for being submissive to their fathers and for fulfilling the roles fathers are expected to fulfill. One daughter reports that her mother is afraid of her father's angry outbursts (and potential physical abuse) and as a result, the daughter feels that she can't rely on either parent (Ellis, 2008). In another family, the father isolates himself in the bedroom and the mother joins him there; the daughter feels that she has lost both parents (Ellis, 2008).

In multiple marriages there may be blended families with stepchildren and half siblings. Multiple children add stress; relationships among stepchildren and stepparents, especially if the children are older, may be strained. A PTSD parent may become angry easily and overreact to a child's self-asserting behavior; the child might become more oppositional or may fearfully withdraw. In one family, the stepchildren of the PTSD parent began to simply disregard him and ignore his attempts to establish rules or discipline. The wife sided with her children against her husband, and divorce soon followed. Blended families are difficult to navigate for most of us; think how much more so they must be for PTSD families.

Some of the coping mechanisms of children have been mentioned, including mimicking the father's symptoms. Others include developing behavioral problems that will bring attention to the crisis in the family (becoming the scapegoat), triangulating against the PTSD parent by joining forces with the other parent, or becoming a parental figure themselves (Matsakis, 1996). Additionally, as children grow older, they may, as stated previously, go out and attempt to fight their fathers' battles or complete their fathers' missions. Children may also be drawn to the "helping" professions (Garland, 1993). As they grow, children may leave home physically but remain bound to their families emotionally (Scaturo & Hayman, 1992). Clearly, the children will have difficulty completing their own developmental tasks as long as they are focused on their families of origin.

While one parent may be the one suffering from PTSD, the family as a whole requires attention. Figley and Sprenkle (1978) note that some families reinforce problems: a veteran who is emotionally numb and in denial may be encouraged by the family *not* to talk about problems. Further, a veteran's outbursts may be met by anger, causing a bad situation to escalate. Craine, Hanks, and Stevens (1992, p.107) note that the following family coping responses mimic individual coping responses:

- Loss of belief in invulnerability
- Family belief that the world is a dangerous place
- Guilt and vicarious experience of pain
- Avoidance behaviors
- Substance abuse
- Difficulty completing family developmental tasks
- Confusion of relationship boundaries
- Isolation

Every family develops patterns; these are reinforced by family rules and norms, and guided by family values (McCubbin & McCubbin, 1989, cited in Craine et al., 1992). Such a system, once in place, is difficult to alter. One child notes that "there were many angry outbursts in my childhood. There was never any violence; however, the yelling was intense" (KW, personal communication, 2002). And the difficulties radiate from the nuclear family to the extended family.

Extended Families

Even the best adjusted among us struggle with our relationships to our extended families. Holiday gatherings with our families of origin can be difficult, as we return as adults yet promptly feel like children again. Old roles, as children and siblings, mingle with new roles, as adults and perhaps parents of our own children. We are surrounded by visions of happy families, good meals in well-furnished homes, a fire in the fireplace and gifts under the tree. Such visions, which seldom match reality, cause us to feel disappointment and tension. Physical closeness intensifies emotional closeness and much as we may love our families, such a gathering can be quite difficult to negotiate.

More difficult might be such gatherings with our in-laws, whose routines, values and beliefs may be quite different from our own. Many of us adapt and endure for the relatively short time of contact, but it may be much harder for the PTSD survivor. Forced to interact when she/he might be accustomed to privacy and space to withdraw, an already low tolerance for people might be expressed in irritability, hostility, outbursts of anger, or even abuse, often directed at those most vulnerable and calling forth protective responses from other family members.

The PTSD survivor might retreat into alcohol or other substance abuse, attempting to deal with overwhelming feelings. Alcohol can be plentiful at family gatherings, or it could be a forbidden indulgence. Rarely does drinking help any situation, as it tends to loosen inhibitions. Loud arguments, tears, and/or frightened children may result from the influence of alcohol at family gatherings.

Certainly, simply not participating in extended family gatherings is another option. Countless anecdotes exist of a wife leaving her PTSD husband at home, and being relieved that she doesn't have to watch out for him while complaining of his lack of participation. A husband may simply refuse to attend or a wife may leave him home, finding the visits more tolerable even though she is a single parent for the duration, fulfilling both parental roles, and frequently having to deflect questions and criticism of the missing partner. A wife who at home complains of her husband's inaccessibility is put in the position of defending him; or perhaps he becomes the elephant in the living room — his presence filling the room while all pretend he doesn't really exist.

Families may also find themselves "sandwiched" between caring for aged parents and caring for children still at home. Financial burdens increase; demands on time and energy, already in short supply, may become overwhelming. A PTSD survivor who is hyper-reactive can find the responsibilities too heavy and retreat, leaving more burdens for the spouse and other family members. Interpersonal tensions may be intolerable. The well spouse may burn out, feeling incompetent and unable to control the situation he/she finds himself/herself in. Without outside assistance, the family may shatter.

But again, families dealing with PTSD may have strengths as well as weaknesses. An extended family can be a great help, providing childcare, financial assistance, job assistance, or simply moral support. The well spouse might seek and receive support from the family of origin and/or in-laws. Children whose PTSD parent is emotionally unavailable may find aunts, uncles, or grandparents to fill the void. Another source of support is the larger community.

Community Participation

A lack of understanding on the part of others exacerbates the difficulties of living with PTSD. Vietnam veterans sometimes point to the lack of a "welcome home" as contributing to their feelings of isolation. Extended family members and the larger society seem to suspect that PTSD survivors are malingerers who should stop feeling sorry for themselves and get back to work. Even the survivors might adopt that attitude towards themselves, and wonder why they have trouble leaving the stressful event behind. Veterans of more recent wars may feel that there is greater societal support yet closer to home, the divide between military and civilian populations may contribute to a feeling of isolation.

Anecdotal reports from across the country tell of Vietnam veterans reaching out to veterans of the Iraq and Afghanistan wars. One Marine veteran of Vietnam has established a close relationship with an Iraq War veteran; his forty years of experience with PTSD have helped his friend understand the symptoms and difficulties of PTSD, and have augmented the care he gets from the VA in a more meaningful way (Miller, 2008). A program at Camp Pendleton in California invites Vietnam veterans to attend debriefings with recently returned Marines; one participant notes that "you are brothers here but there's a lot of uncles that are ready to help," which is a reassuring metaphor for these younger veterans (Elliot, 2007).

Many PTSD survivors limit interaction with their communities. They might do their grocery shopping at night, might work third shift, or might rely on mail-order and delivery services. They may expect or require spouses or children to interact for them with the outside world. One PTSD survivor refuses to use the telephone, and asks her husband to make all necessary phone calls. Another never attends her children's school functions or parent-teacher conferences.

If the outside world is perceived as dangerous, a PTSD individual might experience panic attacks upon leaving his/her home, thus effectively reinforcing the belief that it is safer to stay in. It becomes a self-perpetuating cycle that is difficult to break.

Not only does such avoidance of community create logistical challenges for an individual and family, it also deprives them of a source of support. The community, or groups within the community, can offer acceptance and connections to others, which our families alone cannot completely fulfill. Interacting with others reassures us that we are not alone, that there are others like us, and that there is value and purpose in life. Without such interactions, we deny ourselves friendship and companionship that can give us comfort.

In addition, community service, including volunteer work, also reasserts our value in that we actively contribute to the good of others. Some say that the best medicine for anyone feeling low is to help someone else. A rape survivor states, "Even though I may never be able to legally help myself, maybe I can help other people like me. Helping them, maybe, will give me the catalyst to become a person I can love" (Coffey, 1998, p. 82). Certainly the feeling of giving back to one's community and making unique contributions can only help assure the PTSD survivor that there is meaning to life. The survivor benefits and the community benefits.

Some veterans of different wars and different branches of service volunteer to visit public schools and share their experiences. While it may be difficult for them to talk about specific events, it is enormously beneficial to feel heard by an attentive audience. Survivors of the Holocaust, too, may be welcomed in schools so children can learn about the horrors of the concentration camps.

Speaking publicly may be more difficult for rape or incest survivors, but they may benefit from support groups of other survivors, who can acknowledge and understand the pain and shame a victim feels. Support groups have become quite popular over the past 30 years, and deal with all sorts of topics, bringing together people with similar concerns and enabling them to find acceptance and understanding.

In short, community participation is difficult for many survivors and their families, yet in the community they may find the support that will make their lives more pleasurable.

CHAPTER 7

Can PTSD Families
Be Healthy Families?

For spouses and family members living with PTSD, the battles are indeed tough. They face anti-social behavior, depression, anger, abuse and even suicide. They live with the reality of isolation. They have learned to cross Christmas and birthdays off the calendar because it's too hard to celebrate them alone. And they wake up each day knowing that they may win the battle, but they have made no significant gains on the war (McCarty-Gould, 1998, p. 2).

Some think our guys are insensitive, but I think it is just the opposite. They are extremely sensitive — to their own emotions — to the point of not being able to extend compassion to others. They will even say they don't care. It's a defense (CK, personal communication, 2002).

I no longer feel that I am a wife and partner. Instead I feel that I have become his protector. I feel that he has been robbed of something and I'm helpless. What he's "lost" is something that I can't give back to him (JJ, personal communication, 2002).

All is despair and you soon run out of tears ... until you hear a voice from somewhere above that says "I love you and I want to help you." Those words are the rope you need to climb with (GH, personal communication, 2002).

This chapter describes in greater detail the characteristics of PTSD families and contrasts these with the characteristics of families functioning more successfully. By looking at the two side by side, some roadmaps can perhaps be drawn to help PTSD families learn to function better for all their members.

Because families are systems, they can be viewed as either open or closed systems (Goldenberg & Goldenberg, 1990). An open system allows a variety of opinions, is more adaptable, doesn't insist on one correct way to accomplish tasks, and maintains interactions with extended family and the outside community. An open system feels more flexible to its members, but too much openness can lead to the system breaking apart.

Closed systems are rigid and inflexible, isolated, and threatened by change. They may feel more safe and secure, but too much rigidity stifles individual expression. Healthy families achieve a balance between the two extremes: "both stability and change are necessary for the continuity of any family" (Goldenberg & Goldenberg, 1990, p. 52).

Characteristics of PTSD Families

"A traumatized family ... is struggling to recover from, to cope with, an injury or wound to their system" (Figley, 1989, p. 5). In a sense, as an individual can be wounded by trauma, so too can the family with a traumatized member be wounded. And the family's response to that injury may be more or less dysfunctional, depending on the family. Families are unique, as are individuals, but some generalizations can be made.

Isolation

PTSD families are often isolated to some extent. They may have few interactions with others outside the home, including co-workers and neighbors. They may not attend community functions, church or synagogue, and their choice of recreation might be movies or individual sports, where interaction with others can be controlled or limited. Sometimes, too, the family is isolated from its extended family.

If there are children, the children may also have few friends or activities beyond school, and may avoid extracurricular activities. They may prefer not to bring their friends home, and may avoid going to friends' houses as well. Children often pick up on the atmosphere at home, and may feel the need to be home to take care of other family members. For example, a young man in high school hurries home to provide companionship to his mother, who receives little from her husband and has few or no friends of her own.

Sometimes children have absorbed the family belief that the world is dangerous and vigilance is necessary; these children might feel anxious away from home and prefer to stay home whenever possible. The parents might be overprotective of their children, and insist that they be home during free time. A woman who survived rape might be especially protective of her daughters, and refuse to allow them to date or go to parties.

PTSD families lack the network of couple and family friends that would provide some balance. They don't meet or get to know the parents of their children's friends. They may avoid neighbors as well; one veteran refuses to go out into his yard when his neighbor is working in her garden because he doesn't want to have to talk with her. He denies himself the pleasure he might have working outside because he dislikes having to make even trivial conversation.

Substance Abuse

PTSD families may also experience substance abuse, frequently by the survivor, but possibly also by the spouse or the children. Substance abuse very often creates economic difficulties for the family, uses precious resources, and makes it impossible for the family to function as a unit. The abuser is typically at the center of everyone's attention, and family members either pretend there is no problem, or focus so intently on changing the abuser that there is little time or energy for other members and their needs.

Substance abusers may be trying to self-medicate or escape their pain through drugs or alcohol, but the havoc wreaked by such strategies is widespread. The abuser may be able to hold a job, but wages may be spent disproportionately on the abused substance. The spouse might also drink or do drugs, to assuage his/her own pain that results from the abusing spouse, or to keep that spouse company. Children learn from their parents and may experiment with drugs as a way to deal with their problems or feelings.

In response to an addicted family member, other members may become enablers, helping the individual to maintain his/her substance abuse while seeming to the outside world as though he/she is continuing to function. At the other extreme, family members may rebel to the point of leaving the home. One child might act out, misbehaving at school, in order to obtain some attention and/or deflect attention from the problem family member. The members of a family in this situation can become stuck in roles such as rescuer, scapegoat, enabler, peacemaker, and so on.

Because substance abuse is often found in PTSD survivors, some programs and counselors will not attempt to deal with the PTSD until the substance abuse is resolved. Yet the substance abuse is keeping the survivor from feeling overwhelmed by the PTSD; removing that "help" leaves the survivor with no support at all. Thus, treating both at the same time is more likely to be successful.

Unfortunately, sometimes substance abuse leads to violence in the home. The next section discusses violence in PTSD families.

Violence

Violence, such as spousal abuse or child abuse, may or may not be related to substance abuse. It might be the result of a blaming attitude toward others or an escalation of the rage that some PTSD survivors feel and don't know how to express safely. Violence can be verbal, as when a father's primary communication with his children is to yell at them, or when a mother calls her husband and children cruel names. Because no visible marks are left, and there are seldom any outside witnesses, it may be thought that this sort of abuse is less damaging, but anyone who has experienced it knows how hurtful it can be. A young girl constantly told that she is fat and ugly is more likely to be anorexic, or to engage in sex at an early age, looking for some validation of herself.

Of course, violence can be physical as well. One PTSD survivor systematically threw every single glass from the kitchen shelves onto the patio outdoors. Besides the horrible mess, he frightened his girlfriend who hadn't believed he was capable of such violence. On the one hand, it was only glasses. But on the other hand, the girlfriend had a sinking feeling that she could be the target the next time.

Violence directed at a spouse or child will result in the spouse or child becoming highly vigilant, attempting to prevent setting the violent person off, mollifying him/her in an effort to shorten the violence, begging, pleading, promising to be better. These strategies rarely work, as the violence is beneath the surface, waiting to erupt, and nearly anything can be a trigger. The rage is in the attacker, rather than being a response to a provocation of some sort. The trigger is an excuse to express violence, and there is no way to reason with someone in the irrational state of rage.

For that reason, families are told to physically remove themselves from the home to avoid physical violence. There are women's and children's shelters, and some men's shelters are being established. There are agencies in the community that can help abused families, and the court system can be tapped to obtain restraining orders or legal separation or divorce. Abusers can be required to attend special programs, and to undergo anger-management counseling. And families can seek family counseling to heal the wounds of abuse.

In any case, a family characterized by physical violence may have to separate in order to get together again. Violence is insidious: children learn it from their families of origin and later repeat the violence in their own families. Thus, it becomes the first issue to deal with before any other can be tackled. A PTSD family experiencing such violence needs to get help stopping the violence before addressing the PTSD.

Boundaries

Dysfunctional families tend to have boundary issues. A boundary is the psychological and emotional distance between two people. If two people are too closely entwined — that is, it is difficult to see them as separate individuals (or for them to see themselves as separate) — they are said to be fused or enmeshed. If two people are not close at all, they are detached, and may have little or no interest in each other. Healthy boundaries are like Goldilocks' porridge, "just right." Such a boundary is characterized by both interdependence and independence, concern for each other but respect for each other's differences.

PTSD families tend to have unhealthy boundaries. Family members may be enmeshed and overidentify with each other. For example, the children may feel and express the PTSD survivor's pain in their own lives — staying home, even having nightmares. A spouse might be a shadow to the other spouse, barely differentiated, with no independent interests and desires. Sometimes such a spouse might be attempting to deflect violence, or to give comfort, by identifying so closely with the other. But eventually resentment at such a loss of identity will build and need to be expressed.

Appropriate boundaries are often difficult to establish. Cloud and Townsend (1992), for example, ask where the line is between taking responsibility for a trauma survivor and being appropriately helpful. Are we enabling their behavior? Are we doing too much for them? Are we not allowing them to experience the consequences of their actions? Those who have experienced trauma have trouble trusting others, and may become very compliant (out of fear of loss) or highly controlling (to cope with anxiety). The family may need to set boundaries a little bit closer for the member who has trust difficulties.

In detached families, the members may come and go as separate individuals who happen to share a living space. They may express little or no concern or interest in any other family member, and indeed may seem to feel truly alive only away from home. They are highly independent, but not interdependent at all. In fact, they may seem to be a group of people rather than a family with shared concerns and history.

Boundaries do adapt to changing circumstances appropriate to the growth of the family. Small children are supervised more closely than older children; teenagers take on more responsibility for themselves and negotiate their independence from their parents. Boundaries are flexible to respond to these changes, but in PTSD families, boundaries may be strict and inviolable, thus interfering with or preventing the normal developmental tasks that are the major task of the family. Children who do not negotiate these developmental milestones will be stuck and unable to move on, and they will not be able to model growth for their own children later.

PTSD families may be either enmeshed or detached, depending on how the family solves the problem of PTSD that it is coping with. Caring intensely or not caring at all are both strategies for dealing with the pain. And children who grow up in either will repeat the patterns in later life, having families of their own that have unhealthy boundaries.

Another aspect of boundaries is the boundary between the married couple and the children: sometimes the children in a PTSD family take on roles as surrogate father or mother, and this disrupts the couple boundary. In addition, the family as a whole has a boundary separating it from the outside world. That boundary can be impermeable, as when the family is quite isolated, or it can be nonexistent, as when outsiders come and go in the house freely (as may happen with substance-abuse situations). Boundaries are critical for identifying who the individual is, who the couple is, and who the family is, as well as who they are not.

Related to boundaries is the strategy of "detouring." In detouring, a problem in one area shifts to a different area (Kaplan, 1986), as, for example, when one spouse criticizes the other for not keeping the kitchen clean, and the criticized spouse begins talking about the oldest child's poor school grades. Another well-known example is when a parent has difficulties at work and comes home and yells at the children. Healthy people and families try to handle conflict at its source, rather than shifting it elsewhere. But PTSD families with poor boundaries might not realize they are shifting problems.

Learning new boundaries can cause anxiety, as with all change. But psychoeducation, which focuses on teaching explicitly about how people act and why, is an effective tool for helping people recognize patterns that aren't working well, so that they can try replacing them with more functional patterns.

Communication

Communication in a family is top-down (parents to children), bottom-up (children to parents) and interactional (between spouses and among children). Families will have rules about who communicates to whom when and about what. Children speaking rudely to parents is generally considered bad behavior and will be discouraged. A spouse addressing his wife as if she were a child is also considered inappropriate. Families negotiate and develop these rules within the framework of having both a safe and a happy family.

PTSD families tend to have poor communication skills. The members may communicate primarily through shouting, or through sarcasm, or through silence. Appropriate topics might only include meals and activities, never emotions or ideas. A PTSD survivor might speak to everyone as if they were adults, making no distinction between the spouse and the children (they are all "the audience"). It may be taboo to talk about the original trauma suffered by the PTSD member, leaving children knowing something is wrong but not able to find out what.

PTSD families often do not express a great deal of support and commitment to each other (Figley, 1989), and as a result they lack cohesion. They may be physically together, but they don't feel emotionally close or committed to one another. Both the content of communication (support and caring) and the form of communication (times set aside for talking, calm voices, "I" perspectives) are weak in PTSD families, but both are also learnable. Individual and family counseling can be of great help in teaching communication skills.

Characteristics of Healthy Families

Healthy families also come in all varieties, but some characteristics are typical of families that are navigating life-development stages successfully. Kaplan (1986) describes two common models for viewing a family. The traditional, medical model identifies an illness and its degree of severity, while a growth-development model sees a family with problems as being caught up in patterns that it has trouble changing. The family is not static, but rather moves forward or backward. Seeing the strengths of families can move the family forward.

Tolerance

Tolerance characterizes a healthy family, as members permit each other to express differences safely. The PTSD member is certainly "different," in some sense, and allowing that member to be different rather than trying to change him or her allows other members the freedom to be themselves. Often an unhealthy member becomes the central focus of the family, and all family activities and behaviors are skewed, and revolve around that family member. When this is the case, individuals are not caring for themselves or taking responsibility for themselves, but instead are seeing all aspects of life as colored by the unhealthy member. Tolerant families maintain commitment to one another and appropriate levels of concern without trying to "fix" the perceived problem member. Indeed, families in counseling are advised that there is no reality to a "problem" member, but rather, the system is the problem. Tolerant families focus on the system rather than the individual.

Focusing on one family member tends to result in enabling behavior, compensating for the unhealthy member. In a more functional family, members accept that one of the family is ill or disabled or injured, they express care and support for that individual, yet they continue to take responsibility for themselves and their own happiness. In healthy families, there could be more than one unhealthy member, or the unhealthy member could be the husband one year and a child the next. The family that can accept evolving situations and work with them will be more successful as a unit.

Problem-Solving Perspective

Problem solving contrasts with blaming; unhealthy families tend to try to focus blame on a single individual, and to point to that individual as the source of all the family's difficulties. Healthy families, however, accept that traumatization has occurred and focus on how to respond, work with, or cope with the traumatized individual.

In blaming, the family remains stuck on the individual and his/her issues and cannot move ahead with normal developmental tasks. But a problem-solving perspective seeks solutions and is forward-looking. That family is more likely to find answers or strategies or assistance in dealing with the difficulties, since they are actively seeking them.

Problem solving also lessens the likelihood of violence in the home, or substance abuse. In addition, the healthy family is working together, bringing more commitment and resources to bear on the problem, as opposed to expecting the individual to figure it out and solve it alone.

When a blaming family's injured member does seek help, and seeks to solve his/her problem alone, perhaps through counseling or medication, it can paradoxically cause more stress for the family. Families become habituated to their problems and ways of handling disagreement, and when one member changes, the system must change in response. "Change back" messages are given, either explicitly or implicitly, telling the problem member to go back to the old way of behaving. And sometimes that member does. Change is threatening, even if it might result in better functioning for the family.

For that reason, a problem-solving family is more likely to welcome any individual's efforts to improve, to give that member support, and to successfully adapt as a family to such changes. Healthy families consider the problem; unhealthy families blame the individual.

A problem-solving family can experience dysfunction in response to a crisis, such as the death of a family member. Temporarily, there may be enmeshment or disengagement. In a healthy family, these changes are not permanent, while in a dysfunctional family the patterns of enmeshment/disengagement are more rigid. The family is stuck in patterns that aren't healthy (Kaplan, 1986).

Cohesion and Successful Communication

Dysfunctional families have poor communication skills; in contrast, functional families have good communication skills. Healthy families express themselves as individuals in the context of the family unit; they express support and commitment to one another; they express differences without accusing or blaming. They may be adept at statements such as "I feel sad when you go out every night," as opposed to "You shouldn't go out every night." Making "I" statements keeps the responsibility where it belongs, and doesn't focus the problem on the other person. It also facilitates honesty and vulnerability without making the other person responsible for making the first person happy. (After all, no one can "make" us feel happy or sad; those are choices we make ourselves.)

In using non-accusatory language, individuals open the lines of communication to a more sharing and equitable exchange. Listeners do not become defensive and try to counterattack. Arguments are less likely to escalate when an honest exchange of differences is permitted and encouraged.

Many families can identify with the scenario of frequently finding themselves having the same arguments over and over. Clearly, there is little communication going on, as members resort to familiar complaints and accusations. Many families can see that it is a waste of time to engage in repeated arguments, yet don't see a way out of the pattern. To use Lerner's (1989) "dance" metaphor, if one individual changes his/her steps, the dance cannot continue in the same way. Healthy families permit learning new patterns and accept changes without feeling overly threatened.

Accessing Resources

Perhaps at the basis of healthy families is the ability to find and use appropriate resources. This can be physical, as in finding a doctor or exercise equipment, or psychological, as in seeking therapy or seeing a psychiatrist. Individual and family therapy can be quite helpful in guiding families to discover and change their patterns. Healthy families seek out such assistance and take advantage of it.

Other resources might be support groups in the community, or family friends, or extended family members. These can help with childcare, transportation, emergency situations, and just ongoing contact and communication. The military has gone to great lengths to initiate and promote programs aimed at spouses and families (see recommended links at end of book). Studies show that having relationships with family, friends, and their local communities can help spouses and families manage stress better (Orthner & Rose, 2009). Knowing that the family has outside resources gives a sense of security.

Community resources might include substance abuse centers or programs, VA medical facilities, food banks, social support services, consumer credit counseling, public transportation, and crisis lines. (Two lists of some support services are found in Appendices C and D.) A healthy family might or might not need to take advantage of these resources, but does know something about their existence and is willing to use them without fear of exposing family secrets or failing to be independent.

Some resources are within the family. There might be skills or talents that one member can use to help support the family, such as giving private piano lessons during difficult financial times, or taking on a part-time job, or selling an unused car. Family members may be of help in less tangible ways as well; one member might be a good listener or capable of home nursing. Another might excel at organizing finances or taking over cooking tasks. An unhealthy family, in blame mode, might not consider that there are resources within the family itself that can be called on in times of difficulty. Healthy families seeking solutions are better able to identify these resources.

Healthy families, then, are characterized by tolerance, cohesion, communication skills, a problem-solving perspective, and the ability to access resources. Even in a healthy family, however, it can be difficult to deal with one unhealthy member. How do families cope when one member suffers from PTSD?

Compensating for an Unhealthy Family Member

How do healthy families deal with an injured member? Figley (1989, p. 5) observes that "the trauma experienced by one family member may be experienced by the entire family system." He goes on to point out that the most important factor is how the individuals and family perceive the problem.

Families are helpful in first recognizing a difference in the behavior of one of their members. Sudden silence, lack of participation, low mood, insomnia, irritable outbursts can all be signals that something is wrong. Rather than ignore the changes, the family can point them out, and seek to find the cause of the changed behavior. Finding a cause can be a prerequisite to seeking a solution. An unhealthy response to another family member's difficulties is to compensate for or ennable the individual. One wife reported that "I just wanted peace at any cost.... It is no wonder that I fell into my own version of my husband's illness" and "My life had evolved so much around Jim and his feelings that I had lost my own thoughts" (King, 2010, p. 83, 146). Maintaining a sense of self, apart from the problem or the individual with the problem, is essential. Being responsible *to* rather than *for* another person helps keep the problem in perspective.

For a traumatized individual, the family can help by allowing the individual to express the trauma, talk about it, relive it, work through it, all in a supportive atmosphere of safety and caring. Reliving a traumatic experience can be difficult, particularly if the trauma was repeated, and families should be sensitive to the individual's ability to tolerate such reexperiencing. The individual shouldn't be pushed and prodded into talking about a painful experience, but encouraged to do so when she or he feels it is safe. Sometimes professional expertise is needed, and the family can recognize that and help to find it. Sometimes, family members are so close to one another that they need outside assistance in recognizing their own situation.

Some therapists believe that individuals have the power to heal themselves, and with the support of family, friends, and/or a trained counselor, individuals can find new ways of thinking about their traumatic experience(s) and see them in a different light. For example, a survivor of torture might come to see herself as very strong to have survived, rather than humiliated as a person by the torture. Holocaust survivors see the good they may have done in helping others survive rather than seeing themselves only as victims.

Families, too, have the power to heal themselves. As individuals learn to tell new stories about their experiences, so too can families learn to tell new family stories, seeing not only the problems but also the strengths.

Strengths of PTSD Families

A number of Vietnam veterans profess to be confused about PTSD diagnostic criteria, specifically "hypervigilance." Why is it seen as a problem? Isn't it better to be aware of your surroundings, alert to danger, and thus able to deal with it? And in fact, being vigilant in a dangerous world is a strength. It is valuable to be alert and aware, and one has a much better chance of avoiding danger by being so alert. Thus, one strength of PTSD individuals and families may be that they are more aware of their surroundings and correspondingly more careful.

Of course, the PTSD criterion is *hyper*vigilance, not just vigilance, and refers to the tendency to respond to innocent triggers as though they were dangerous. Still, some level of vigilance is valuable, and taming hypervigilance may best be directed at overreactions.

Another strength of a PTSD family is its resiliency. True, some families do fall apart; couples divorce or separate. But many hold together and continue to travel life as a unit, however dysfunctional. And in that resilience is strength of commitment, loyalty, support for others, and courage. "He may be imperfect, but he's my husband." "He is hard to live with, but I promised to stay with him and I will" (personal communication, 2001). These families have weathered many storms, yet stay together and continue to support one another. Even if their communication of such support is weak, the physical fact of their staying reveals their commitment to the family. Resiliency can be tapped to help the family more actively seek better ways of living, giving hope and optimism to the family members.

PTSD families are often adept at handling crises (they may go through many crises and thus have experience). A PTSD individual has survived a trauma through some sort of survival skill and strategies, and these are called on to deal with family crises as well. For example, who better to have around if a child cuts her foot open? Her medic father will know what to do and he will, indeed, do what is necessary. Similarly, to a survivor, crises like losing electricity or water or heat might be challenges rather than disasters. Success in handling crises can be mental or emotional as well, as when those who have survived trauma have the ability to remain calm in a crisis, thus calming and reassuring others. They may become leaders in crisis situations, as others look to them for help. And they serve as models, demonstrating that crises are survivable.

Related to resiliency is determination, a belief that surviving previous trauma signals success for handling current situations, which are seldom as severe or life-threatening as the original trauma. Many PTSD survivors and their families are determined to stay together and make their system work. It may seem unconventional to outsiders, but if the family is determined to move forward, it may not matter to them how they appear to the larger society. That determination of will can overcome times of emotional volatility, and enable the family to feel safe with one another.

Some have wryly noted that dysfunctional families are more the norm than functional ones — indeed, that virtually all of us come from some sort of dysfunctional family. The PTSD family need not see itself as alone and unique in its difficulties. Families can assess what their strengths are, and what they are doing well, as they seek to do better. Realizing that they are already successful in some ways is strong motivation and reassurance. Everything is not "broken" and not everything needs to be "fixed." When the task of healthier living is seen as improving on what is, families are more likely to try to move forward.

CHAPTER 8

Treatment for PTSD: Counseling

[A torture survivor] clings to his identity as a victim, drawing a secondary gain from perpetuating his state of illness and his suffering. "At least I'm still a hero in my suffering" (Pross, 2001, p. 138).

When they saw how much we wanted to listen to them, they talked—about their struggles and the pains that they have had to endure for so long, and about hopes and victories and little happinesses (Faderman, 1998, p. 253).

When my husband returned from Viet Nam he suffered from PTSD, among other illnesses, until the day he died at 53. As he was dying he said to me, "I cannot die yet; I am not worthy," so haunted was he by the atrocities of the war (RM, personal communication, 2002).

I thought that if I could learn how to help others maybe I could help myself. It has sort of worked out that way. I'm still screwed up but now I have an idea why (WH, personal communication, 2002).

PTSD is not like an infection that can be cured with antibiotics, or a cold that clears up after a few days. It is, in fact, a chronic condition resulting from a moment or moments in time that irrevocably change the way the individual's body and mind function. "Managing" PTSD might be a more useful concept, in which individuals, families, and friends recognize the pervasive nature of PTSD and seek ways to cope effectively with the idiosyncratic constellation of symptoms that accompany it. But given the often devastating effects of PTSD, it has been noted that efforts should be made to prevent the disorder from developing in the first place. Friedman (2001) asserts that "early intervention for traumatic stress disorders helps to abort the onset of a serious mental disorder, reduce the severity and duration [of] PTSD once it has taken hold, or prevent Acute Stress Disorder (ASD) from progressing to chronic and incapacitating PTSD (p. 39)."

Typically, early intervention occurs quickly and on-site, and provides some sort of debriefing experience, often involving support in a group format. The participant is encouraged to share thoughts and feelings associated with the trauma in a safe and confidential environment, and is reassured of the normality of his/her reactions. After exploring the trauma itself, participants learn what to expect in the future and discuss how to recognize and cope with post-traumatic stress symptoms (Friedman, 2001). During World War II, the military employed "Critical Incident Stress Debriefing," in which leaders would guide a group to discuss both what occurred and what they thought about it. Members learned about how stress might affect their lives, and how to respond to it. The Israeli Defense Forces have also used this model, which draws heavily upon peer support (McCammon and Allison, 1995).

During the Vietnam War, military policy was designed to lessen the development of stress disorders. Perceiving length of exposure to combat to be a contributing factor, the military instituted a policy of limiting tours to one year (or 13 months, in the case of the Marines). Upon arrival in Vietnam, a combat soldier knew his "DEROS" (Date Expected to Return from Overseas) (Kormos, 1978). This well-intended policy, however, led to individuals being rotated into and out of units of men they hadn't trained with, and weakened morale within the unit. Further, men would create "short-timers' calendars" on which they recorded how many days they had left "in country." Men who were new to units were not battle-tested and were therefore considered less reliable; they were mixed with men who were "short," with less than a few months of duty remaining, and who tended to be cautious in battle. The resulting unit had little cohesion, an important aspect of military success; thus the attempt to limit stress disorders may have unintentionally contributed to the development of those same disorders.

Efforts to intervene on the battlefield (unconventional as that battlefield was) seemed to reduce the incidence of stress disorders among Vietnam War combat soldiers, and men would be rotated out of the field to base camps to work with psychiatrists and chaplains, and then returned to their units. This approach seemed to cut down on the rate of stress-related problems during the war, but the large number of Vietnam veterans reporting problems after the war was a major factor in the articulation of PTSD as a psychiatric diagnosis; thus, the long-term success of intervention in this case is questionable.

Perhaps, too, chaplains were not well equipped to deal with problems reported by combat soldiers. One Vietnam veteran recalls his conviction early in his tour that the war was wrong, and that he could not morally kill another person except in self-defense. Because he was also a squad leader, and felt he couldn't order his men to shoot when he himself wouldn't, he was sent to an army chaplain, who encouraged him to see killing as a necessity of war, not as a breaking of one of the Ten Commandments. This answer did not satisfy him or change his mind, so he was reassigned to a mortar unit, where killing was less certain and much less visible. In some cases, the military would rotate such an individual back to the U.S., or to a larger base and out of direct combat, which shifted the problem to a different setting but didn't necessarily "cure" it.

Prevention has been employed with survivors of natural disasters, as well. Many institutions, including schools, businesses, and government offices, have crisis plans in the event of a traumatic event, from unnatural events like mass shootings or bombings, to natural disasters such as flooding or earthquakes. These plans typically include having counselors immediately available to individuals to help them process the experience as soon as possible. In 1999, when much of North Dakota experienced terrible floods, people were encouraged to call crisis centers to get counseling support, recognition of stress symptoms, and suggestions for dealing with these symptoms. Adults were also given advice on how to help children deal with their fears and reactions (FEMA, n.d.). In fact, children's reactions to stress are often influenced by how the adults around them respond; adults who attempt to shield children may be exacerbating children's fear and anxiety, resulting in regressive behaviors in the children. Being prepared, and talking honestly and openly with children, seem to better allay their fears.

Therapists and those who work with trauma victims are considered to be at risk for developing secondary PTSD and thus are candidates for preventative measures. Dutton and Rubinstein (1995) distinguish between crisis workers, such as firefighters and emergency medical workers, and trauma workers, such as therapists, who have longer-term exposure. Either group can experience depression, grief, emotional numbing, arousal, intrusive memories, and difficulty with work or home life, and both groups are candidates for early intervention. Often education is seen as a valuable tool, providing information about symptoms and teaching coping skills. On-site counseling, providing rest breaks, consulting with other professionals, and offering support may help prevent or ameliorate PTSD symptoms for these workers. Sometimes, of course, the trauma is so overwhelming that taking a break or knowing what to expect might be wholly insufficient. Rescue workers at the World Trade Center in New York who witnessed people jumping from the towers to their certain deaths could not have been prepared for the horror that they experienced. And therapists working with such traumatized individuals may find themselves feeling overwhelmed, helpless, and upset. Sometimes having teams of therapists may work well, as exposure can be rotated or shared, and therapists can find support in the team.

Since it is not possible to predict who may go on to develop PTSD as a result of a trauma, early intervention is necessary but may not be sufficient. What kinds of resources and approaches are available to help those who do develop this disorder?

Individual Counseling

Individual mental health counseling is often assumed to be a standard treatment for PTSD, but may not be the most successful. PTSD survivors often have difficulty trusting others, and the intensity of one-on-one counseling may feel very threatening. In addition, a counselor who has not personally experienced a serious trauma might be viewed with great distrust. Accordingly, group therapies might be more effective, at least at the beginning. Groups of combat veterans, rape survivors, or survivors of the same natural disaster might find great value in sharing their difficulties with one another, somewhat as they shared their specific traumas. One of the great benefits of groups is the realization that someone else feels the same way, a "normalizing" response that says, "You are not alone in your feelings."

One common goal of therapeutic approaches is to educate the client, to explain that symptoms have a name, that the client is normal in his/her reactions, and that these reactions can be considered a normal response to the trauma suffered. This helps alleviate the shame or blame that victims sometimes feel, and reassures the victims so they can move forward in their understanding and treatment goals.

Counseling requires participation to be effective, and obstacles must be anticipated and removed if trauma survivors are to attend sessions. At some VA clinics, for example, doctors, therapists, nurses or other personnel may be Filipino, Vietnamese, Thai, or from another Asian background. Some Vietnam or Korean War veterans feel uncomfortable interacting with people who look Asian. Other possible obstacles include distance and transportation to the clinic or center, meeting times that conflict with work or child care, and expenses associated with treatment. If recognized, such obstacles can be dealt with.

In this section, individual counseling approaches, group counseling, and couples and family counseling for treating PTSD and secondary PTSD are discussed.

Traditional Individual Counseling

Individual therapies are often a reflection of a therapist's philosophy of counseling. In fact, some counselor training programs direct their students to explicitly consider and spell out their personal philosophies. In general, approaches may be Freudian, cognitive, humanistic, behavioral, or some combination of all of these.

Freudian therapists seek the roots of problems in the client's past. Leading the individual to introspection about early family experiences and interactions may reveal long-standing patterns. Freudian psychotherapists often believe that discovering past patterns leads to understanding, and with understanding comes change. This type of therapy tends to be long term, even lasting for a period of years. While many dispute some of Freud's claims about early familial causes of neuroses, there are still many who find value in this kind of introspection. For PTSD, seeking problems that existed before the trauma was suffered might lead to insights about patterns of response or coping. However, the PTSD itself, by definition, dates from the trauma suffered. Leading the client to discuss pre-trauma experiences might be interpreted as meaning that the trauma itself was not as serious, or that the individual's responses after the trauma are not conditioned by it at all. On the other hand, those who might work with an individual by starting at the point of the trauma and then moving forward in time might be missing valuable insights and information.

The Veterans Administration encourages the tendency to view the individual as post-trauma only. After all, if any disability existed before traumatic experiences in Vietnam, for example, then the VA might not be responsible for disability benefits. The effect of this perspective is to discourage a potential claimant from seeing his or her situation from a larger, life-long perspective.

Humanistic therapists take their cue from Carl Rogers, who popularized this approach to therapy in the 1960s. Rogers believed that the relationship between the therapist and the client was all-important, and that if the therapist views the client with unconditional positive regard, the client will feel accepted enough to explore the reasons for his/her own difficulties, and further, will be able to find the most appropriate solutions. A humanistic therapist doesn't tell the client what to do, but instead listens nonjudgmentally. It can be enormously affirming to be accepted so completely, and many find it liberating to be able to say anything at all without risking the loss of the therapist's acceptance. For PTSD sufferers, this acceptance is welcome and comforting, since many fear what others will think of them if they speak honestly of their rage or shame.

Further, a humanistic therapist believes that the client already has the answers she or he needs, and that the unconditional positive regard will naturally bring about insight and change. For some, though, this seems a curiously passive approach to therapy. It is seen as too non-directive and perhaps too unstructured. On an interpersonal level, the acceptance is a wonderful basis for further work, and many therapists include humanistic aspects in their practices, using behavioral and cognitive techniques as well.

Cognitive therapists typically focus on how the client perceives the trauma and subsequent events. Such a therapist might explore irrational beliefs that the client has that result from the trauma. For example, a rape survivor might feel that she invited the rape by dressing in a provocative way. The therapist might lead the woman to consider whether the rapist is not expected to have any self-control, or whether every woman who wears high heels should be considered to be "asking for it." Indeed, it is cognitively irrational for the victim to take all the responsibility for the attack while not ascribing any responsibility to the attacker. Another example is the sometimes debilitating "survivor grief" experienced by combat veterans and other survivors of accidents or disasters. One Vietnam medic worries that he didn't do enough to save a man who was instantly killed by a mine, though rationally there was nothing at all he could have done to stop it. Another spends a great deal of time wishing that he were dead and his friend had survived. But it simply isn't possible in combat to notice that someone is about to die and step into his place. Sometimes it might just be luck, or an individual might find a satisfactory answer in religious faith.

In the film *Saving Private Ryan*, the dying Captain tells Ryan to "earn this," essentially guaranteeing that Ryan, well aware of the sacrifices made to find him and send him home, will experience survivor guilt. And Ryan indeed leads his life trying to make the sacrifices worthwhile, asking his wife at the end of the film if she thinks he has been a good man. All of us are responsible for finding the meaning in our lives, for answering the question, "Why am I here?" For PTSD survivors, finding that meaning can be quite difficult. A cognitive therapist might guide the client to consider the question rationally and find his/her own answer.

The cognitive approach recognizes that sometimes it is our beliefs and interpretations of trauma that cause us difficulty and result in dysfunctional symptoms. For example, many PTSD survivors believe that the world is a dangerous place. Some are afraid to leave their homes. Some leave lights on at night for safety; others turn lights off at night so they can better see any approaching danger. One Vietnam veteran insists he will never again allow himself to have a close friend because he lost those he became close to in Vietnam. This is so pervasive, in fact, that even in Vietnam, new men to a unit would be given nicknames. Not knowing someone's name is a way to not know the person. (Years later it has become nearly impossible for some of these veterans to find those they served with, but at the time, it was the way they coped with the overwhelming fears of loss.) A cognitive therapist helps the individual to re-examine his/her reactions to the trauma, perhaps to recognize that a useful coping mechanism at the time (numbing) is no longer serving him/her well. Having achieved the rather abstract recognition, however, how does the individual learn a new way of reacting?

Often cognitive therapy is combined with behavioral techniques. Behavioral psychology, popularized by B. F. Skinner in the 1940s, is especially concerned with people's behavior, and how that behavior is shaped by either positive or negative responses (reinforcement). Behavioral techniques might involve reconditioning; for example, a combat veteran who startles at loud noises might be exposed to repeated noises so that he becomes accustomed to them and loses the startle response. Or the noises might be soft at first and gradually louder, habituating the hearer to the feelings generated by those noises. The combining of cognitive and behavioral therapies can both take advantage of an individual's typical behavioral patterns and influence his/her thinking about those patterns.

Rational-Emotive-Behavioral Therapy (REBT), developed by Dr. Albert Ellis in the 1950s, combines elements of cognitive, humanistic, and behavioral approaches. Difficulties are seen as the result of irrational thinking that is in our power to change, and that we must take responsibility for. How we feel both derives from and influences how we perceive events, and our behavior follows naturally from our thoughts and emotions. By recognizing and changing how we think about events, we also change how we feel and thus how we act. REBT focuses on the present rather than the past, and is considered by its proponents to be capable of helping individuals in a relatively short period of time (Ellis, n.d., www.threeminutetherapy.com). Thus, it is often employed for brief therapy, discussed next.

Brief Therapy

Because of the need for PTSD survivors to establish a trusting relationship, "brief therapy" might be inappropriate. Brief therapy is defined as short-term (six to eight weeks) therapy focusing on problem-causing behaviors and problem-solving techniques, often behavioral. For example, an individual is not led to understand his/her problems so much as to change them. Typically, the focus is on symptoms, not underlying causes. An incest survivor who is afraid to confront others might be given specific assertiveness techniques (buying an item and returning it). There is some value to this, as oftentimes when we change our behaviors we succeed in changing our thinking. However, regardless of its popularity with HMOs and insurance companies, brief therapy works better for targeting specific individual problems than for the more deep-seated constellation of difficulties many PTSD survivors confront in their lives.

Exposure techniques. Several techniques are available in individual counseling that focus on revisiting the original trauma or traumas in order to lessen their effects on the survivor. These techniques include exposure therapy, Traumatic Incident Reduction, and Eye Movement Desensitization and Reprocessing.

Exposure therapy is an example of a therapeutic technique whose purpose is to reduce reactivity and intrusive memories. The client is led to recall the traumatic event or events and recount them to the therapist. Typically, the client will be highly upset as the events are recalled. The therapist reassures the client that these are memories and no longer represent immediate danger or pain. Sessions are repeated, and as the trauma is remembered each time, the anxiety decreases until the client is able to recall the event without the associated distress. Ideally, the client can then remember the event without it triggering a flashback, and therefore no longer becomes emotionally upset because of the flashback (Friedman, 2001).

A similar technique is Traumatic Incident Reduction (TIR) (Schiraldi, 2000), in which the client is asked to review a traumatic incident as if it were being shown on videotape (p. 209). The client then tells the therapist what he/she saw and how he/she felt while seeing it. The therapist then guides the client to go through the event again, again describing it and the emotions accompanying it. Sometimes greater detail will emerge with subsequent viewings, and distressing emotions decrease. Even better, the client might discover some insight as a result of reviewing the traumatic events, such as a rape victim who recalls that she did call out for help or resist. Such an insight often provides a rush of positive emotion. TIR, like exposure therapy, interrupts the triggering cycle of PTSD.

Eye Movement Desensitization and Reprocessing (EMDR) is founded on the belief that by changing physical eye movements, the brain can be reprogrammed to respond differently to a traumatic memory. The procedure involves asking the client to recall a traumatic memory and negative feelings or thoughts associated with it while also associating a positive belief that counters the negative. During the recall, the client focuses on the practitioner's finger movements. Afterwards, the client recalls both the traumatic memory and the positive belief; theoretically the positive belief becomes strengthened. Friedman (2001) reports that the eye movement seems to be unnecessary for beneficial results; in fact, he states that it is merely another form of cognitive behavioral therapy. Proponents argue that the eye movements are integral and effective.

Anecdotal accounts from Vietnam veterans' wives suggest a variety of opinions on this approach. Some report that their husbands improved greatly after EMDR treatment; others adamantly argue against it, stating that their husbands were worse after treatment than before, presumably because reexperiencing their traumatic memories made them more symptomatic. Therapies like exposure therapy and traumatic incident reduction also bring memories to the forefront, thus lending some support to recalling as a valid treatment. EMDR, then, may be considered as one of the treatments using recall as a strategy.

Anger Management

Anger-management counseling can be offered in conjunction with other therapies or may be offered as a stand-alone, focused intervention. Since PTSD survivors often experience ongoing anger with outbursts of rage, anger management may be specifically recommended as a therapeutic approach.

Anger-management classes attempt to accomplish two goals. The first is to reduce the general level of arousal and anger that the individual feels. Triggers for anger and rage are explored and examined in a safe and dispassionate environment, and individuals are encouraged to recognize those triggers. Contextual factors that might contribute to the anger are also explored; these may include fatigue, hunger, noise, or physical pain. After identifying such triggers, individuals might be instructed to delay the emotions of anger and consider both the trigger and the consequences of acting on the anger. Keeping a journal is a good technique for both learning what precipitates explosions and creating space between the trigger and the expression of anger.

The second goal is learning to control anger as well as to express it more appropriately. Again, recognizing the triggers helps the individual exert some control as he/she realizes that acting upon angry feelings is potentially within his/her control. Family upbringing might be discussed, since the way the family of origin handled anger is likely to be repeated. Techniques for calming down are offered, such as deep breathing, listening to music, physically walking away from the environment briefly, or doing some physical activity such as sports, hobbies, or other physical exercise.

One veteran recalls his anger-management classes, in which he learned that anger may be a cover emotion for fear. His anger masked fears of abandonment, of being unable to provide for his family, of being taken advantage of by other people. Realizing that fear was the source of some of his anger enabled him to address the fears he had, thus alleviating the anger he felt. Coping with fear or anger through alcohol or other substances is a common strategy, but ultimately unsuccessful, because it doesn't deal with the sources of these emotions.

Anger management can be an individual therapy or can be explored in group therapies.

Group Counseling

An early treatment that continues to be effective today is group therapy. Robert Jay Lifton, a psychiatrist, began a series of "rap groups" in 1970 in which Vietnam veterans met together to discuss their problems that the larger society couldn't — and seemingly didn't want to — understand. Distrustful of others, they trusted each other and found the camaraderie of the battlefield recreated in these groups. It became a safe place to rage, cry, and share deeply personal feelings and experiences (Lifton, 1973). In the post–Vietnam war period until the establishment of the diagnosis of PTSD in 1980, the lack of diagnostic criteria resulted in a lack of established treatments. Rap groups were an early effort to provide some sort of help to Vietnam combat veterans.

These groups were so successful that the VA began employing them. In late 1979, finding that Vietnam veterans distrusted the bureaucracy of the VA, vet centers were opened in storefronts and other locations away from the VA medical centers and hospitals (populated by veterans of other wars and doctors who may have had no war experience themselves). Even more effective, Vietnam combat veterans were recruited to work (along with trained counselors) with other Vietnam veterans. From relying on their "brothers" in combat, these veterans could come to rely on their brothers in treatment and recovery.

For another perspective on support groups, imagine a rape survivor who fears to tell her story, expecting questions like "Why didn't you fight back?" or "Why were you out at night that late?" Whether these would actually be asked is not as important as that the individual anticipates them. She needs to trust others before feeling free to talk about the experience. A study of women with PTSD who had experienced multiple traumas found that cognitive behavioral group therapy was successful in reducing their PTSD symptoms (Lubin et al., 1998). Survivors of the September 11, 2001 attacks might feel that only another survivor can know what she/he went through. A group of people who have had similar experiences would be more likely to offer the unconditional acceptance necessary before the individual feels it is safe to share.

Another benefit of support or rap groups is that individuals in a group develop a sense of responsibility to the other group members (Fujishin, 2001). Some PTSD survivors feel they have nothing to offer, but when they become part of a group and feel responsible to both the group and its members, they realize that they do have something to offer. In any group, confidentiality is essential. If confidentiality cannot be assured, members will not be honest or self-disclosing. Thus, maintaining confidentiality becomes a shared responsibility in the group as well.

Rap groups can be primarily support groups, or can focus as well on cognitive and behavior changes in group members. Breast cancer patients have been found to have more positive outcomes by participating in support groups. Groups such as Alcoholics Anonymous have become quite popular for dealing with addictions and their pervasive effects on lives. Groups similar to AA but with different philosophical foundations, such as Rational Recovery (developed in part to counter the perceived overly religious focus of AA), have also attracted participants. AA has several spinoffs that focus on family members of alcoholics or other addicts. Since PTSD survivors may also be substance abusers, these groups may be part of a larger treatment plan.

Some therapists have warned that rap groups in which survivors focus on traumatic events might have negative effects, for example in provoking aggression. Many participants may reject talking about their traumas, feeling it better to leave them in the past and learn to go on. Family members of Vietnam veterans have reported that their husbands' symptoms seem to worsen after group meetings, rather than improve. This may well be a case of getting worse before getting better. Reopening psychological wounds is hard work, but necessary for healing to take place.

One important task of a group is to help members learn to communicate better and to handle conflict. Communication means expressing views clearly without becoming angry, and allowing others to express themselves similarly (Fujishin, 2001). Learning communication skills in the safety of the group is easier, and those same skills may then transfer to home and family life. Conflict, too, is an important aspect of groups, not in the sense of avoiding conflict, but in learning to handle it. Successfully managing conflict leads to growth and change, and again, skills practiced and learned in groups, with supervision, can be employed outside the group, at work, home, or in the community.

Some groups may become comfortable and nonproductive. The members may be content merely to be together, and not challenge each other to get better. A counselor, too, might become attached to the group and enable it to remain static. Such a group becomes primarily social rather than therapeutic. But with careful handling and effective leadership, rap groups have been a mainstay of many PTSD treatment programs.

Therapy for secondary PTSD is similar to treatment for PTSD; individual counseling and rap groups can help an individual become "unstuck" in unhealthy patterns of coping. Munroe et al. (1995) provide this definition: "Secondary trauma refers to effects in people who care for, or are involved with, those who have been directly traumatized" (p. 210), and the authors cite several studies showing how wives and children can exhibit symptoms similar to PTSD. It is helpful for those with secondary PTSD to be able to unravel feelings about themselves from feelings about the trauma survivor, to explore their own pasts and recognize what might be contributing to their own difficulties, and to treat themselves as well as they might seek to treat the survivor. Such self-attention includes caring for one's physical needs, including good nutrition and exercise; addressing spiritual needs, including relaxation or meditation; and attending to social needs by seeking support from family and friends.

Certainly therapy for couples and families may be an appropriate choice for helping to resolve dysfunctional patterns.

Couples Therapy

Couples therapy, or marital therapy, addresses the problems that a couple experiences as a result of one or both partners' PTSD issues. Some of the problems that bring couples into therapy are treated much as any couple's difficulties might be; with PTSD, there might well be individual therapy for the trauma survivor separately. Sometimes team therapists are suggested for couples therapy; a female counselor might be suspected of being on the wife's side, for example, whereas having both a male and a female counselor provides balance. Since this is not always practical, O'Leary (1999) comments that the therapist should not be neutral, but rather should be on both partners' sides.

Couples therapy may be approached from a variety of philosophical standpoints, just as individual therapy is. Many therapists take a systems approach to both marital and family counseling, recognizing that we often find ourselves in unproductive patterns of interaction, and that no one individual is responsible for the problems in the system. Frequently one partner is more interested in marital therapy than the other; and, sadly, it is common for one partner to see all the problems as being caused by the other. The blaming partner seeks marital therapy in order to recruit the therapist to "fix" the blamed partner. The therapist is faced with disappointing both partners; the blamer by not taking sides, and the blamed by attending to the problem behaviors.

Many therapists take a person-centered approach to couples therapy, in which the counselor is advised to give up expectations and listen. Sometimes the couple brings in expectations of the outside world, and if the therapist confirms them, intentionally or not, the therapy will not be successful. For example, a wife who worries that outsiders think she is foolish for staying in a marriage (whether they do or not!) may well feel despair if the counselor confirms that view rather than helping to explore the strengths of the relationship. When people feel judged, they tend to become defensive, and if they are busy defending themselves, they won't be focused on resolving problems.

The diversity of backgrounds and approaches to counseling may lead a counselor to seek patterns in the past, with families of origin, or to focus on problem interactions in the present. It is important that therapists not have a predetermined agenda for the couple, and instead be open to what the couple is saying. By listening and asking questions, the therapist might recognize a theme of disengagement, for example, in which distance is the pattern in a parent-child relationship from the family of origin. We often repeat the patterns that we grew up with. An only daughter who had a very close relationship with her mother might seem to her husband to be still spending too much time with her mother, and not enough with her husband. Or one partner in a marriage might have angry outbursts, alarming the other, who grew up in a home where anger was not expressed. We internalize these patterns and may assume they are universal, or at the least we may interpret angry outbursts to mean a crisis of huge proportions rather than a venting of frustration. Marital therapy may, by exposing these patterns, enable partners to view each other more empathetically.

Harriet Lerner, in *The Dance of Intimacy* (1989), discusses the ways that couples participate in the "dance" of their relationship, pointing out that both partners are following steps. There is not an individual whose steps are out of balance; instead, both are maintaining a familiar pattern and contributing to it. She points out that women in U.S. society are often expected to take care of personal relationships, and a common pattern is the woman who seeks emotional closeness while the man distances himself. In this dance, as the woman pursues, the man flees. This may be a dance that was present in the original families, so it is a familiar and comfortable one. Further, a couple can become unbalanced as one partner (often but not always the woman) expresses emotions for both partners, as the other maintains calm objectivity. In truth, all of us have needs to be weak and strong at different times; when one is the "strong" partner and the other the "weak," there is no opportunity for each to "own" weakness or strength. In fact, qualities such as "emotional" or "objective" have both positive and negative aspects, and it is often the positive aspect that draws couples together, only to become the focal point of their difficulties. A rape victim who marries a man she feels is strong and protective might later come to feel that he is too controlling, although that is the very characteristic that appealed to her originally.

In identifying the issues within a relationship, couples are encouraged to focus on themselves as individuals as well as on their partnership. With PTSD, the trauma survivor tends to be seen as the problem to be fixed — understandably so, as the PTSD survivor may exhibit a range of symptoms that are debilitating and certainly can cause stress in a close relationship. Long-time wives of veterans may find that early patterns of ignoring symptoms, or enabling them (by tiptoeing so as not to disturb their partner's sleep, for example), are difficult to break years later. We prefer not to see our own contributions to problems, yet such insight is necessary for growth and change to occur.

A common complaint in couples therapy is that one partner is not paying enough attention to the other. With a PTSD survivor who has difficulty with intimacy, distancing is a coping technique for managing strong emotions. Lerner points out that distancing may be a way of handling overwhelming anxiety. In some couples, physical distancing occurs; a veteran may avoid sleeping in the same bed with his wife because of fears of flashbacks or nightmares that might cause him to actually physically harm her. The partner who can understand the "why" behind the behavior, and realize that the distancing actually expresses attachment, is better able to deal with her own fears of abandonment.

Underfunctioning and overfunctioning may be both emotional and environmental. Intimacy and distancing are common roles played out in couples, but partners may also over- and under-function with respect to household chores or employment. A survivor who is disabled by PTSD may be unemployed, may be unable to manage the family finances, and may have difficulty helping around the house or raising the children. We all have multiple roles, as parents or partners or employees or friends, but in some PTSD couples, one partner takes on more roles and may take on roles being unfulfilled by the other partner. In one marriage between a Vietnam veteran and his wife, the wife is the breadwinner, the mother, the wife, the housekeeper, the financial organizer, the grocery shopper, and so on. The husband is, well, the husband, and a father, and an occasional chore-doer. The wife seethes with resentment at taking on so many roles as she perceives him to have so few. The more she does, the less he does, and the angrier she becomes. Stuck in an overfunctioning/underfunctioning pattern, the couple has little sense of common goals and working together for a shared future. Worse, they seem unable to break out of the pattern. If she does less, she becomes angry as some things go undone. From her perspective he is the problem, and she focuses her energy on getting him to change. From his perspective, she is choosing to take on these roles, or she is nagging him just as his mother used to, or he distances himself to escape her anger.

A couple's therapist who took sides would merely perpetuate unproductive patterns. Instead, he/she might encourage the couple first to express their respective angers and frustrations, then to listen to each other and recognize how their communication patterns impede their ability to resolve problems. He/she might suggest techniques such as using "I" statements rather than the blaming "you" statements, and might make assignments involving times set aside to talk and listen to each other. Behavioral techniques might be suggested to promote intimacy or to help the couple negotiate tasks and roles with the goal of solving a problem rather than polarizing the relationship into a "good guy-bad guy" dichotomy.

Certainly, some couples seeking therapy may also be dealing with significant practical issues, such as a physical disability or aging parents. Attention needs to be paid to these critical stresses on a relationship. The Veterans Administration has programs to help with physically disabled veterans, for example, and communities may offer social services such as transportation for the elderly or adult day care. A therapist who is aware of the community resources can be of great assistance.

Couples therapy, therefore, is most effective when individuals are recognized both as individuals and as part of a system. A systems approach is also employed in family therapy.

Family Therapy

Family therapy is not individual therapy with multiple individuals. Though a family might seek therapy because of a problem member, it has long been recognized that any individual's environment greatly influences his/her behavior. O'Leary (1999) gives the example of a man who was quite disorganized in one-on-one therapy, but when he came in with his family, he was quite the opposite. Just as a single leaf doesn't tell us what the entire plant looks like, an individual seen out of the family context is similarly just one small part of a larger picture. In family therapy, the whole is greater than the sum of its parts.

While an individual may seem to be the presenting problem for a family, therapists today often operate from a systems perspective: if one member is having difficulties, the entire system is affected. O'Leary further states that one individual's problem may be "a kind of language which leads to awareness of all the pressures, internal and external, which result in only one observable symptom" (p. 27). The therapist's task is to come to understand that language.

Another aspect of a systems approach to family therapy includes the concept of circularity, i.e., how one person's action results in a response, which provokes a repetition of that action. Neither person is to blame, as each contributes to the ongoing pattern. For example, an over-functioning partner takes on additional tasks, resulting in the under-functioning partner doing less, and as he/she does less, the spouse steps in to do more. Rather than blaming either, the therapist helps the couple understand the pattern they are in.

In other words, there is no single scapegoat. "There is no identified patient to be cured in the midst of an otherwise healthy family (O'Leary, 1999, p. 27). Families are led to both recognize their patterns of behavior and interaction, and to identify the often unstated assumptions that behavior is based on. Mothers, for example, are expected to take their daughters shopping for clothes, yet a woman who was raped in a mall parking lot might refuse to fulfill this expectation. Realizing that it is the violation of expectation, rather than the shopping itself, that is causing resentment for the daughter and father could lead to creative solutions, such as catalog ordering, or a grandparent taking the daughter. This is an example of how families often operate according to rules, which they may be unaware of. These family rules could be carried over from families of origin, or adopted from the larger society ("it makes me happy to spend money") or might be created by the existing family in its efforts to function.

Unwritten Family Rules

Rules reflect family beliefs and values, and might be discovered when family members use words like "should": "Parents should take their children to church." "Children should be seen and not heard." "Boys should do sports, girls should learn to cook." Further, rules often underlie communication patterns. Fathers talk to mothers, who talk to children. Girls shouldn't yell. Boys shouldn't cry when they get hurt. These rules may be more or less explicit, but typically they are internalized by children as they grow up, and thus not perceived as open to challenge or change.

Families may cling to their rules even when they don't seem to be working very well. A mother who works outside the home may feel that she is still required to make a home-cooked dinner every evening, even when she arrives home late and has little time, and even when the father or children are available to make dinner. Perhaps home-cooked dinners every night are causing such stress that sandwiches might be more pleasant for the family. One task the therapist has is listening closely and helping families see how these rules are controlling their behavior. It is not the therapist's job to assign dinner-making to another member (though perhaps the mother wishes that were possible) but instead to point out the shared rule and expectations so that the family can solve its own problem. They might prefer frozen pizza to sandwiches!

Family Roles

Rules are closely intertwined with roles. Adler's extensive work on birth order is a helpful start to understanding family systems. Oldest children are responsible, youngest children tend to be more sociable. Single children are natural leaders, while middle children sometimes feel lost or overlooked. Gender roles are also important, as boys are expected to be more active and aggressive while girls are supposed to be more compliant. Certainly no individual can be assumed to be a typical example of his/her birth order; examples abound of younger daughters becoming the responsible sibling, or oldest children being the most outgoing. Nevertheless, birth order does provide a useful framework for looking at family roles. Some therapists believe that we bring our sibling and parental relationships into our new families, and both repeat and attempt to resolve early conflict in a new family setting.

Lerner (1989) gives a personal example that illustrates how birth-order roles might become polarized in a crisis situation. When her mother was diagnosed with cancer, her older sister became very competent while she herself became the problem child; both daughters were responding to their high levels of anxiety, but in quite different ways. Further, by acting out, Lerner focused the family's attention on her, thus deflecting anxiety from the very real fears about the mother. It might be said that by acting out, she was providing a needed outlet for the worries that could not be expressed directly. Indeed, her mother's focus on Lerner's problems may have been instrumental in her battle against cancer, as she felt that she needed to live because her daughter needed her so much.

Labels and Family Relationships

The roles that are fulfilled in a family may also be seen as labels: breadwinner, disciplinarian, problem child, smart child, troublemaker, and peacemaker. Labels limit us because they impose expectations, and we often try to live up to these expectations. The child who is labeled "the smart one," for example, feels pressure to measure up with good grades and may either fulfill the expectation or reject it, perhaps becoming "the problem child." Roles certainly may change over time or in response to a crisis, as when a child becomes a parent to his/her own parent. Temporarily, this can be a strength at a difficult time, but when the crisis has passed, it may be come dysfunctional for the family as well as the individual. In highly flexible families, the roles and shifting of roles may be so extreme as to be chaotic; in overly rigid families, the impossibility of evolving roles may be equally detrimental.

If one member of the family has PTSD, she/he might be labeled "the sick one," and the family system might be configured to revolve around that individual. Everyone in the family focuses on the sick individual, and all the family tasks are organized around that individual. In a healthy family, each member would have a self-focus, relationships with other family members, and relationships with individuals outside the family. But in a PTSD family, all relationships might be uni-directional, toward the sick person, who might become dependent (childlike) and one of the children might become a surrogate parent. The parent might become overly enmeshed with that child (often the oldest child), creating a pseudo-couple that interferes with the parents forming a more balanced partnership with each other, and with their children. Individuals lose sight of their own personal development, and relationships with others in and out of the family are neglected. Triangles might develop, where two family members become a team focused on a third. In a PTSD family there might be multiple triangles. A mother and daughter might become a team focusing on a PTSD father while at the same time two daughters might become a team acting against the mother. Triangles are common ways that we avoid dealing directly with our personal relationships; it is so much easier to commiserate with mom about dad's drinking than to deal directly with our fathers. And because triangles are easier, they are also stable and difficult patterns to break. Yet they act to prevent change and growth.

Sometimes in a PTSD family, the parents will try to shield the children from one parent's illness. Hinshaw (2002), writing about his father's bipolar depression, notes that there should be some "middle ground" between exposure to chaos on the one hand, and deafening silence on the other; a middle ground that would involve the parents' ability to create a meaningful story, in words that the child or adolescent could comprehend, to help explain the home situation (p. 203). Patience Mason has developed guidelines and suggestions for explaining a parent's PTSD to children; this valuable information is available on her website, patiencepress.com (see Appendix C). Children recognize difficulties even when they don't understand them, and so should be included in family discussion and therapy.

Boundaries

Boundary issues are another aspect of family counseling. Boundaries exist between family members and between the family and society. Appropriate boundaries, neither too close nor too distant, characterize a healthy family; family members are both individuals and members of a larger system. In struggling families, there might be too few boundaries between individuals and other family members, resulting in an enmeshed relationship in which family members have little autonomy and are too involved with each other. Family members might seek to meet each other's needs and expect reciprocation, rather than meeting their own needs. On the opposite end of the continuum is disengagement, where individuals operate so independently that they are essentially a group of individuals rather than a family system. As mentioned in Chapter 6, Goldenberg and Goldenberg (1990) describe family systems as either open or closed. Open systems allow for a variety of viewpoints, with no one "correct" way to think, and foster interactions with extended family members and the outside world that are more adaptable and flexible. Closed systems, on the other hand, are rigid, inflexible, isolated, and threatened by change. Closed systems feel more secure but may also seem stifling to family members; open systems are more flexible but could give rise to subgroupings. Either may occur with PTSD families: there can be so little attachment that family members have little interaction with or commitment to each other. Members might seek closeness outside the family, leaving home early to get married, or forming alliances outside the family. Some families of veterans report that their husbands essentially stay "bunkered" at home and do not welcome visitors. Wives may have extensive relationships with other women, at work or church, yet complain about not feeling close to their husbands. Other families might be too closed; children are encouraged to see the outside world as hostile, and the entire family is isolated from the larger society. Neither type of system reflects a balance between intra-family closeness and outside relationships.

How Family Therapy Can Help

The goal of therapy is not to impose some idealized version of a "perfect family," but to help families to recognize their natural needs for both intimacy and distance and find their own ways to meet these needs.

The importance of listening is highlighted when we realize that families may be experiencing "anniversaries" which they may not even be aware of. A father's sudden overprotectiveness of his daughter may be related to the death of his sister at about the same age. Or a woman might become highly fearful about her child's health at about the age her own mother had an unexpected heart attack. These anniversaries are part of our memories and affect us even when we are unaware of them. At other times an unacknowledged feeling of loss could manifest itself years later. For example, a woman who feels sorrow about giving up her career to raise children might not even be aware of the feelings of grief. Vietnam veterans may unconsciously still feel betrayed by officers or their government in an unpopular war, or an incest victim may mourn the loss of feeling safe in her own home. The therapist listens carefully both to what is said and what is not said.

Developmental family tasks are often a time of stress. When a child leaves home, or a wife goes to work outside the home, the entire family system shifts. A younger child might suddenly get more attention than before; a husband might be threatened by his wife's new source of income. When the system fails to change appropriately for these developmental stages, it may seek assistance.

Rules, roles, boundaries, communication patterns all combine to create family stories. Historical events are interpreted through a filter of these unspoken family rules and values, and the retelling of these stories reinforces the rules. Because these stories, to some extent, are created and not merely remembered, they can be recreated. Families might be directed to find strengths in their history and tell new stories that build on strengths and express hope for the future. We can learn to interpret differently; we can change our filters.

Therapists working with PTSD families must be aware of the dynamics of family systems and listen to the family to understand what rules and roles govern the family's functioning. Again, the goal is not to change the family into some idealized societal vision but to help the family seek and find ways of interacting that meet the needs of the family members. After all, there are many different models of successful families, and no one "right" way.

Cross-Cultural Considerations

Today it is also crucial for therapists to understand something about cultural diversity. In the United States there are many cultures and sub-cultures (and some would say that each family is a mini-culture in itself). The term "family" itself is defined differently by different cultures, with a Spanish-speaking family including extended family members while a traditional Anglo family limits itself to just a couple and their children. Therapists dealing with other cultures might need to invite in the grandparents, for example, who may be the heads of the family and the source of family wisdom and authority. Rules and roles may be quite distinct in other cultural traditions, and crises may lead to role reversals that threaten the integrity of the family.

Kaplan and Girard (1994) point out a problem many of us have in understanding other cultures and lifestyles. They describe a client who buys a dress when she has an electric bill due, and the social worker doesn't understand why, as she would not behave this way herself. In this case the social worker is judging the action according to her own values; she doesn't recognize the futility the client might feel about bills that never end, or that the client is accustomed to dealing with her electricity being turned off.

When Indochinese refugees fled to the United States after 1975, it was not uncommon for the children to acquire English more quickly than their parents, and to become the mediators of the new language and culture. Furthermore, the children acquired American attitudes about independence and rebelled against their parents. The result for many families was children who were more powerful than their parents, disrupting the traditional patterns of authority. In an earlier chapter, reference was made to a Hmong family with an epileptic child. The medical specialists insisted on treating the child to control the seizures; the Hmong considered epilepsy not an illness to be cured, but a natural, even God-given, resource. Unfortunately for all, the state's social services became involved and removed the child from the home because the parents were not administering the medication as ordered. The child later was returned, but family traditions had been severely affected by the mismatched cultural expectations.

Cross-cultural therapy also must take into account differing communication styles. Anglo Americans are said to have a rather direct style, stating what they think and feel. In contrast, Japanese communication tends to be more indirect and more polite. Hispanic Americans may use more gestures and touch than Anglo Americans. Smiling is interpreted differently in different cultures. Rules of eye contact and physical distance between speakers are also culturally determined (Sue & Sue, 1999). Therapists are adept at interpreting verbal and nonverbal communication, but if they are not familiar with the client's cultural background, they may well misinterpret the message. Between a typically Western definition of PTSD itself and traditional Anglo-American therapists, PTSD survivors from other cultural backgrounds may not receive appropriate care — if they seek it in the first place, also a potential problem with culturally different populations.

Dealing with a System

In family therapy approaches, does awareness of family patterns lead inevitably to change? While earlier client-centered therapies may have believed so, more recent views suggest more is needed. A therapist might take the view that family patterns that are not working are in fact a sign that the family is attempting to overcome problems, and seeking strengths is a productive way to begin to approach change. Change is never easy, since our patterns tend to be so ingrained, and efforts to change are frequently met with "Change back!" reactions. When one family member chooses a different response, other family members often react anxiously and may consciously or unconsciously attempt to reinstate familiar patterns. Counselors also need to be aware of their own baggage that they bring to family therapy, and need to be aware when they themselves are responding to old memories rather than to the family they are working with (O'Leary, 1999). O'Leary also comments on how complex family counseling is, and how difficult it can be to keep track of all the information, interactions, and so on — another reason to let the family lead the way. The counselor can never know everything and so instead tries to empower the family, seeing the family as the best expert on itself.

O'Leary suggests that effective family counselors are active, structuring meetings for the family, seeking input from all family members, and then using a reframing technique: suggesting a different way to look at the issue, for example, or suggesting that some underlying need is being expressed but not heard. Sometimes such reframing implies a different way to act, thus allowing a possibility for change but keeping the power in the clients, not the counselor. For example, a therapist might reflect that avoiding intimacy is related to a fear of getting close to someone that you might lose, as in the case of combat. This reframing could lead to the possible alternative value of enjoying closeness with someone when you have the opportunity. PTSD survivors who experience debilitating panic attacks might be led to consider how an irregular heartbeat might in fact be caused by the panicked feelings rather than the other way around. A skilled therapist might use reframing techniques to suggest alternatives without giving direct advice, which might provoke defensive reactions.

Families generally seek counseling when their established patterns are causing them more pain than joy; that is, when the equilibrium is disturbed. Often one member might be cited as the problem, but in a systems approach it is understood that the system needs attention, not just the individual. The fact that a change in one area of the system will result in changes elsewhere in the system is a source of possible strength. Rather than addressing the presenting problem directly, the therapist might suggest a change in a less-charged area that is not as threatening to the family members. That change, then, can lead to positive changes elsewhere. For example, a child might act out in response to tensions between her parents, unconsciously attempting to keep them together by keeping them focused on her. Rather than directly confronting the problems in the couple, the therapist might suggest they go out for an evening, without the child and without focusing on the child's issues. In doing so, the couple pays more attention to each other and takes a step toward dealing with their interpersonal problems. This in time may result in a better relationship, freeing the child from attempting to diffuse marital problems by acting out.

Troubled families do exist in a larger environment, one that might include a weak economy with the possibility of job loss or pressures to conform to a particular lifestyle. Even as the environment can be a source of stress, it can also be a source of support. Religious institutions, parent-teacher organizations, social services, and certainly extended family members can all be resources for families and family members. Therapists who work with families are tireless in pointing out the importance of seeking strengths, within and outside the family, to provide that sense of hope that leads to changes that promote healthier functioning. Families in distress often do not see their own strengths, yet these can be considerable and can be engaged to help families see their own power to effect appropriate changes. For PTSD families in particular, the existence of a very real disabling condition requires a balanced approach to address the needs of the PTSD individual as well as the members of his/her family.

Veterans Administration PTSD Programs

The Veterans Administration offers both outpatient and inpatient programs to treat veterans with PTSD. Outpatient programs typically include individual and group therapy for PTSD, may address substance abuse problems, and incorporate education into therapeutic approaches (Parrish, 1999). Some centers also offer group counseling for wives or other family members; these vary widely in availability and success.

Inpatient programs offered by the Veterans Administration may be short term (two weeks) to longer term (90 days) and similarly incorporate individual and group counseling with education, recreation, and vocational activities in a controlled and supportive environment (Parrish, 1999). Sometimes a veteran will need or want to repeat an inpatient experience, and this can be done. Again, some centers have excellent reputations for their programs while others are perceived to be of poor quality.

Some individuals who are totally disabled by PTSD or a combination of PTSD and other problems may live in Veterans' hospitals or homes. As the veteran population shrinks, these hospitals and residences are under great financial pressure. In Iowa, veteran health services were consolidated into one VA hospital rather than being scattered about the state. Nationwide, there is discussion of eliminating the Veterans' health system altogether, and referring veterans to civilian doctors. This hasn't happened as yet, but as finances become ever more scarce, it is a real possibility.

Counseling is an effective treatment for PTSD. Counseling for the individual might be one-on-one or a rap or support group. If the family is having problems, and it is feasible, family counseling is a good adjunct. In deciding to seek counseling, an individual or family should take the time to meet with potential counselors and find someone they feel comfortable with and can trust. One middle-aged male PTSD survivor went to a counseling office with very specific requirements: he wanted someone of his age who had particular political beliefs. He was certain that he would be unable to speak honestly with someone who didn't share his views.

Referrals from medical doctors or friends might be helpful in finding a therapist to work with, and therapists will often spend some time deciding whether they think they can be of help to a particular individual or family. So it is really a case of finding a good match, if possible.

For families and individuals with limited budgets, there are agencies and medical establishments that offer varying amounts of free counseling or support. Some of these are listed in Appendix C.

While counseling is an important treatment for PTSD, medications may also be used. Sometimes a combination of therapy and medication is the best way to manage PTSD. The next chapter describes the medications prescribed for PTSD and its symptoms.

CHAPTER 9

Treatment for PTSD: Medication

The afflicted person may come to be blamed for susceptibility to having become "ill," especially given that the symptoms of the illness are disturbed emotions and behavior patterns, over which people are typically held to exert control (Cicchetti, 2000; cited in Hinshaw, 2002, p. 177).

I was in the uncharted territory of healing (Kim, 2000, p. 209).

One of the things that makes it hard for us to handle our own problems and to help others with theirs is that we have so much trouble accepting pain (Kusher, 1989, p. xi).

There is no magic pill that will "cure" PTSD, but treatment has expanded considerably with the increased recognition of PTSD as a distinct psychological diagnosis, not only in combat veterans (ongoing military operations, a volunteer army, call up of the National Guard and Reserves, and recruitment/retention issues) but also in the general population (natural disaster traumas such as recent earthquakes and floods; crime or accident traumas). As with medicine in general, researchers continues to seek and develop new drug regimens of benefit to PTSD sufferers.

Drug treatments for PTSD are typically focused on relieving symptoms; for example, sleep medications may be prescribed in order to address insomnia and nightmares. Psychiatric medicines usually intended to treat psychotic disorders may be used for combat veterans having flashbacks, which might be interpreted as experiencing a split from reality. PTSD survivors with symptoms of depression would be candidates for antidepressants. The early antidepressant medications often included a variety of unpleasant side effects; these have been superseded by newer medications, including selective serotonin reuptake inhibitors (SSRIs) that target specific chemicals in the brain with fewer side effects. Recent additions to the arsenal are blood pressure medications, which help the heart beat more slowly, or the blood vessels to relax, thus calming, in a sense, the nervous system. Anti-epilectic medicines are also found to dampen the limbic system kindling associated with PTSD. All of these will be discussed in greater detail in this chapter.

Of course, medications should not be used to merely cover up problems or to help people deny their problems. Instead, these drugs should assist a PTSD sufferer to be better able to understand and manage his/her PTSD. And rarely are medications alone sufficient. Group and individual therapy, as well as a variety of alternative approaches, should be part of the overall treatment plan as well.

The Importance of Assessment

Some assessment of the individual's current state of functioning is required before considering the most appropriate treatment strategy. For example, the treatment of an incest survivor who seeks help because some event has triggered past memories may be different from the treatment of a combat veteran who has endured for several decades before deciding life is too difficult to go on without help. In the first, an acute reaction is the compelling factor while in the second, chronic issues the focus.

In some cases, symptoms must be dealt with before the underlying PTSD can be addressed. Substance abuse is a good example. While alcohol or other drugs might be used to numb oneself from painful emotions, or to help with sleep, it is difficult to work on the issues provoking the alcohol abuse until the abuse is stopped. Additionally, many medications should not be mixed with alcohol or other medications because of the risk of serious side effects. But it is also important to recognize that alcohol may be helping a person cope, and simply removing the "crutch" without offering something else to stand on will not be successful. Dealing with substance reliance while also addressing the underlying PTSD has more likelihood of success than does either alone. If the abused substance is an illegal drug, it is even more important, since being arrested or straining family finances may be incapacitating the individual's and the family's resources, financial and personal.

It may also be the case that comorbid psychological conditions, such as bipolar disorder or anxiety disorders, exist. Medical professionals must determine whether to first treat the preexisting disorder in order to make it possible for the individual to then focus on the PTSD that exacerbates the disorder.

Furthermore, assessment must be targeted and individualized. Many drug studies may use middle-aged white males as subjects, and then generalize the results to the larger population. African Americans, for example, have different responses to treatment (both therapy and medication) for depression and panic attacks, although cognitive behavioral therapy for PTSD has been found effective both for African Americans and whites (*Mental Health Care for African Americans*, n.d.). Similarly, women's responses to therapy and medication may be different from men's. Individuals are known to have differing reactions to medications. For example, an individual with clinical depression may have to try several medications, or combinations of medications, before finding relief. There may be physiological bases for these differing responses to drugs. As research reveals these distinctions in more detail, it may be possible to select the best medications for an individual without the lengthy trial and error period often found today.

Finally, assessment is critical because PTSD survivors might also have an array of physical wounds or illnesses; some Vietnam veterans suffer from Agent Orange–related problems, while veterans of combat since Vietnam may be amputees, suffer acquired deafness, or have other little-understood physical problems (such as Gulf War Syndrome). If medications are prescribed for physical ailments, these may interact with psychiatric medications. They may also be abused; painkillers in particular are susceptible to misuse. Doctors sometimes advise that painkillers be taken before or at the onset of pain, which may be therapeutic for the pain, but invites a cycle of anticipation and treatment that can be difficult to break. Oxycontin is one narcotic medication that has been hailed for its effectiveness in treating chronic pain, but has quickly become widely abused. Thus it is essential for medical practitioners (and for those taking medications) to recognize that drugs for the treatment of physical disabilities may interact with PTSD medicines; and that, while they may be legal, the potential for drug interactions, overdose, or addiction (dependence) is as serious as with illegal substances.

All of this confirms the necessity of doctors and psychiatrists to spend time in accurately assessing the individual's current state of physical and mental functioning before designing an appropriate treatment program. A number of assessment tools are available, from standard interviewing techniques to exposure scales to self-reporting instruments (Friedman, 2001). Clinicians may also use psychological tools such as the Minnesota Multiphasic Personality Inventory (MMPI) or the Rorschach Ink Blot Test (Friedman, 2001). A psychiatrist trained in the use of the diagnostic tools and with experience in PTSD is probably best able to conduct a thorough assessment. Although these tools aid in the diagnostic evaluation, ultimately the criteria that must be met for a diagnosis of PTSD are established by the DSM IV. And since a revision of the DSM is underway, practitioners need to stay up to date on diagnostic criteria and tools (the proposed revisions are described more fully in Chapter 2).

Treatment for PTSD ultimately begins when the survivor decides the benefits of treatment outweigh the benefits of PTSD. While programs are in place that seek to identify and treat PTSD in active duty soldiers, the individual still must be invested in the treatment. Odd as it may seem, many PTSD survivors have become accustomed to their pain and how they deal with it. Schiraldi (2000) notes that a combat veteran might feel loyal to his dead comrades, or an abuse survivor justify past failures, by keeping traumatic memories alive; these individuals need to address the value that they find in PTSD. An outsider may view the coping strategies as dysfunctional, but they are familiar and comfortable to the survivor. Resistance to change is natural. No one can convince the sufferer to abandon familiar problems for the unfamiliar goal of possible improvement. The survivor must come to a point of recognizing that the results are worth the risk.

Schiraldi (2000) suggests that a PTSD survivor might compare a list of the benefits of PTSD with the disadvantages to help the individual realize the source of his/her resistance to treatment. Understanding that she/he finds value in having PTSD can help the individual see the value in recovery. The benefits may not only be psychological: a combat veteran may depend on a disability check and recovery may mean seeking employment. Or perhaps the survivor might fear, with some reason, that a wife or parent may leave if unneeded to help the survivor. These are very real fears; by noting the potential benefits (self-sufficiency, self-esteem, more satisfying personal relationships) the survivor may come to choose the risk of treatment and the resulting change.

A therapist working with a PTSD sufferer must be aware of this dynamic and walk a delicate line of encouraging recovery without pushing the client to do too much too quickly. The client sets the pace of recovery. Although medications alone may be used to treat PTSD, the author believes that counseling is an important adjunct, and that counseling ought to begin before or at the same time medications are prescribed. The rest of this chapter details the array of drugs that might be used in treating PTSD. Brand names are given first, with generic names in parentheses, merely because the brand names are probably more familiar to readers.

Medications for PTSD

Medications can be helpful in treating the symptoms of PTSD; however, not all survivors will agree to take them. One Vietnam veteran says he simply doesn't like to take pills, and he fears that the side effects will be worse than his PTSD symptoms. He also thinks using a "drug" means giving up control, a control that has long been a focus of his daily life. Many people consider taking a prescribed psychotropic medication synonymous with personal failure or character weakness. Fear of dependence may also be a factor. Others believe using psychiatric medications is a sign of cowardice or a lack of self-control; our society does tend to see mental problems as a lack of strength or character and the survivor might as well. It is "OK" to take heart, cholesterol, or antibiotic medications, but "not OK" to take psychiatric medications.

Finally, personal identity might be a reason to resist drugs; one Vietnam veteran who refused any drug therapy for decades explained that he knew who he was without any medication, and he feared a loss of self. When he began taking Zoloft, he felt that he was indeed a different person, and he had to get to know that new person, and to integrate both views of himself into a whole. He stubbornly stayed with the medication against his own impulses to quit, and came to appreciate it, but only after a full six months. Many survivors might not have the patience to stay with a medication that long. The use of medications is a highly personal choice, and the individual should understand the purpose and goal of the medication and the possible unpleasant side effects. Medications for PTSD are assistive, not curative.

In addition, the number and variety of medications has increased enormously in the past few decades. Several medications prescribed for the same disorder or symptoms may have quite different effects on individuals, so that if one medication doesn't seem to help, another might work better. For example, Prozac, Paxil, Celexa and Zoloft are all Selective Serotonin Reuptake Inhibitor (SSRI) antidepressants and work in approximately the same ways, but an individual might respond to one and not another. Some affect serotonin and dopamine; others affect seratonin and norepinephrine. Having this flexibility is valuable, as there is always hope that a slightly different medication might be helpful. Unfortunately, the effects of some of these medications may not be felt for several weeks. Imagine someone living with despair and suicidal intentions being told to be patient, give the drug time, discover if it works, and if it doesn't, then change drugs and go through the process again. It would not be uncommon for months or even years to pass before an optimal medication and dosage were established.

At this time, there are only two medications specifically approved for the treatment of PTSD: Zoloft (sertraline) and Paxil (paroxetine). Zoloft and Paxil (first approved for panic disorder) are two of the SSRI antidepressants and seem to also lower anxiety and alleviate obsessive-compulsive disorder (OCD). That these drugs are prescribed for both anxiety and mood disorders is part of the general picture for use of medications with PTSD: antianxiety and/or antidepressant drugs are the usual choices. It should not be assumed that either are uniquely effective for PTSD.

Antidepressants

There are several classes of antidepressants currently available; those primarily prescribed today include tricyclics, Monoamine Oxidase Inhibitors (MAO inhibitors or MAOIs), SSRIs and more the newer SSNRIs (Selective Serotonin and Norepinephrine Reuptake Inhibitors). These drugs target the chemicals in the brain that transmit messages to neurons, that is, neurotransmitters. Older antidepressants seemed to work on multiple systems, thus resulting in more side effects. SSRIs and SSNRIs target specific neurotransmitters in the brain (serotonin, norephinephrine, dopamine) and thus have fewer side effects. However, intolerance of a side effect leads to discontinuation of a medication, so side effects must still be taken into account.

The tricyclic class of antidepressants is older, and includes the brand names Anafranil (clomipramine), Elavil (amitryptiline), Norpramin (desipramine), Sinequan (doxepin), Pamelor (nortripyline), Tofranil (imipramine), Surmontil (trimipramine), and others. Some might be used for bed-wetting problems in children, Obsessive Compulsive Disorder (OCD), narcolepsy, and Attention Deficit Disorder (ADD) in addition to general antidepressant use (Griffith, 1999). Tricyclic antidepressants tend not to be as effective as other antidepressants for PTSD, and they tend to alleviate symptoms of flashbacks better than other symptoms (such as numbing or hyperarousal) (Friedman, 2001). The effects of the drugs may not be seen for some weeks, which is a long time to someone who is severely disabled. In addition, tricyclic medications should be discontinued under the supervision of a doctor as there may be withdrawal symptoms. Some of the common side effects include tremor, headache, dry mouth, constipation or diarrhea, nausea, fatigue, anxiety or insomnia, and sedation. Generally the side effects wear off over time, but again, it can be diffi cult for a depressed person to tolerate the lack of immediate improvement along with dealing with side effects. As with other drugs, there are also contraindications (thyroid disease, asthma, liver or heart disease, high blood pressure), and patients need to be aware of drug interactions (in particular, patients need to avoid using alcohol). A higher risk for overdose exists with the tricyclic antidepressants.

Another class of antidepressants is the MAO (monoamine oxidase) inhibitors, brand names Nardil (phenelzine) and Parnate (tranylcypromine). These may also take several weeks to take effect. Used for depression and panic disorder, the drugs increase levels of norepinephrine, serotonin, and dopamine in the brain and have been found to be helpful with reexperiencing symptoms and insomnia. They seem less helpful for numbing and hyperarousal symptoms (Friedman, 2001). Common side effects include weakness, fatigue, possible dizziness, restlessness and dry mouth. MAO inhibitors block an enzyme that breaks down serotonin and norepinephrine, thus increasing levels of these neurotransmitters within the brain (Friedman, 2001). MAOIs have risks associated with particular foods, with over the counter and prescription medicines, with supplements, and with illegal drugs and so should be carefully monitored by a physician. Patients on MAOIs need to be more careful with drug interactions and accompanying medical problems; in particular, a patient changing medications must wait several weeks after discontinuing an MAOI and before beginning another medication. In fact, life-threatening conditions can develop if SSRIs and MAO inhibitors are used together or if there is not sufficient time between stopping one and starting another. Restrictions on diet are also important (Griffith, 1999). However, these drugs may be effective when the SSRIs are not, so they are an important contribution to the available medications for those with PTSD.

The SSRIs were first introduced in the late 1980s and were characterized by having a better safety profile. They specifically target serotonin, which seems to be closely related to moods. SSNRIs are more recent, and while they typically affect primarily serotonin, they also affect norephinephrine, a neurotransmitter associated with focus and alertness. SSRIs are popular today because they have been widely prescribed and studied, and because they are also useful for treating problems that are comorbid with PTSD — depression, panic disorder, OCD, and alcohol dependence (Friedman, 2001). The SSRIs also seem to help with a wider range of PTSD symptoms, including numbing, hyperarousal, and flashbacks (Friedman, 2001). Effectiveness has been noted for "rage, impulsivity, suicidal intent, depressed mood, panic symptoms, and obsessional thinking" (Friedman, 2001, p. 73). The most well-known SSRI is Prozac (fluoxetine); others include Paxil (paroxetine), Celexa (citalopram), and Zoloft (sertraline) (Griffith, 1999). Newer SSRIs include Luvox (fluvoxamine) and Lexapro (escitalopram). SSNRIs include Cymbalta (duloxetine) and Effexor (venlafaxine). These medications take several weeks for full effect and should only be discontinued under medical supervision, but their side effects are fairly mild, and include dry mouth and insomnia. However, 10 to 30 percent (depending on the study) of users may experience sexual dysfunction. For a depressed individual with perhaps limited sources of pleasure, this may well lead the individual to quit taking the drug. There is some controversy over just how many users might experience this side effect; those who estimate close to 30 percent suggest that many people are uncomfortable reporting this problem to their doctors and will simply quit taking the drug. But the patient should be encouraged to be honest about the problem, because other antidepressants can be just as therapeutic without that particular side effect. Among them are Wellbutrin (bupropion), also marketed as the smoking-cessation medication Zyban (Griffin, 1999). Considered an atypical antidepressant, it influences the neurotransmitters dopamine and norepinephrine. It too may take several weeks to work and have similar side effects, except for the sexual dysfunction. Side effects may also diminish or disappear over time.

It should be noted that studies have looked at the possible increase in suicidal ideation with SSRIs; the FDA recommends that doctors pay particular attention to this risk with children and adolescents, but adults should also be monitored closely.

With SSRIs and SSRNIs, there is the possibility of what is called serotonin syndrome, a condition in which there is too much serotonin in the system. This can be caused by raising the dosage, by taking too many doses, or by interaction with other medications, both prescription and over the counter. Serotonin syndrome is potentially dangerous: if symptoms are observed, the individual should seek medical attention immediately. At least three of the following symptoms may indicate serontonin syndrome: fever, shivering, poor coordination, agitation, twitching or trembling, confusion, rigidity, restlessness, diarrhea, sweating, unstable vital signs (http://www.mayoclinic.com/health/serotonin-syndrome/DS00860).

The newer antidepressants that specifically target neurotransmitters in the brain have fewer broad systemic effects compared to the older tricyclics and the MAOIs. Effexor (venlafaxine), for example, targets the neurotransmitters serotonin and norepinephrine. It has shown success in relieving the symptoms of major depression.

Desyrel, Trazon, Trialodine (brand names for trazadone), Serzone (nefazodone), and Remeron (mirtazapine) are antidepressants that also influence chemicals in the brain. Trazadone has not been shown to be very effective in studies, but it has sedative properties and so is helpful for inducing sleep. Serzone (nefazodone) seems to be more effective for PTSD. Both alleviate the symptoms of intrusive memories, avoidance/numbing, and hyperarousal. Both are non-habit-forming, take several weeks for maximum effect, and should not be discontinued without medical supervision. Side effects include clumsiness, lightheadedness, odd dreams, headache, dry mouth, and sleep disturbance (either more or less) (Griffith, 1999). Remeron (mirtazapine) seems to be helpful for depressed individuals with anxiety, and helps with sleep; increased appetite and weight gain are side effects.

As mentioned previously, many antidepressants take several weeks to relieve depression, and it may be necessary to change dosage or switch medications if one drug doesn't seem to work well. A depressed individual may find it quite discouraging to go through the potentially lengthy process of finding the correct drug at the correct dosage.

Antianxiety Drugs/Tranquilizers

Anxiety may be seen as a normal human reaction to stressful situations, the "fight or flight" response. In times of danger or crisis, our bodies release adrenaline and cortisol (the so-called stress chemical), which give us a burst of energy while temporarily damping down other systems in our bodies. PTSD individuals may experience a fight-or-flight response to a threat that is perceived rather than real. Their bodies are flooded with these chemicals although there is no real threat. Some of the neurotransmitters in our brains mediate the fight-or-flight response, particularly noradrenaline and adrenaline (also known as norepinephrine and epinephrine). Thus, antidepressant medications that affect these neurotransmitters can help, as described in the previous section. These are fairly recent additions to the arsenal of medications used in psychiatric treatment, however.

One of the earliest antipsychotics used in psychiatric medicine was Thorazine. One of a group of phenothiazines, Thorazine was (and is) used to reduce anxiety and agitation, particularly in patients with psychotic disorders. Some side effects include dry mouth, constipation, dizziness, and sedation, and doctors must supervise the discontinuation of the drug. One stereotyped view of Thorazine is its use to make difficult patients more compliant for the benefit, perhaps, of the medical staff rather than the patient.

Sedatives and tranquilizers have been in use since the mid–1950s (Preston et al., 1999); common medications include Valium (diazepam), Librium (chlordiazepoxide), Ativan and Restoril (temazepam), and Xanax (alprazolam), which are all benzodiazepines. These drugs affect the limbic system of the brain, which controls emotions. The side effects of these drugs are not serious if the dosage is correct. However, too high a dose might cause an individual to become sleepy, stumble over words, and have difficulty walking steadily, resulting in the individual being suspected of being drunk. An overdose causes a life-threatening respiratory depression or arrest. Naturally, operating a car or other heavy machinery would be dangerous. Dosage can be adjusted so that symptoms are relieved while limiting side effects. Many of these medications will take several weeks to reach full effect (Griffith, 1999). These drugs are considered to be fairly safe and effective, but they do have the strong potential to be habit forming. Friedman (2001) warns, too, that there may be withdrawal symptoms upon discontinuing the drugs. For this reason the tranquilizers might best be considered for temporary use.

In the same class of sedative and hypnotic medications is Halcion, one of several brand names for triazolam. Used for anxiety and insomnia, it also works on the limbic system of the brain. However, its effects may be realized in as few as thirty minutes (Griffith, 1999). Ambien (zolpidem) is also classified as a sedative hypnotic agent, and is to be used only for short-term treatment of insomnia. It also works quickly, within an hour or two. It depresses the central nervous system, causes drowsiness, and is not to be discontinued without the supervision of a doctor. Unfortunately, it may have a rebound effect of sleeplessness after discontinuing use. Since sleep difficulties are often a problem with PTSD, and since sleep deprivation worsens other symptoms, these sedative-hypnotic medications can play an appropriate role, but only for short periods of time.

A newer medication, specifically classified as an antianxiety (anxiolyptic), is BuSpar (buspirone). It is less sedating, non-habit-forming, and less likely to be abused. BuSpar helps reduce aggressiveness and irritability. Common side effects of BuSpar include lightheadedness, headache, and nausea, but not sedation. How it actually works is unknown, but it is believed to act on brain neurotransmitters. Patients do not have to discontinue its use under supervision of a doctor (Preston et al., 1999).

With many of the drugs used to treat anxiety, the possibility of addiction is a concern. While some are less likely to be abused, in most cases patients using antianxiety medications are advised to taper off under the direction of a doctor (this is true for many antidepressants as well). But patients may feel so relaxed with the medication that they don't want to stop using it. It might be difficult and meaningless to distinguish between a dependency and a full-blown addiction. But some doctors, and patients, feel that dependence on a drug merely substitutes one problem for another.

Other Medications

Antipsychotics were used early for the treatment of PTSD when it was seen as a psychotic disorder; psychotic diseases such as schizophrenia are characterized by marked thinking disturbance with an impaired view of reality, perhaps with paranoia. Some PTSD symptoms such as hypervigilance, agitation, and aggression seem to fit into a distorted view of reality, thus the rationale for the use of antipsychotic medications. Early drugs such as Clozaril and Leponex (clozapine), Haldol (haloperidol), Moban (molindone) and Navane (thiothixene) are classified as antipsychotics and indicated for treatment of schizophrenia in particular. These drugs may have sedative effects and seem to reduce anxiety and agitation by affecting nerve impulse (Griffith, 1999). Some are specifically not to be taken by a depressed individual, however, and the side effects of dizziness, constipation, restlessness, and dry mouth may be troublesome, especially when relief might not be felt for one to six weeks or more. Worse, prolonged use may result in the development of tics (involuntary sudden jerky motions). As with many previously mentioned medications, these drugs should be discontinued only under the supervision of a doctor. Because of their undesirable side effects, most doctors would try other medications before resorting to these.

More recently, so-called atypical antipsychotics have been developed which can be helpful for hypervigilance, aggression, and isolation. Some of these are Risperdal (risperidone), Zyprexa (olanzapine), and Seroquel (quetiapine). All are classified as antipsychotic drugs, non-habit-forming, for use primarily with schizophrenia or nervous or emotional problems. They take from one to seven days to take effect and act by antagonizing the effects of dopamine within the brain. Some of the side effects include anxiety or agitation (the symptoms that are supposed to be reduced!), drowsiness or insomnia, vision problems, possible sexual dysfunction (with Risperdal). These medications are usually considered if other drugs don't seem to work well for the patient.

Mood stabilizers are a category of drugs that generally are used for bipolar disorder; they dampen the agitation of the manic phase, and help with depression. As the category suggests, they are used to even out a person's moods. Lithium (brand names Carbolith, Duralith, Eskalith, Lithone, Lithonate, and others) is perhaps the best known, having been used since the 1970s (Preston et al., 1999). Two anticonvulsants are also used as mood stabilizers; these are Tegretol or Novocarbamaz (carbamazepine) and Depakote or Epival (divalproex). Tegretol is similar in structure to the tricyclic antidepressants. It inhibits transmission of nerve impulses within the brain cells that are susceptible to seizure activity. Depakote seems to influence the levels of a neurotransmitter called GABA, reducing manic symptoms.

Other anticonvulsants may be used for PTSD to help with hyperarousal or reexperiencing symptoms; some may also be used to help with numbing and avoidance. They may work by damping the reactions of over-sensitive nerves, reducing excitability of nerve fibers (Griffith 1999). Neurontin (gabapentin) and Lamictal (lamotrigine) are newer anticonvulsants that may be therapeutic. The side effects of all of these drugs include blurred vision, confusion, headaches, fatigue, fainting and more, and the drugs should be used with care for patients with high blood pressure, glaucoma, or diseases of the kidney, liver or blood. For PTSD, anticonvulsants are not the first drug of choice and are considered when other drugs do not work well or when PTSD symptoms specifically match these drugs' therapeutic effects.

Interestingly, antihistamines can be used to lessen anxiety and induce drowsiness; they are non-habit-forming and have sedative properties. These are available over the counter, but their ease of availability does not mean they should be used freely, without the advice of a doctor, to aid with sleep for any length of time.

Beta blockers such as Lopressor and Betaloc (metoprolol), Inderal and Novopranol (propranolol), Tenormin and Apo-Atenolol (atenolol), and many others, are normally used to treat high blood pressure, but seem to counter (oppose) the effects of adrenaline. Because they help with irregular heartbeats, they may also be helpful in treating panic symptoms. They are not considered habit-forming, but, because of their effect on blood pressure, a patient should not discontinue use suddenly.

Finally, Catapres (clonidine), another drug prescribed for high blood pressure, seems to have antianxiety effects and thus may be helpful in relieving some PTSD symptoms, particularly intrusive memories and hyperarousal.

Glucocorticosteroids are another new area of treatment. Cortisol is the most familiar one, and has widespread systemic effects on the immune system, metabolic system, and more. Cortisol seems to inhibit the retrieval of traumatic memory, thus decreasing symptoms (de Quervain, 2008). Because these drugs have such system wide effects, as opposed to highly targeted effects, it is important to consider the larger physical and emotional context in using them.

New drugs are always in development, and medications that dampen the excitation in the brain are being investigated for treatment of anxiety. Still in clinical trials, they are not yet approved for marketing.

In summary, Friedman (2001) notes that medications should be chosen with consideration to particular symptoms. He groups these into three categories: intrusive memories, avoidance/numbing, and hyperarousal. For each group, some medications are more effective than others. For intrusive memories, the best drugs include the SSRIs, Trazadone and Serzone, the MAO Inhibitors, the tricyclic antidepressants, clonidine, and the anticonvulsant carbemazepine.

For symptoms of avoidance and numbing, the SSRIs, Trazadone, and Serzone are indicated. For hyperarousal symptoms, doctors may consider the SSRIs, Trazadone and Serzone, Clonidine, Alprazolam (an antianxiety) and the anticonvulsants carbamazepine and divalproex.

Drug Combinations

It is not uncommon for doctors to provide some combination of drugs to ease an individual's particular constellation of symptoms. Some drugs, such as antihistamines, might increase the effects of an antidepressant, such as amitriptyline, making it possible to keep the dosage of the antidepressant low while achieving a better result. On the other hand, there are potentially life-threatening drug interactions that must be avoided. For example, using MAO inhibitors with other antidepressants can cause serious blood pressure elevation. Indeed, prescription drugs, alcohol, illicit drugs, and over-the-counter medications can all interact, so any combinations of drugs must be used under medical supervision.

Those taking medications, whether over the counter or prescription, must inform their doctors (and pharmacists) of all the medicine they take, so that such interactions can be anticipated and avoided.

Major issues involve the actual mechanisms of the drugs, the side effects, and the potential for abuse or addiction. In general, it is believed that the goal of medication should be to support an individual as she/he progresses to health without the need for drugs. Short-term use, particularly of non-benzodiazepine anxiolytics and antidepressants, is usually ineffective. It is generally recommended that after satisfactory results are achieved, use should continue for at least six months, more usually a year, before discontinuation is contemplated. We take antibiotics, painkillers, steroids, and other drugs to help our bodies deal with illness, and then we stop. Somehow, we may expect that drugs for mental illnesses should similarly be short-term.

But doesn't this reflect our bias about mental health problems? An individual taking thyroid medication to compensate for inadequate levels of the hormone would not be told that the goal is to heal sufficiently to get off the drug. In fact, may people will use anticholesterol medications, high blood pressure medications, or antiseizure drugs their entire lives, with no societal disapproval. Why then shouldn't it be OK to continue using psychiatric medications for mental disorders, such as PTSD or depression?

Perhaps the difference is that we believe it is possible and important to address the underlying sources of anxiety or depression. In other words, these psychiatric drugs may be seen as treating symptoms rather than diseases. Yet the developing awareness of PTSD as a bona fide disease suggests that these medications may in fact be necessary on a lifelong basis. Certainly some doctors feel that Prozac, an antidepressant, can be and perhaps should be continued for years; the decades of use have not shown any major problems developing over time. Perhaps the best goal of PTSD medications may be selecting the lowest dosage of the most appropriate drugs to promote healthy living.

CHAPTER 10

Complementary Techniques for Treating PTSD

If you look at the names of the most popular categories of drugs in use today, you will find that most of them begin with the prefix "anti." ... This is truly antimedicine ... (Weil, 1995 p. 14).

Without awareness we have no choice (Levine, 1997, p. 186).

The first step, for me, was simply to feel.... I was afraid that if I really let myself sink into all those feelings, they'd engulf me and I'd drown in them. But that didn't happen. Amazingly, after the first terror had passed and I was still alive, I found that not only had I survived, I was finding unexpected comfort in simply relaxing into the pain (Kim, 2000, pp. 212–213).

There is no separation of mind and body (Weil, 1995, p. 38).

Laughter feels to me like a life force that bubbles up in the darkest moments (Turner & Diebschlag, 2001, p. 87).

In addition to mental health counseling and medications, a number of complementary techniques may be effective for PTSD. These include naturalistic approaches, such as relaxation, meditation, herbal supplements, expressive therapy, and hypnosis. Some, such as relaxation, can be done by anyone, without a doctor or specialized training, while hypnosis requires a trained professional. And nothing precludes combining these techniques with drug or counseling therapies. The following is a brief introduction to additional treatments or techniques that may be considered for PTSD.

Physical Activities

Physical activities are not only a part of general good health, research has shown that exercise can help alleviate some symptoms of depression and lower stress levels. Sports, housework, regular walks, gym equipment or exercise classes are ways to incorporate exercise into daily life. Some PTSD survivors "bunker" in their homes or apartments, and encouraging them to go out, even if quite briefly, can help them expand their horizons.

Exercise also represents doing something for yourself, taking time to take care of yourself. While it may not be consciously realized, exercising is a way of communicating to yourself that you are important enough to spend time and energy on. The result is not only better physical health but improved emotional health as well.

Exercise can also be a form of play, an activity that is done for the pleasure of it rather than for some other goal. PTSD survivors carry emotional burdens, and play can redirect attention to pleasurable activities. Playing sports is one example; a PTSD survivor might think about sports that he or she enjoyed as a child, and rediscover them. Some prefer individual sports, such as ice skating or swimming, while others enjoy team sports, such as doubles tennis or basketball. The U.S. Paraolympic Team includes Iraq/Afghanistan combat veterans who have lost limbs but have found another way to participate in competitive sports. Rediscovering pleasurable activities helps a PTSD survivor (or members of the family) reconnect with a time before the trauma, thus bringing happy memories into the present as a counterbalance to traumatic memories.

Aerobic exercises (especially low impact), strength training and weights are excellent ways to direct adrenaline into safe activities. There are many gyms available, some with personal trainers, as well as home equipment that can be used for organized exercises.

Getting out into nature can also be therapeutic for many PTSD survivors. Sunshine helps develop vitamin D, and getting fresh air and appreciating the beauty around us are great mood elevators. Being outdoors literally provides a different view of life. Nature refocuses our attention on objects and activities outside ourselves. Water, whether still water in a small lake or moving water in a river, has a calming effect. Wind feels as though it is blowing away anxiety, and provides white noise that masks the ruminations in our minds. Some people feel safer when they are outside, and thus freer. Combining nature with exercise increases the benefits of both.

Yoga and tai chi are two physical activities which focus on calm, controlled stretching and balance, resulting in a calmer physical and thus emotional/ mental state. Tai chi done in nature can be additionally valuable. In some countries in Asia, for example Vietnam and China, people join together outdoors in a park or plaza to do tai chi together. DVDs and classes are readily available for both.

Some people with PTSD find dance (also an expressive activity) or martial arts to be most appealing. Both include balance, rhythm, exercise, and perhaps some spiritual components. Most important, perhaps, is that the individual choose an activity that appeals to him/her and that he/she will be likely to stay with.

Hydrotherapy is yet another physical approach to PTSD, though it may seem rather marginal. Warm water, eg with baths or hot tubs, promote muscle relaxation and blood flow in the body. Cool water lowers inflammation. Switching from warm to cool and back to warm is generally stimulating to the body.

Finally, swimming can be an organized or free activity, a way to simply exercise or a therapeutic low impact activity. It can be a group or team activity as well, and can include competitive swimming, endurance swimming, or just playful swimming. Since swimming is easier on the joints of the body, veterans with physical limitations may find swimming a useful and pleasurable physical activity.

Exercise also helps promote appetite, and healthy eating is also helpful for individuals with PTSD.

Nutrition, Vitamins, and Herbal Approaches

One important aspect of treatment that is sometimes overlooked is the importance of good nutrition. Poor nutrition exacerbates problems: a lack of carbohydrates (breads, pasta, rice) can lead to low energy levels, insufficient fruits and vegetables can lead to constipation, too much fat makes us sluggish. Vitamins and minerals contribute to overall health. Some foods may interact with medications, increasing or decreasing effects, so being aware of the foods we eat is important. For example, MAO Inhibitors interact with caffeine to raise blood pressure. Foods such as cheese, smoked salmon, bologna, and Chinese pea pods, among others, should also be avoided (see Preston et al., 1999, for more complete information on food and drug interactions). Some level of personalization is called for in nutrition; for example, some Vietnam veterans hate to eat rice because of its associations with their Vietnam experience.

A sufferer of PTSD may not pay attention to his or her nutrition. If depressed, preparing and eating healthy food can feel like an overwhelming chore. Fast food or junk food is easier and may temporarily elevate mood but is not good nutrition. It can be more expensive to eat healthy foods as well. And a PTSD victim who lives alone may find it particularly challenging — as do many who live alone. We are inundated with health messages telling us how to eat better, but it is still hard for many of us to do. An effective approach is to identify the healthy foods that one likes — bananas, or grapes, for example, or favorite meats — and then begin to eat better by incorporating more of these foods. Convenience can be a help, too; we can now buy salad greens prepackaged, dried fruits have a longer shelf life. And eating with other people encourages us to eat more regularly. As with most aspects of a healthy lifestyle, it is rarely easy or natural; it takes time to develop new habits. But starting small is still good, and can motivate us to continue to make changes.

Vitamin supplements can help ensure that our bodies get the vitamins and minerals we need. Many formulations are available on the market, and most are just fine. It is fairly easy to look at federal guidelines and compare product labels. Some PTSD sufferers take megavitamins, including B-Complex vitamins, vitamins C, E, beta carotene, B6, zinc, fish oil, and others. These help to modulate a possibly overactive nervous system (Plesman, 2010) and regulate the body's metabolism. Vitamin and especially megavitamin supplements should always be reported to one's doctor, as individual physiology and drug interactions must be considered.

A number of herbal medicines have been described for the treatment of PTSD symptoms. For example, valerian, lemon balm, and kava kava are suggested for anxiety and insomnia, and feverfew is said to calm nerves. Ginkgo biloba and St. John's Wort are said to help with depression, and verbena is said to be a sedative. Lemon balm is a relaxant. Mints made into teas are effective for calming upset stomachs. Chamomile tea helps with sleep (but should not be used by pregnant women). Ginseng and peppermint increase energy.

Combinations of herbs may also be considered, as a tea, or as a pillow, or in pill form. It should be noted that there is little clinical evidence on the efficacy of these herbal treatments, and herbs, while natural compounds, are not always harmless, particularly when taken in large doses. Anyone considering using herbals as the primary or a supplementary treatment for PTSD should consult a medical professional.

Melatonin, a naturally occurring hormone in our bodies, has recently been promoted as a sleep aid for travelers or for those who have trouble sleeping. Its role is to help regulate the body's internal clock, and it can help those who have irregular sleep schedules, falling asleep during the day but being awake at night. It seems to be safe and effective (Weil, 1995). Sleep is critically important to our overall health, and those with PTSD often report difficulty sleeping. So herbal treatments that help promote better sleep should be considered in the treatment of PTSD.

Homeopathy is not a new approach, but has become more popular in the U.S. in recent years. Homeopathic medications are highly diluted doses of treatments derived from natural substances, such as herbs or other medicinal plants. Because they are so diluted, they are unlikely to be harmful. Some suggest that they are equally unlikely to promote health or healing, and that those who take them improved because of the placebo effect (the medicine itself has no value, but believing the medicine will heal, the person experiences improvement). Aconite, ignatia, gelsemium are several that are used for anxiety.

Herbal medicines, vitamin therapy, and homeopathic formulations should all be considered in the total context of treatment. The industry is not well regulated and there is potential for interaction with prescribed and over-the-counter medications. Consultation with a medical professional is strongly advised.

Massage, Acupuncture, and Other "Touch" Therapies

Massage and other touch therapies can help the body, and thus the mind, relax. Touch itself may be difficult for a trauma survivor, but massage can be adapted to the individual's needs. For a sexual assault survivor, having a light massage while fully clothed can be a good starting point. A variety of massage techniques exist, some with aromatic oils that also invoke the sense of smell in influencing how we feel. Massage promotes physical pleasure, which some survivors may get very little of. Again, the message that we are communicating to ourselves is that we matter, and that too is valuable mental health treatment.

Massage therapy can be targeted to areas of the body that are particularly stiff or tense, and a licensed therapist is a good place to start. There are massage centers, and there are massage therapists who are associated with physical therapy centers. For those with concomitant physical therapy needs, these are excellent places to find appropriate massage therapy.

Shiatsu is one type of massage therapy that uses the fingers, thumbs, and palms to apply pressure to areas of the body associated with the nervous system. Developed in Japan, practitioners are familiar with areas on the body to apply massage. There are different types of shiatsu, in particular a western version and an eastern version. While there is little western clinical research showing the efficacy of shiatsu, it nevertheless is a type of massage that can help calm and relax an individual.

Reiki is another method of massage that rather than focusing on centers of energy, focuses on the energy field as a flowing system, blocked in areas because of emotional difficulties. Reiki proposes to open the pathways to allow energy to flow more easily and thus restore emotional balance.

Reflexology is a massage technique that focuses on the feet; zones on the feet correspond to body systems and thus applying pressure to particular zones helps relieve problems in other parts of the body.

Acupuncture, in which thin needles are inserted into various parts of the body, or acupressure, in which particular spots are pressed or massaged, are intended to help realign energy in the body. Both are used for physical pains and emotional pain. For anxiety, acupuncture helps to release tension in the muscles, thus allowing the flow of energy. Anger, too, is said to bottle emotions into certain parts of the body, impeding the balance of energy in the body. Generally, acupuncture or acupressure require a series of treatments over time. An additional benefit may be, again, taking the time to care for oneself, thus communicating to both the body and mind that one is worth caring for.

Finally, some individuals find chiropractic treatments to be helpful.

These focus on the structural system of the body, particularly the spine; when the spine is appropriately aligned, the muscles are also appropriately aligned and thus less tense.

All of these therapies may be useful parts of an overall, more holistic, approach to treating PTSD.

Relaxation, Breathing, and Aromatherapy

While relaxation therapies by themselves may be inadequate in the treatment of PTSD, they can be helpful in managing anger or anxiety, and in improving sleep patterns. Thus they should be considered potentially valuable parts of an overall treatment program.

Perhaps the most fundamental relaxation technique is breathing. Turner and Diebschlag (2001, p. 72) suggest imagining breathing as nourishment. When we breathe shallowly, we are not taking in enough nourishment to "feed" our bodies. When we breathe more deeply, which will also be more slowly, we more fully nourish our bodies.

A variety of audio recordings can be helpful in relaxation therapies, as well. Soft music, a soothing voice, instructions to breathe, can help a survivor imagine a calmer state. Guided imagery might describe a soothing scene. Image Paths, Inc., offers an audio recording specifically for PTSD in which the listener is led through a relaxation sequence and then to remember aspects of the trauma with the goal developing a calm response to the traumatic memory. Also included are affirmations designed to help the listener focus on inner strengths and resources (www.healthjourneys.com).

Another relaxation technique is relaxing all the muscles of the body, progressively. The individual consciously focuses attention on the feet, for example, and then the lower legs, and then the thighs, and so on until all the major muscle groups of the body are relaxed. One can imagine that the muscles are becoming heavy, sinking into the floor or bed. Breathing typically slows. The mind, focused on the muscles, is not focused on the worrying thoughts that sometimes seem to race endlessly. Similar to biofeedback, progressive relaxation takes note of our own nonverbal signals, the physical signals that we are often not aware of. By learning to recognize our own signals of distress or anxiety, we can respond to those signals with relaxation techniques that will calm both the body and the mind.

Another source of relaxation, not traditionally considered a relaxation technique, is taking up a new — or old — hobby. More than a frivolous distraction, a hobby encourages focusing on something besides ruminating thoughts, and often results in tangible products of our own making. People who enjoy words may work crossword or other word puzzles. Crafts or woodworking are enjoyable for some. Gardening, again, or organizing family photos, or researching a family genealogy can be engrossing. Any hobby that is of interest to the individual can be relaxing, and individuals not sure where to start can investigate community classes or workshops, books, television or video programs, or friends and family.

Aromatherapy has become popular recently for influencing moods. Scented candles, incense, warm oils are all different ways of introducing mood-altering aromas. In general, aromatherapies may be calming or stimulating. Calming oils include bergamot, chamomile, frankincense, geranium, lavender, orange blossom, sandalwood, and ylang ylang. Oils that improve mood include basil, gergamot, geranium, juniper and lavender. To alleviate stress, geranium, lavender, marjoram, peppermint, and sandalwood are recommended. Some oils are more targeted; for example, jasmine and lemon are recommended for depression, lavender and rosemary are suggested for stress related disorders, and sandalwood and lavender for insomnia (www.holisticonline.org). Creams in various formulations can be used as well, putting a small amount of cream under the nose or on the wrists. Some individuals may find some of these oils to be irritating (either physically or emotionally!), and some may find there are associations with particular oils that promote or lower effectiveness (if lavender reminds one of one's mother, this could make lavender either a positive scent or a sad and grieving one). Since most are readily available and not very expensive, it is worth experimenting to see if any may be of help in relieving symptoms.

Hypnosis and Biofeedback

Some practitioners discuss hypnosis as a treatment for PTSD. In hypnosis, the client is brought to a deep state of relaxation and given one or more suggestions. The client might be led to reimagine a traumatic experience; the therapist might suggest picturing a different ending, or seeing the experience as an observer. Frequently the session will end with some positive suggestion, for example, that upon conclusion the client will feel safe and relaxed. Hypnosis may not be effective for all PTSD survivors; traumatic memories may be too intense, or the survivor may resist, fearing a loss of control. It should not be the only treatment considered for PTSD, and does require a trained practitioner.

Cardeña et al. (2000) note that hypnotic techniques may be especially helpful for "patients who exhibit such symptoms as anxiety, dissociation, pain, and sleep problems, for which hypnosis has been effective" (p. 270). In their review of research, they also suggest that hypnosis can be a useful additional technique, used in conjunction with other treatments.

Biofeedback can be very helpful for a PTSD sufferer. It focuses the survivor's attention on the signs of emotional distress in his/her body. For example, when we are angry our hearts beat faster, our muscles tense, and we hold our breaths or breathe rapidly and shallowly (even to the point of hyperventilation). All of these mirror the fight-or-flight response, useful in times of danger but an inappropriate reaction that can severely stress the body at other times. Biofeedback techniques help us recognize these physical events and direct our attention to them by the use of machines which visually record symptoms such as a fast heartbeat. The individual is instructed to watch the physical monitors while intentionally relaxing tense muscles and taking deep and measured breaths (perhaps counting slowly at the same time). By recognizing and internalizing the visual signal, an individual can learn to reproduce the effects without the machine.

Expressive Therapies

Expressive therapies are helpful for clients who have difficulty approaching memories directly, or who find it difficult to articulate feelings. Children in particular might be good candidates for expressive therapies, which may include drawing, telling stories, dancing, drama, or virtually any activity of creative expression. A specific example might be asking a combat veteran to create a visual memorial to a lost comrade (Schiraldi, 2000), or writing a poem to oneself, noting positive qualities. Writing a story can involve rewriting the traumatic event, or writing a fiction piece in which themes might be explored — the theme of feeling abandoned, for example, or frightened and in an unfamiliar place. Often the art created is an indirect expression of the fears or anxieties of the individual, and insight can be gained by recognizing the truth expressed by the creation.

Johnson (2000) notes that creative art therapies are fairly recent as professional approaches, beginning in the 1940s and developing further in the 1950s and since. Their use in treating trauma has been helpful particularly, but not only, with children. Trained professionals may be employed to design creative arts therapies to accompany traditional medical treatments for PTSD.

Journaling is a useful strategy, with or without additional expressive techniques. Journaling is like keeping a diary, but without the association diaries have with femininity and secretiveness. In keeping a journal, the writer simply spends some period of time regularly writing down in a notebook what is happening and how he/she feels about it. Journaling can relieve stress and anger as these emotions are expressed on paper. It can also lead the writer to self-discovery, as when a PTSD survivor finds that loud noises or flashing lights are triggering a traumatic memory. A journal becomes something of a historical document, as well, enabling an individual to go back and observe change, progress, strengths, and major events over time.

Playing a musical instrument is an expressive technique. A survivor might play an instrument previously learned, or might learn a new instrument. Making music taps our creative energies, and composing music does so even more. Music can be both melody and lyrics; Bob Dylan considered himself a poet who set his poems to music. For those who find it difficult to play an instrument, listening to and/or singing along with favorite music can also help express emotions, whether cathartically (as will an angry protest song) or finding expression for emotions difficult to express, such as love or longing.

Again, expressive therapies might best be considered an adjunct to other treatments. Certainly these might be useful in assessing the survivor's current state of emotional and mental health, and should be among the tools that a professional might use to understand and help his/her client.

Animals

Interacting with animals seems to have a number of therapeutic effects. Caring for another encourages us to take the focus of ourselves and connecting to another living creature is a relationship and even social support device. A number of programs and activities show the value of caring for or working with animals: disabled children with horses, prisoners training service animals. Being responsible for another creature requires us to maintain some sort of schedule; a depressed or anxious individual may not want to get out of bed, but the dog must be fed and taken outside. Animals also give back to us; they show attachment, acceptance, and respond to our moods. There are programs in many communities, but certainly not all. While an organized program might be very helpful, simply owning and caring for an animal can also be helpful. No animal should be chosen and given to a PTSD sufferer (or anyone else!); the individual needs to be allowed to choose. Many humane societies have numbers of animals to bond with and choose from.

Spirituality and Meditation

Meditation is an increasingly popular technique for relaxation, and has different styles. In one, the individual empties the mind by concentrating on a particular word or image. Such singular focus calms both the mind and the body, but takes practice to develop. Mindfulness meditation begins with clearing the mind, and then moves to observation, gaining a sense of distance and perspective about ourselves, allowing us to see ourselves as perhaps an outsider might. There is no effort to judge or change, merely observe. The benefit is that we have a clearer view of our situation if we can view it from the outside rather than from within our turbulent thoughts and feelings.

Anyone can meditate: no special equipment, location, or clothing is required. An anxious or worried individual can simply sit quietly, without distractions. Of course, it sometimes feels quite unnatural to just sit, and even a few minutes can seem like a long time. But beginning with just a few minutes and practicing to lengthen the meditation time can result in real benefits. Some individuals find that it is easier to fall asleep after the deep relaxation of meditating. Classes and books on meditation are widely available.

Similarly, mindfulness is an approach to daily living in which we focus on here and now. One of my favorite quotations from Jon Kabat-

Zinn's books on mindfulness is "Be. Here. Now," which I find to be an effective reminder to stop worrying about the past (what I should have said or done) or the future (what may or may not happen tomorrow) and focus on where I am and what I am doing. It is true that we can't change the past, and our worrying about the future doesn't do much to influence it. All we can really change is what is in our present. Kabat-Zinn has several beginning books that are quite approachable and understandable, and I recommend them highly.

As human beings we look for meaning in life, and a purpose for the good and bad events that befall us. For some people, belief in a higher power helps to explain these life events. Survivors and their families may find comfort and community in a religious environment, a church, synagogue, or mosque. Religious leaders may provide one-on-one, couple, or family counseling. Special classes may be held in religious groups addressing parenting skills or personal growth. These are opportunities that may be offered and taken advantage of.

Other religions may not focus on a God, per se, but rather on explaining the meaning of life. Buddhism, for example, points out that our desires lead to suffering, and by learning to limit desire, we can limit pain. Meditation leads to enlightenment and inner peace.

Caring for others is often a part of many religious practices, and focusing on helping others often makes us feel better about ourselves, as well as distracting us from our own problems. Balance must be sought, however, so that in caring for others we do not neglect ourselves.

Prayer, reading spiritual texts, spending time in introspection, and considering our role in a larger world are all activities that help promote calm, acceptance, and balance. For those who reject organized religion, these can be done privately. For some families, worshipping together becomes a strength and resource, helping the family to face its problems.

On a practical level, PTSD survivors may find it beneficial to practice and/or create rituals, for example, making an annual or more frequent visit to a gravesite with seasonally appropriate flowers. One wife of a deceased veteran made a habit of drinking a Pepsi in his memory on special occasions. Reviewing documents (newspaper or books) about the 1993 flood in Iowa helps some recall how difficult it was, and how far they have come since then.

For some survivors, tangible favorites can be reassuring. Native Americans carried small leather bags with symbolically important contents, and this could be done by a survivor today as well. Polished rocks that can serve as worry stones, a favorite key chain, dog tags, a locket, a birthstone, or a photograph can be a talisman of a sort. Larger items, too, can be anchors for our emotions, including a favorite article of clothing or a piece of furniture (Turner & Diebschlag, 2001).

In addition, survivors can create memorials of their own. Perhaps planting a certain type of flower, tree, or bush in the yard could become a living memorial. One veteran has a small shelf with a can of Blatz beer, a military can opener, an M-16 shell, and a photograph; this shelf is his memorial to his friends who didn't come home from the war. Alternatively, there are organizations which plant trees in national forests in honor of someone special, and certainly a survivor could dedicate a memorial to him or herself. In a sense, such a memorial externalizes the trauma and/or pre-trauma individual, and is a concrete step towards honoring the self that has survived.

While complementary techniques are likely insufficient for treating PTSD, they can be valuable adjuncts to more traditional approaches. They are largely benign or positive, are individually developed, and can be privately practiced.

Since each individual's combination of physical and psychological symptoms of PTSD is unique, a psychiatrist working with a primary medical doctor may be best positioned to consider effects and interactions for an optimal combination of treatments. Relaxation techniques are potentially helpful and unlikely to be dangerous. (The PTSD audio recording mentioned previously advises against listening while driving, as one might become too relaxed!) Herbals and alternative medicines should be considered with caution, and always in reference to other treatments. Techniques that entail some level of recalling a traumatic event might be quite helpful but should be employed by a qualified practitioner, and usually as part of an overall plan of treatment. Finally, developing spiritual insights can provide a sense that there is meaning to life and a reason for suffering, as well as a reason for healing.

CHAPTER 11

Living with PTSD

The strongest principle of growth lies in human choice (George Eliot, *Daniel Deronda*, 1885).

[My birth mother said] life is made up of ten thousand joys and ten thousand sorrows. I realized ... that every moment, if fully savored, could take its place [with the ten thousand joys] (Kim, 2000, p. 210).

God grant me the serenity to accept the things I cannot change, courage to change the things I can, and the wisdom to know the difference (The Serenity Prayer).

In some ways, being diagnosed with PTSD can be a great relief, as there is finally a name for the constellation of difficulties that beset an individual and hence his/her personal relationships. At the same time, considering that there is no cure for PTSD, that it is a chronic and disabling condition, such a diagnosis may seem like a life sentence. Indeed, while there are many treatments, there is no magic pill or surgery that will eliminate PTSD. But that is not to say that there aren't ways to live with it, and to live a fulfilling life. There is hope for the family and friends, too, in learning about PTSD, recognizing their own boundaries, allowing for both intimacy and independence. As one cartoon noted, very very few of us come from "functional" families. Seeking to create some sort of idealized relationship or family is to ignore the reality that while our problems are not all the same, we all have problems. And problems that we refuse to face now we may well meet again in the future.

Healthy Coping Strategies

For the survivor of a traumatic event, there are some cognitive and behavioral strategies that the individual can implement to help deal with

PTSD symptoms. A common characteristic of PTSD is all-or-nothing thinking: the trauma was all bad, the person's response to trauma was all wrong, there is no hope for the future. A helpful technique is to write down the aspects of the traumatic event that were or are positive, along with those that are negative. For example, the house burned down but the individual escaped it. The plane crashed but there were survivors. The firefight was fierce but the soldier faced fear and lived through it. The survivor has become a different person as a result of the traumatic event, but that new person is not all bad either; perhaps she or he has learned to use distancing during an emergency as a tool for acting effectively. By putting these aspects down on paper, it is easier to see that most events have both positive and negative sides.

Often with PTSD the individual has distorted thought processes, believing that others can or should be able to read one's mind, expecting that a friend or family member "should know" that she gets upset watching horror movies, or that he can't handle large crowds. Those thoughts can be challenged; why should anyone know what we are thinking unless we tell them? An argument can quickly escalate when it focuses on what one should know about the other; such an argument is short-circuited with a simple explanation. Other distorted thoughts might be related to self-blaming — "I should have known that I would be attacked." Challenging such thoughts can lead to the inevitable conclusion that in fact, it was not predictable. This is demonstrated, in Scott and Stradling (1992), by a police officer who was assaulted and felt it was his own fault. But realistically, he had been in similar situations that did not result in assault, so how could he have known that, this particular time, it would happen?

This same officer was quite concerned about being the victim of another, similar assault, and could not go back to his normal activities because of his fear. The therapist asked him whether it was more likely that he would have an automobile accident or be assaulted, to which he replied a car accident was more likely. Yet he didn't fear driving a car. Seen in that perspective, the officer was able to make more realistic judgments about both what had happened and what was likely to happen in the future (Scott & Stradling, 1992). Rather than remain imprisoned by worrisome thoughts, the officer was able to rationally consider his underlying assumptions and recognize that these were not logical. As a result of changed thinking, behavior can change as well.

Another cognitive strategy for PTSD survivors is to become aware of intrusive or continual thoughts and images and find ways to stop or control them. One technique is to recognize an intrusive memory and physically respond, by pinching oneself or snapping a rubber band around one's wrist (Scott & Stradling, 1992). This changes the focus from the mental thought to the physical touch, and also helps the survivor realize just how often these thoughts occur. As a result, the thoughts might lessen in frequency.

When intrusive thoughts are debilitating, an individual might try countering negative images with an equal number of positive ones. For example, if a soldier regularly relives a grenade exploding, he can remember a pleasant memory from around the same time, perhaps of sharing a meal with another solider in the mess tent. Each time he remembers the grenade, he calls to mind the meal. For each negative memory, a positive one is generated, and when the negative memories come to mind, the individual calls up the positive ones as well. Both polarized thinking and distorted cognition can be helped with this technique.

Another technique for debilitating images or thoughts is to set aside a time each day to devote to just that topic. Rather than have such thoughts or images distract the individual all the time, he or she might promise to devote fifteen or thirty minutes to just that issue at some scheduled time during the day. Knowing that the images or thoughts will be given attention may make them less intrusive or easier to brush aside. When the time comes to focus on them, the individual indeed devotes the allotted minutes; over time, fewer and fewer minutes may be needed. It should be emphasized that severely disabling thoughts or hallucinations can not be resolved this simplistically; those require the attention of a professional with a more complete treatment plan. But for worrisome or repetitive thoughts, this technique can be quite helpful.

Yet another strategy is to finish unspoken thoughts (Scott & Stradling, 1992). Often, PTSD survivors tell themselves "I could have been seriously injured..." (p. 62) yet fail to complete the thought: "...but I wasn't." Rather than brooding over what might have happened, the survivor recognizes that it didn't, in fact, happen. This has the effect of focusing attention on the concrete rather than the unfulfilled possibility.

It might be seen that distorted thoughts or distorted thinking often incorporate words like *could, should, might, ought to,* and *have to.* These are expressions of moral imperative and suggest that an individual is demanding a high level of expectation that, in most cases, the individual would consider inappropriate for any other person. In other words, it is not uncommon for PTSD survivors to acknowledge that any other person need not feel guilty or worried, but then expect themselves to meet the higher standard. This too can be pointed out as an example of irrational thinking, and is part of the "normalizing" of feelings that counselors often provide, for example by noting that anyone would feel frightened in such a situation. This normalizing helps the individual to treat him or herself as simply another human being, no stronger or better or worse than another.

These cognitive and behavioral strategies can be seen in a larger context in answer to the question of how we might live with PTSD. Since PTSD is a chronic disability, treatment goals might focus on coping with symptoms in strategically wise ways. Developing such strategies requires recognizing one's symptoms and strengths. A PTSD survivor who is highly anxious and loves carpentry might take up woodworking as a stress reliever, not only producing his/her own creations but also lessening arousal at the same time, leading to a calmer family life. A Korean-American adoptee says that "The first step, for me, was simply to feel" (Kim, 2000, p. 212). An incest survivor with flashbacks might paint her feelings on a canvas, objectifying her terrors and making them easier to confront. Survivors of natural disasters may plant gardens, or tend a single plant, nurturing life within as well as without.

Recognizing the triggers that provoke PTSD outbursts is another goal, as some of these triggers, such as 4th of July fireworks or crowded places, can be avoided or eliminated. One veteran, for example, goes camping in a state park on the 4th of July, avoiding the loud bangs and explosions taking place in the park in town. Another useful strategy is recognizing and anticipating anniversaries, those dates upon which significant events occurred. Rather than becoming deeply depressed every October without knowing why, one survivor discovered that the October 1968 ambush that killed his friend was cropping up every year without his knowing it. He then began to expect the anniversary and prepare for it, honoring the memory of his lost friend by lighting a candle. His family respected his need for solitude on that date, and he was able to handle the anniversary without debilitating depression.

PTSD survivors may manage their anxiety by attempting to control everything around them. One survivor states, "I found that if I just acknowledged the feelings, the panic abated ... the temporary balms eventually ate away at me and created their own acidic pain. The permanent balm seemed to be just letting the pain come to the surface where it could breathe and heal in its own way and time" (Kim, 2000, p. 205). PTSD survivors seek to control their own emotions, generally by pushing them away or refusing to recognize them, but until feelings are freed from such rigid control, they continue to fester.

PTSD survivors also attempt to control their environments, homes, workplaces, families, and so on. While control makes us feel safe, Beck (2002) notes that it is an illusion. There is much we cannot control, and, with PTSD, a sense that we cannot even control ourselves. Rather than seeking control, we might accept our lack of control and instead focus on the present and living in the present.

In particular, we cannot control others. The more we try, the more frustrated we will become, because in truth, we can only control ourselves and how we react to events and people around us. Spouses and family members of a PTSD survivor must abandon the idea that he/she can be "fixed," and stop attempting to love the survivor into health, or force the survivor to behave as if he/she does not have PTSD. By focusing on the other person as the one who needs fixing, we avoid recognizing that we have our own problems that need work. It is much easier to point out someone else's difficulties than to admit to our own. But it results in neither person changing for the better.

Steps Toward Life with PTSD

Thus a necessary first step in living with PTSD is simple acceptance, acceptance of the PTSD and its symptoms, acceptance of the care and commitment to the PTSD survivor, and acceptance that the PTSD won't disappear in response to a magical medication. In fact, we cannot get anywhere without knowing where we are starting from; we cannot go somewhere else until we know where we are now. By accepting what is, we can plot a course toward the future.

Acceptance of PTSD and its effects on the individual and family can be a liberating experience. A great deal of energy is consumed by wishing the PTSD didn't exist, that the trauma had never occurred, that the survivor wasn't so affected by his/her past. Simple acceptance frees up that energy to be directed elsewhere. Acceptance also frees us from blaming others for their illness or for their failure to make us happy, and refocuses our attention on ourselves, our choices, our decision to change.

Acceptance can also help us recognize the value of the pain we feel. Pain can force us to give up hopes that are unrealistic (Beck, 2002). Pain can encourage us to seek help, whether professional counseling help or support from friends and family. Pain and anger are both signals that something is wrong; if we try to deny or suppress either, they will find expression in ways that are probably not very helpful. If we recognize them, however, and seek to understand what is causing the anger or pain, we may be able to deal with the causes and find effective ways to manage them.

A second useful step in living with PTSD is to recognize that life with a PTSD survivor is a process. Rather than focusing on future goals such as "when she gets better" or "after the children are grown," we should focus on present processes. Living with PTSD is a day-by-day experience; there will be good times and bad times. There will be stages of some functionality and dysfunctionality; there will be the seesaw effect of mood swings, of intimacy struggling with independence. By looking to some future when life might be different, we miss the only time we have to live, which is the present. Being committed to the present and the process doesn't mean that we have no goals, only that we focus on working toward the goals each day rather than dreaming about achieving the goals in the future. If we commit to the process of living with PTSD and with a PTSD individual, the end product will take care of itself, and will likely be better than what we can imagine. But we need to focus our energies on making the present the best it can be.

A third valuable step is to seek balance. The PTSD is not the person; the person is much more than the disability. PTSD survivors should not see themselves as being defined by PTSD and neither should their families. They are neither all PTSD nor only PTSD. Families, too, should not be defined by the PTSD of one or more of their members. We should not focus so much on the PTSD that we miss the rest of the story, the strengths, abilities, and talents of both the individual and the family. Within a family, no one member should be the focus of everyone; instead, each member needs and receives attention and each member gives attention to others.

Families and individuals can easily become unbalanced with a difficult diagnosis like PTSD, but by paying attention to the health of each member and the family as a whole, some balance will be achieved.

Like balance, moderation is a helpful step. Avoiding excesses helps keep the family and individual balanced. Too much food, or alcohol, or anger, or fear is very difficult to live with. An entirely deprived life is barren. Each individual and family has to determine what moderation means, and what an ideal balance is, but having done so, they will be able to experience good times along with the hard times. Individuals with and without PTSD need to pay attention to both their needs and their wants, to care for themselves and to care for others. We can only care for ourselves and others when we know them well, which means we may need to spend time with ourselves to know what we like and dislike, and spend time with others listening and observing their personalities. That enables us then to know what we need to do to take care of and care for ourselves and others.

Acceptance, focusing on process, balance and moderation are goals that we can attempt to implement every day, with ourselves, our PTSD survivors, and our families. Each of us can interpret and apply these as we believe best, and we will see positive results. PTSD need not be the albatross around the neck of the family, and we can learn to live better lives even with the disorder.

CHAPTER 12

Trends in PTSD
Research and Treatment

He was in Rwanda just once, for six or eight months. Like I said, he's still in treatment for that, and the military keeps sending him overseas (Chad, ate 17, *Off to War: Voices of soldiers' children*, 2008).

When you use equipment, you expect it to need maintenance and wear out and at some point need replacement.... But when it comes to human beings, there seems to be an expectation of infinite, infinite usability ... (Shay, 2010).

A survivor of trauma is a victim, certainly; but "victim" does not comprise the totality of her, or anyone else's, identity (Stout, 2001, p. 213).

There is life after PTSD. I'm a survivor. I'm not holed up in a room with an M-4. Yes, you can acknowledge the issue and get through it (Speakes, 2010).

Perhaps the most positive trend in PTSD research and treatment is the growing public awareness and acceptance of PTSD as a bona fide "wound," one which does not result from weakness of character or poor personal judgement. While it is true that public awareness can, ironically, lead to overdiagnosis, or to individuals claiming to have PTSD simply because it is newly noted in the media, the trend toward removing the stigma is a positive one.

Still, there is much work to be done. The Department of Defense is devoting considerable resources (which are never enough) to address PTSD, but civilians for the most part are still responsible for seeking treatment on their own, treatment which may be expensive and time-consuming, and which may not be covered by health insurance plans. Below are detailed some of the current trends in the recognition, understanding, and treatment of PTSD.

Biological and Neurological Research

Research on brain neurotransmitters and chemical hormones in the body are a promising field of research. It is known that during the course of a traumatic event, stress hormones increase sharply and remain elevated (Porterfield, 1996). Could medicines be developed which would lower the levels of these hormones? Or could intervention techniques be taught and learned in order to be employed as soon as possible after a traumatic event?

Brain neurotransmitters such as serotonin also increase dramatically during a traumatic event, and then become depleted. Lower levels of serotonin in the brain may result in irritability and depression. Could medication be given that would restore a normal level of serotonin?

The incredible surge of brain and body chemicals can be intoxicating, leading to individuals seeking to recreate the "high"—the so-called adrenaline junkies who deliberately seek dangerous situations. Would it be possible to channel this behavior into safer ways of experiencing the sense of well-being? Exercise has been shown to increase endorphins in the brain; perhaps a range of physical activities could be made easily available for individuals to choose from.

Treatment Programs

Treatment programs have become both broader in scope and more individualized. In several of the programs described in Chapter 3, a variety of classes and activities are offered in hopes that one or more will prove to meet an individual's needs. At the same time, some treatments are more effective for a given individual than others, and if we can discover why, we can treat PTSD in a more meaningful, not to mention efficient, way.

For example, while Cognitive Behavioral Theory and rap groups seem to help most people, EMDR and hypnosis certainly do not. How can we identify those who will benefit from one and not the other? Does simulated exposure therapy, such as playing a realistic combat video, help those who have enjoyed video games? Would verbal re-enactment work better for others? We simply do not know at this time, but studies are underway that may help us tailor treatment to particular individuals.

Treatment programs that focus on teaching resiliency show promise; these again are typically cognitive behavioral programs, which have been widely studied. Cultural sensitivity training may also be a good "preventative"; for Marines who were deployed to Haiti after its massive earthquake, cultural training helped them connect with the community they were working with, understanding differences in hierarchies and values, for example. As a result, these Marines felt that they were helping the population. Similar training is being implemented for those serving in Iraq and Afghanistan as a strategy for limited the enemy's appeal to local populations. These can reduce the incidences of attacks and perhaps the trauma of those attacks which do occur (Gerson, 2010).

Finally, treatment programs have been successful when they take a systems approach, and include the families in the treatment protocol. This is a highly promising area to pursue, in breaking the cycle of PTSD, in helping to heal both the individual and his/her major support group, and in helping families become stronger as a result.

Public Education

Beckett (2002) notes that responding to any mass casualty event may be beyond the resources of any health system; efforts may better be spent on prevention. In that vein, he suggests our efforts should be devoted to removing the causes, seeking peaceful solutions rather than war, for example. Though it may seem idealistic or naïve, his point is worth serious consideration.

There may still be something of a "don't ask, don't tell" culture in the military regarding PTSD, showing that there is still a stigma associated with it. Recently, however, high level pentagon officials and upper echelon military officers have begun speaking out, sometimes about their own struggles, sometimes to bring openness to the topics of PTSD and suicide (Abdullah, 2010). Besides the content of their message, their willingness to speak publicly also sends the message that it is ok, normal, understandable, to suffer after a traumatic event, and there should be no shame in seeking help.

Along the same lines, President Obama has changed a long-standing policy of not sending condolences to families of service members who have committed suicide. The previous policy was in place in order not to appear to approve of suicide. Obama's change may seem minor, but speaks volumes about the willingness to be open about the struggles faced by active duty and veteran soldiers.

Ursano (2002) argues that community wide awareness and prevention has succeeded in changing attitudes about skin cancer (more of us wear sunscreen now), lung cancer (fewer people smoke), seat belts (now required of drivers), and other health concerns. Perhaps a similar public campaign could increase awareness of PTSD? What behaviors might we change if we were better informed about the risks of and treatments for PTSD?

I believe that our approach to PTSD needs to be addressed on two fronts. First, mental health issues in general are still stigmatized. People don't want to be known to have them, insurance plans often don't cover them, and getting help is equated to being weak. Perhaps a public campaign should focus on this issue. Second, the divide between our military and civilian populations has grown with the volunteer army. Many of us don't know anyone who has served or been in combat. The line between "us" and "them" should be eliminated; what affects one, affects all. We should seek a unity of purpose such that we realize our responsibilities to the individuals and families suffering from PTSD.

Conclusion

PTSD can affect anyone. It doesn't seek out the weak, the lazy, the introspective, or the unlucky. It doesn't target a particular gender, generation, social class, or ethnic group. It doesn't pass over rural villages in favor of large cities. It doesn't favor the educated over the uneducated, the poor over the rich. It is not the result of bad thoughts, unkind actions, or negative feelings.

Instead, it results simply from surviving one or more traumatic incidents. Such incidents are unfortunately quite widespread. They include natural disasters, such as floods, earthquakes, tornadoes, hurricanes, mudslides, volcanic eruptions, blizzards, tsunamis, typhoons, wildfires, and avalanches. Disasters that result from human actions can also be traumatic, including automobile or plane accidents, home or other building fires, torture, rape, incest, combat, violent attack, terrorist attacks, forced slavery or forced military participation, attacks by animals, and disease epidemics. While many will survive traumatic events without developing PTSD, it is estimated that 30 percent of those experiencing such trauma will go on to develop the disorder. That is, 30 percent of *us*, our families or friends, would go on to develop PTSD.

We know that multiple traumas are more likely to result in PTSD than a single event. Soldiers exposed to repeated combat, sexual abuse that lasts for years, or imprisonment in concentration camps are all multiple traumas that accumulate and increase the possibility of developing PTSD. We know that natural disasters are less likely to cause PTSD than the so-called man-made disasters, perhaps because natural disasters are clearly beyond our control and thus we don't blame ourselves for causing or contributing to the traumatic events. Though the abuse survivor, combat sol-

179

dier, or Holocaust victim were similarly not in control of their traumas, it is not uncommon for them to ascribe some blame to themselves for being victimized or failing to avoid the traumas. One recovering survivor notes, "I've learned it wasn't my fault for relaxing my guard; I could never have prevented any of it" (Kim, 2000, p. 202).

We do not know why some who experience trauma will not develop PTSD, but personal characteristics of resiliency and flexibility seem to be protective. Resiliency means we are not incapacitated by traumatic events and can "bounce back." Flexibility involves being able to modify our own reactions or actions in response to trauma. The individual who cannot see alternative ways of being or behaving is more influenced by trauma.

We know that spouses of PTSD survivors can develop secondary PTSD. Secondary PTSD symptoms are similar to PTSD symptoms, and include emotional numbing, hypervigilance, difficulty sleeping, depressed mood, and irritability. In their response to the PTSD survivor, they may find ways of coping that are certainly functional, but perhaps could be more functional. The wife or husband who leaves the PTSD survivor, or who seeks help in extramarital relationships, might be resolving some issues of emotional distancing, but in doing so exacerbates the problems rather than addressing them. Understanding PTSD symptoms and causes can help a spouse avoid personalizing the difficulties and instead focus on ways of dealing with them.

Children, too, may develop secondary PTSD, and may show symptoms such as sleeplessness, irritability, hypervigilance, and so on. Children do imitate what they see, and in particular model on the same-sex parent. Their symptoms need to be seen as their own efforts to deal with home and family issues, a sign of caring and commitment. However, they too need to be able to distinguish themselves from the PTSD survivor, understanding the origins of the disability, and developing their own strengths and characters independently. Some children will attempt to compensate for the PTSD parent by becoming too competent and responsible (missing their own childhoods), or by parenting the PTSD parent rather than being parented, or by becoming the scapegoat and behaving badly, thus deflecting attention from the PTSD parent. Family therapy may be very helpful in reestablishing appropriate roles and responsibilities.

In addition to parents and children, we know that emergency workers and those who work with disaster survivors may also develop secondary

PTSD symptoms. Emergency room doctors, paramedics, police officers, firefighters, and so on, typically experience a great deal of adrenaline and stress on the job. Seeing and treating victims of accidents and crimes can become emotionally wearing. Similarly, those who counsel trauma survivors, who may not be working in emergency situations but are working with traumatic events on a regular basis, are at risk for developing symptoms of secondary PTSD. Without treatment, the potential for these symptoms to damage individuals and families is much higher than if we find ways to intervene and help both individuals and their families.

We know that early intervention after a traumatic experience may help prevent the development of PTSD. The use of crisis counselors, emergency plans, and preparation for anticipated difficulties can help people process trauma and their responses to it, thus relieving some of the horror and fear. We know that cognitive therapies can help by challenging irrational thinking ("It is my fault he abused me." "I should have died, not she.") and all-or-nothing thinking ("I will never get over it." "All men are bad."). We know that behavioral techniques can also help; desensitization can dampen triggers, can help memories become less intense.

We know that group therapies can be effective for PTSD, particularly if the group has experienced similar traumas. Rap groups with combat veterans was an early use of group talk therapy that helped participants to know that they are not alone, and that they can count on each other for support. We know that trust is a major prerequisite for successful counseling, whether individual or group. Sharing tales of trauma is in itself highly stressful, and a safe and supportive atmosphere is required. Time is needed for trusting relationships to develop, so brief counseling is less likely to be successful than longer-term therapy.

Counseling for couples and families is also valuable, especially when it incorporates the existing strengths of the family and provides specific assistance in communication skills. Behavioral techniques, recognition of patterns of behavior, explicit discussion of family values and goals, all help a family deal with the PTSD in its midst. Recognizing that families are made up of individuals, with needs for both togetherness and separateness, is an important realization. We know that mental health counselors may also need individual or group counseling to help them avoid burn out and stress symptoms themselves.

We also know that there is no magic pill that can cure PTSD, or eliminate the symptoms. We know that some medications can help with a variety of symptoms. Medications have side effects which vary from person to person, so the growing array of medications offers greater hope for survivors. We have a number of drug treatments available for PTSD symptoms, such as anxiety and depression, and currently one medication, Zoloft, specifically for PTSD. No doubt more medications will be developed for different collocations of symptoms. Combinations of drugs may be most helpful, particularly when multiple symptoms are being treated. Drug treatments can be valuable in helping survivors function, and a combination of medicine and mental health counseling is better than either alone.

We know that nontraditional approaches can be helpful as well. Basic nutrition and exercise help the physical self, and thus enhance the overall health of the individual. Spending time in nature, in creative pursuits, in journaling or handcrafts are tools. One survivor notes, "For me there was a real, earthy comfort to be found in poetry, whether it was my own fumbling verses or exquisite Shakespearean sonnets" (Kim, 2000, p. 89). Volunteering to help others is therapeutic. Having and caring for pets also gives a sense of satisfaction and service.

Paying attention to our spiritual selves is also important. Amy Snow, an ordained minister, addresses the spiritual aspect of PTSD in *The Endless Tour: Vietnam, PTSD, and the Spiritual Void* (2002). She observes that "God seems absent from [veterans'] lives" (p. 20) and encourages viewing God as loving and forgiving rather than judgmental and distant. By God, she means some higher power, by whatever name. Whether an individual joins a traditional religious community or spends time in solitary meditation, devoting time to the soul's needs adds a sense of emotional peace. An organized group can become a supportive community, and can help the PTSD survivor reestablish relationships and trust. Focusing on personal spiritual fulfillment helps a PTSD survivor see him or herself in a larger context, as part of a whole, and is also a powerful way to communicate to the self that the self is worthy of love and attention.

We know that our western view of trauma and survival is rather narrow. For the survivor, learning about other cultures' perspectives broadens an understanding of trauma and how it affects life. Survivors might avail themselves of approaches to trauma from other cultures; for example, noting animal totems, or rituals of memorializing. For caregivers, therapists, doctors, and others, recognizing that other cultures may see trauma as a natural part of life, or as recompense for a failure in religion or life, implies the need for a different approach to understanding and treatment. Noting that in other cultures the extended family is an important part of the picture suggests the need to address treatment in that larger context.

Finally, we know that much as we might wish it to be different, trauma and tragedy are part of our lives on earth. We can work to lessen the occurrences of rape, assault, torture, forced migration, ethnic cleansing, plane crashes, or war; and we should seek to better predict and survive natural disasters like floods, earthquakes, fires, and hurricanes. Yet for the foreseeable future, these human and natural events will continue to occur. As we know more about trauma and how it affects individuals, their families and communities, we can better understand how to assist members of the human family that are suffering.

PTSD has been much studied, and will continue to be studied; the diagnostic criteria might change, the treatments may improve, and our understanding of just what physical changes occur in PTSD will become better known. With the advance in knowledge, we will have more options for prevention and treatment. Yet we do not need to wait until answers are fully spelled out. We can live fulfilling lives today as individuals and families with PTSD.

Diagnostic Criteria
for PTSD (DSM IV)

A. The person has been exposed to a traumatic event in which both of the following were present:

    (1) The person experienced, witnessed, or was confronted with an event or events that involved actual or threatened death or serious injury, or a threat to the physical integrity of self or others.

    (2) The person's response involved intense fear, helplessness, or horror. **Note:** In children, this may be expressed instead by disorganized or agitated behavior.

B. The traumatic event is persistently reexperienced in one (or more) of the following ways:

    (1) Recurrent and intrusive distressing recollections of the event, including images, thoughts, or perceptions. **Note:** In young children, repetitive play may occur in which themes or aspects of the trauma are expressed.

    (2) Recurrent distressing dreams of the event. **Note:** In children, there may be frightening dreams without recognizable content.

    (3) Acting or feeling as if the traumatic event were recurring (includes a sense of reliving the experience, illusions, hallucinations, and dissociative flashback episodes, including those that occur on awakening or when intoxicated). **Note:** In young children, trauma-specific reenactment may occur.

    (4) Intense psychological distress at exposure to internal or external cues that symbolize or resemble an aspect of the traumatic event.

(5) Psychological reactivity on exposure to internal or external cues that symbolize or resemble an aspect of the traumatic event.

C. Persistent avoidance of stimuli associated with the trauma and numbing of general responsiveness (not present before the trauma), as indicated by three (or more) of the following:

(1) Efforts to avoid thoughts, feelings, or conversations associated with the trauma

(2) Efforts to avoid activities, places, or people that arouse recollections of the trauma

(3) Inability to recall an important aspect of the trauma

(4) Markedly diminished interest or participation in significant activities

(5) Feeling of detachment or estrangement from others

(6) Restricted range of affect (e.g., unable to have loving feelings)

(7) Sense of a foreshortened future (e.g., does not expect to have a career, marriage, children, or a normal life span)

D. Persistent symptoms of increased arousal (not present before the trauma), as indicated by two (or more) of the following:

(1) Difficulty falling or staying asleep

(2) Irritability or outbursts of anger

(3) Difficulty concentrating

(4) Hypervigilance

(5) Exaggerated startle response

E. Duration of the disturbance (symptoms in Criteria B, C, and D) is more than 1 month.

F. The disturbance causes clinically significant distress or impairment in social, occupational, or other important areas of functioning.

Specify if:

Acute: if duration of symptoms is less than 3 months

Chronic: if duration of symptoms is 3 months or more

Specify if:

With delayed onset: if onset of symptoms is at least 6 months after the stressor

(DSM IV, 1994, pp. 426–429).

Appendix B

Global Assessment of Functioning (GAF) Scale (DSM IV)

Consider psychological, social, and occupational functioning on a hypothetical continuum of mental health — illness. Do not include impairment in functioning due to physical (or environmental) limitations.

Code (*Note:* use intermediate codes when appropriate, e.g., 45, 68, 72)

100 | Superior functioning in a wide range of activities, life's problems never seem to get out of hand, is sought by others because of his or
91 | her many positive qualities. No symptoms.

90 | Absent or minimal symptoms (e.g., mild anxiety before an exam), good functioning in all areas, interested and involved in a wide range of activities, socially effective, generally satisfied with life, no more than everyday problems or concerns (e.g., an occasional argument
81 | with family members).

80 | If symptoms are present, they are transient and expectable reactions to psychological stressors (e.g., difficulty concentrating after family argument); no more than slight impairment in social, occupational, or school functioning (e.g., temporarily falling behind in school
71 | work).

70 | Some mild symptoms (e.g., depressed mood and mild insomnia) OR some difficulty in social, occupational, or school functioning (e.g., occasional truancy, or theft within the household), but generally func
61 | tioning pretty well, has some meaningful interpersonal relationships.

60 Moderate symptoms (e.g., flat affect and circumstantial speech, occa-
| sional panic attacks) OR moderate difficulty in social, occupational,
| or school functioning (e.g., few friends, conflicts with peers or co-
51 workers).

50 Serious symptoms (e.g., suicidal ideation, severe obsessional rituals,
| frequent shoplifting) OR any serious impairment in social, occupa-
41 tional, or school functioning (e.g., no friends, unable to keep a job).

40 Some impairment in reality testing or communication (e.g., speech at
| times illogical, obscure or irrelevant) OR major impairment in several
| areas, such as work or school, family relations, judgment, thinking, or
| mood (e.g., depressed man avoids friends, neglects family and is unable
| to work; child frequently beats up younger children, is defiant at home,
31 and is failing at school).

30 Behavior is considerably influenced by delusions or hallucinations OR
| serious impairment in communication or judgment (e.g., sometimes
| incoherent, acts grossly inappropriately, suicidal preoccupation) OR
| inability to function in almost all areas (e.g., stays in bed all day; no
21 job, home, or friends).

20 Some danger of hurting self or others (e.g., suicidal attempts without
| clear expectation of death; frequently violent; manic excitement) OR
| occasionally fails to maintain minimal personal hygiene (e.g., smears
| feces) OR gross impairment in communication (e.g., largely incoherent
11 or mute).

10 Persistent danger of severely hurting self or others (e.g., recurrent
| violence) OR persistent inability to maintain minimal personal hygiene
1 OR serious suicidal act with clear expectation of death.

0 Inadequate information

(DSM IV, 1994, p. 32).

Resources for PTSD Survivors and Families

The American Academy of Experts in Traumatic Stress
368 Veterans Memorial Highway
Commack, NY 11725
Phone: 631-543-2217
Fax: 631-543-6977
http://www.aaets.org

American Psychiatric Association
1400 K Street N.W.
Washington, DC 20005
Phone: 888-357-7924
Fax: 202-682-6850
e-mail: apa@psych.org
http://www.psych.org/public_info/ptsd.
cfm

American Psychological Association Online Help Center
http://helping.apa.org/daily/traumatic
stress.html

Anxiety Disorders Association of America
11900 Parklawn Drive, Suite 100
Rockville, MD 20852
Phone: 301-231-9350
http://www.adaa.org

Articles and Support for Trauma Survivors and Caregivers
www.giftfromwithin.org

Australian Veterans and PTSD
www.ncptsd.unimelb.edu.au

Complementary Treatments
www.holisticonline.org

Disabled American Veterans
www.dav.org

General Information about PTSD
www.duke.edu/~vunico/pcaad/ptsdpage.
htm

International Society for Traumatic Stress Studies
60 Revere Drive, Suite 500
Northbrook, IL 60062
Phone: 847-480-9028
http://www.istss.org

Medications for Combat PTSD
www.dr-bob.org/tips/ptsd.html

National Center for PTSD
www.dartmouth.edu/dms/ptsd/index.
html

National Center for Post-Traumatic Stress Disorder
215 North Main Street
White River Junction, VT 05009
Phone: 802-296-6300
e-mail: ncptsd@ncptsd.org
http://www.ncptsd.org

National Center for Victims of Crime
2000 M Street NW, Suite 480
Washington, DC 20036

Phone: 1-800-FYI-CALL (1-800-394-2255)
TTY/TDD: 1-800-211-7996
e-mail: webmaster@NCVC.org
http://www.ncvc.org

National Institute of Mental Health
6001 Executive Boulevard, Rm. 8184, MSC 9663
Bethesda, MD 20892–9663
Phone: 301-443-4513
Fax: 301-443-4279
TTY: 301-443-8431
http://www.nimh.nih.gov/anxiety/ptsd
menu.cfm

Pointman International Ministries
www.geocities.com/Pentagon/Bunker/2092/

PTSD and holidays
http://patiencepress.com/samples/PTSD
andholidays.htm

Rape, Abuse, and Incest National Network (RAINN)
635 B Pennsylvania Ave. S.E.
Washington, DC 20003
Phone: 1-800-656-HOPE (1-800-656-4673) (24-hour confidential hot line)

To reach an on-line counselor: http://rapecrisis.txcyber.com
http://www.rainn.org

The Sidrian Foundation
(nonprofit organization for trauma survivors)
www.sidrian.org

Sons and Daughters In Touch
(for children of veterans)
www.sdit.org

Suicide Website
www.metanoia.org/suicide/index.html

Veteran Resource Network
www.veteransresources.net

Veterans and their Families/The Crow's Nest
http://tmkc.netfirms.com

Vetwives and Families
www.vietnamveteranwives.com
www.angelfire.com/ok/VetWives/Home
page.html

Vietnam Veterans of America
www.vva.org

Appendix D

Resources for Veterans

Active Military and Veteran General Information
http://www.military.com

Agent Orange Reports
www.gao.gov

The Center for Women Veterans
810 Vermont Ave. NW
Washington, DC 20420
Phone: 202-273-6193
Fax: 202-273-7092
http://www.va.gov/womenvet

Department of Veterans Affairs
Washington, DC 20011
http://www.va.gov

Dissociative Disorders and Trauma Program
McLean Hospital (Harvard Medical School affiliate)
115 Mill St
Belmont MA 02478
Phone: 1-800-333-0338
http://www.mclean.harvard.edu/patient/adult/ddtp.php

EMDR Institute, Inc.
PO Box 750, Watsonville, CA 95077
Phone: 831-761-1040
www.emdr.com

EMDR International Association (EMDRIA)
PO Box 141925
Austin, TX 78714–1925

Phone: 512-451-5200 or 866-451-5200 (in U.S.)
www.emdria.org

Links for Veterans
www.VetsOutreach.com

Military Archives and Records
www.nara.gov/regional/mpr.html

National Center for Post-Traumatic Stress Disorder
http://www.ptsd.va.gov/
U.S. Department of Veterans Affairs
810 Vermont Avenue, NW
Washington, DC 20420
For More Information on PTSD *Email:* ncptsd@va.gov or *Call:* The PTSD Information Line at 802-296-6300

National Center for Trauma-Based Disorders
Two Rivers Psychiatric Hospital
5121 Raytown Road
Kansas City, MO 64133
Phone: 816-382-6300 or 1-800-225-8577
http://www.tworivershospital.com/

The National Center for Victims of Crime
2000 M Street NW, Suite 480
Washington, D.C. 20036
Phone: 202-467-8700
http://www.ncvc.org/ncvc/main.aspx?dbID=DB_GettingHelp189

National Veterans Legal Services Program (NVLSP)
http://www.nvlsp.org

PTSD Benefits, Vietnam Veterans of America
www.vva.org/Benefits/ptsd.htm

Sheppard-Pratt Health System
Trauma Disorders Program
6501 N. Charles St.
Baltimore, MD 21285
Phone: 410-938-3000 or 1-800-627-0330
http://www.sheppardpratt.org/sp_html code/sp_locations/sp_loc_balt_sp.aspx #4

There and Back Again
Nonprofit describing alternative and complementary medicine for veterans
http://www.thereandback-again.org/

Youth Crisis Hotline
800-HIT-HOME (800-448-4663)
www.youthcrisisnetwork.org/

State Benefits
www.nasdva.com

Veteran Lost and Found Listings
http://grunt.space.swri.edu/armylf.htm

Veteran Organizations and Support Groups
http://grunt.space.swri/edu/vetorgs.htm

Veteran Service Organizations
www.va.gov/vso/view.asp

Veterans Administration: Forms
www.va.gov/forms/default.asp

Veterans Administration Guidelines for Diagnosis of PTSD
www.nvo.org/vv98/phygde.initial.htm

Veterans Education Benefits
Washington, DC
www.gibill.va.gov/education/benefits.htm

Veterans Family Insurance and Benefits
www.va.gov/opa/pressrel/

Veterans Health Administration
810 Vermont Avenue NW
Washington, DC 20420
Phone:202-273-5400
http://www.va.gov/health_benefits

Vietnam Veterans Memorial
www.vvmf.org

Vietnam War Personal Websites
www.angelfire.com/ny3/Vietnam Memories
www.angelfire.com/ny2/SGTFATS/index. html
www.illyria.com/dustyhp.html

Toll-Free Numbers for Contacting the VA

VA Benefits: 1-800-827-1000
• Disability
• Medical Care
• Life Insurance
• Sexual Trauma
Health Care Benefits: 1-877-222-8387
Telecommunications Device for the Deaf (TDD): 1-800-829-4833

APPENDIX E

Recommended Books

Trauma and Treatment

Achilles in Vietnam: Combat Trauma and the Undoing of Character.
J. Shay, M.D., Ph.D. (1994). New York: Simon & Schuster. A Veterans
Administration psychiatrist draws parallels between the Greek epic *The
Illiad* and his work with Vietnam veterans suffering from PTSD.

Aftermath: Violence and the Remaking of a Self. S. J. Brison (2002).
Princeton: Princeton University Press. A woman relates the process of
her recovery after rape and attempted murder. This first-hand account
illustrates how trauma affects our very concept of self.

First They Killed My Father: A Daughter of Cambodia Remembers. L.
Ung (2000). New York: HarperCollins. The autobiography of a girl
whose family was forced to leave Phnom Penh and work in the country.
Eventually the author and surviving family members resettled in the
U.S., where the author is currently National Spokesperson for the Campaign
for a Landmine Free World.

*Flashback: Posttraumatic Stress Disorder, Suicide, and the Lessons of
War.* P. Coleman. (2006). Boston: Beacon Press. This book records stories
of and by women related to Vietnam war veterans.

Home from the War: Learning from Vietnam Veterans. R. J. Lifton
(1973). New York: Simon & Schuster. Veterans Administration psychiatrist
Jay Lifton describes his pioneering work with Vietnam veterans
using rap groups.

The House of Purple Hearts. P. Solotaroff (1995). New York: HarperCollins.
Solotaroff describes a house and program for homeless veterans, detailing
both the issues of its clients and efforts to enable them to cope with PTSD.

Man's Search for Meaning. V. Frankl (1959). New York: Simon & Schuster. Frankl's classic describes the horrors of concentration camps and explores how humans find meaning and purpose in their efforts to survive.

Odysseus in America. J. Shay (2002). New York: Scribners. Shay's follow-up to *Achilles in Vietnam* explores the difficulties of the combat veteran and suggests fostering a sense of unit community in order to decrease psychological stresses.

Unspeakable Truths and Happy Endings: Human Cruelty and the New Trauma Therapy. R. Coffey (1998). Lutherville, Md.: Sidran. Coffey describes the suffering of survivors of traumatic events, including incest and rape, and explores ways mental health professionals might help victims help themselves.

Women and Self-Esteem: Understanding and Improving the Way We Think and Feel about Ourselves. L. Tschirhart Sanford & M. E. Donovan (1984). New York: Penguin. A practical book aimed at helping women understand and overcome low self-esteem, thus enabling them to act on their own behalf. Wives of PTSD survivors may find encouragement here to recognize their own needs in the context of a PTSD marriage.

Couples, Families, and PTSD

Back from the Brink: A Family Guide to Overcoming Traumatic Stress. D. R. Catherall (1992). New York: Bantam. This book describes and explains PTSD as well as discussing treatment options. It is especially useful for its focus on the family, not just the individual.

Crisis and Chaos: Life with the Combat Veteran. C. McCarty-Gould (1998). Commack, N.Y.: Kroshka. McCarty-Gould helps clarify how specific symptoms of PTSD (hypervigilance, anger, fear) may be manifested in a family context. By doing so, she reassures families that they are not alone, and suggests strategies for coping.

The Dance of Intimacy. H. G. Lerner, Ph.D. (1989). New York: Harper & Row. Lerner, a mental health therapist, describes how couples' interactions may inadvertently perpetuate the behaviors we seek to change. While not about PTSD, it is nevertheless useful, particularly for women, in revealing our own contributions to the "marital dance."

The Endless Tour: Vietnam, PTSD, and the Spiritual Void. The Rev.

A.L. Snow, M.A. (2002). Victoria, B.C.: Trafford. Snow, an ordained minister, focuses on the journey to recovery of her husband, a Vietnam veteran, with particular emphasis on spiritual issues, both wounding and healing.

Facing the Wall: A Mission. 2nd ed. M. S. King (2010). U.S.A.: Xlibris. *www.Xlibris.com* Memoir by the wife of a Vietnam veteran, detailing the difficulties of dealing with PTSD and its effects on their family. The author makes many observations that will sound familiar to those living with PTSD.

An Operators Manual for Combat PTSD: Essays for Coping. A. B. Hart II, Ph.D. (2000). San Jose, Calif.: Writer's Showcase (presented by *Writer's Digest*). This book is a collection of essays discussing PTSD, its symptoms and characteristics. Those suffering from or living with PTSD have found it valuable for understanding how PTSD affects daily life.

Recovering from the War: A Guide for All Veterans, Family Members, Friends, and Therapists. P. H. C. Mason (1998). High Springs, Fla.: Patience Press. Mason discusses the difficulties of families living with PTSD. She reviews aspects of the Vietnam War and PTSD, and offers suggestions for coping. She also includes resources for further information.

Trust After Trauma: A Guide to Relationships for Survivors and Those Who Love Them. A. Matsakis, Ph.D. (1998). Oakland, Calif.: New Harbinger. Matsakis, a psychotherapist specializing in PTSD, not only discusses difficulties faced by survivors of trauma in their personal relationships, but also offers practical exercises for the reader to help clarify and manage some of these difficulties.

Vietnam Wives: Facing the Challenges of Life with Veterans Suffering Post-Traumatic Stress. 2nd ed. A. Matsakis, Ph.D. (1996). Lutherville, Md.: Sidran. Matsakis details numerous examples of survivors, couples, and families within the context of PTSD itself. We not only hear the survivor's voice, but also the voices of those interacting with the survivor, which helps reveal the complexity and challenges of living with PTSD.

When Bad Things Happen to Good People. 2nd ed. H. S. Kusher (1989). New York: Schocken. This *New York Times* bestseller, written by a rabbi, explores our thoughts about God and suffering, and seeks to explain how one can believe in God in spite of tragedies. It is straightforward, easy to read, and ultimately reassuring.

Cross-Cultural Perspectives

The Middle of Everywhere: The World's Refugees Come to Our Town.
M. Pipher (2002). New York: Harcourt. Pipher describes her work with
refugees, from all corners of the world, resettling in Lincoln, Nebraska.
Besides coping with attempting to learn an entirely new way of living,
many of these refugees are also attempting to make sense of their traumatic pasts.

Mutant Message Down Under. M. Morgan (1991). New York: Harper-
Collins. The author learns to appreciate and understand a different culture's worldview as she participates in a walkabout in Australia. The
process through which she becomes able to interpret this different perspective may help readers understand how very Western our views and
treatments of PTSD are.

We Wish to Inform You That Tomorrow We Will Be Killed with Our
Families. P. Gourevitch (1998). New York: Picador. This book describes
the genocide against the Rwandan Tutsis in the mid–1990s. The author
weaves together past (roots of conflicts) and present, and puts a human
face on the suffering of the people in this African country.

Collected Stories / Autobiographies / Memoirs

A Child Called "It." D. Pelzer (1995). Deerfield Beach, Fla.: Health Communications. Pelzer writes about being abused by his alcoholic mother
as a child, including being starved, beaten, burned, and other undeserved
acts. Pelzer was removed from the home at age 12, and his next book
describes being in foster care.

Finding Fish. A. Q. Fisher and M. E. Rivas (2001). New York: Harper-
Collins. Fisher details his traumatic childhood, growing up in a foster
family, and goes on to describe how he joined the Navy to escape the
abuse. This is the book on which the film *Antwone Fisher* is based.

For Rouenna. S. Nunez (2001). New York: Farrar, Straus & Giroux. This
book of fiction narrates the memories of an Army nurse in the Vietnam
War, and her postwar experiences, illustrating how the past continues
to influence the present and future.

Home Before Morning: The True Story of an Army Nurse in Vietnam.

L. Van Devanter (1983). New York: Warner Books. Linda Van Devanter describes how she felt as a nurse in the Vietnam War, and details the difficulties she had readjusting. While sometimes painful to read, it is nevertheless still a classic. Van Devanter died in 2002, at age 55, of a disease she attributed to her exposure to Agent Orange during the war.

I Am a Soldier, Too: The Jessica Lynch Story. R. Bragg (2003). New York: Alfred A. Knopf. Jessica Lynch was wounded and taken prisoner of war in Iraq. While this biography says little about Lynch's post-war experiences, it does show the trauma that may well lead to PTSD.

I Begin My Life All Over: The Hmong and the American Immigrant Experience. L. Faderman (1998). Boston: Beacon. The author presents the results of interviews conducted with Hmong refugees to the United States. The refugees remember life in Laos, fleeing to refugee camps in Thailand, and resettling in the U.S. The interviews reveal the sharp contrasts between genders, generations, and traditional Hmong vs. American values and beliefs.

I'm Still Standing: From Captive U.S. Soldier to Free Citizen — My Journey Home. Shoshana Johnson with M. L. Doyle (2010). Touchstone, a division of Simon & Schuster. New York, NY 2010. Johnson details her story of being ambushed and taken prisoner of war in Iraq; her treatment by Iraqi medical professionals, and her rescue. She describes her PTSD symptoms and treatments upon returning to the U.S.

Long Time Passing: Vietnam and the Haunted Generation. (2nd ed.) M. MacPherson (2001). Bloomington: Indiana University Press. MacPherson reviews the Vietnam War in a historical context, and then describes the war's effects on those who fought in it and their families, political changes, and continuing effects on American society.

The Lost Boy: A Foster Child's Search for the Love of a Family. D. Pelzer (1997). Deerfield Beach, Fla.: Health Communications. Pelzer recalls the multiple foster families he was housed with after being removed from his abusive home. From the original traumas of his early life, through the difficulties of foster care, Pelzer describes his struggle to survive.

Out of the Night: The Spiritual Journey of Vietnam Vets. W. P. Mahedy (1986). New York: Ballantine Books. An Army Chaplain explores the religious faiths of men during and after the Vietnam War, and suggests how religion can help veterans heal.

Ten Thousand Sorrows. E. Kim (2000). New York: Doubleday. The daughter of an unmarried Korean woman and an American serviceman sees her mother killed by her uncle and grandfather to restore the family's honor. She is then left at an orphanage and later adopted by an American fundamentalist Christian family, who arrange her marriage at age 17 to an abusive leader of their church. The author describes her efforts to face her early traumas and move beyond mere physical survival.

The Things They Carried. T. O'Brien (1990). New York: Penguin. Tim O'Brien's book of short stories helps us understand how ordinary people may be transformed by war, in this case Vietnam War soldiers and veterans. Easy to read and profoundly revealing.

Tuesdays with Morrie. M. Albom (1997). New York: Doubleday. While not strictly about surviving a traumatic event, this book inspires the reader with the strength of character and spirit of Morrie, who is dying of Lou Gehrig's disease. Over the course of months, the author visits and discusses with his mentor issues of life and love, friendship and death.

The Unwanted: A Memoir of Childhood. K. Nguyen (2001). Boston: Little, Brown. This is the memoir of an Amerasian boy (Vietnamese mother, American father), both before and after the end of American involvement in the war. As a "half-breed" and the child of a "capitalist," he and his family suffer and must learn new survival skills.

Veteran's Day (1990). R. Kane. New York: Orion. A combat medic traces his experiences in war, his displacement back home, his growing understanding of why he is the way he is, and his efforts to recover from PTSD.

For Young Readers

Abby, My Love. H. Irwin (1985). New York: Atheneum. A teenage boy, Chip, tries to understand why the girl he is in love with seems so distant at times. When she finally confides that her father sexually abuses her, both Abby and Chip have to work through a process of overcoming the trauma. For middle school and junior high, early to middle teen years.

Alan and Naomi. M. Levoy (1977). New York: HarperCollins. A young boy befriends a French girl who has escaped from Nazi-controlled France. By establishing a personal relationship, he hopes to draw her out of her trauma.

Coping with Post-Traumatic Stress Disorder. C. Simpson & D. Simpson (1997). New York: Rosen. A straightforward discussion of PTSD — causes, symptoms, and treatments. Appropriate for teens and older readers.

Lost in the War. N. Antle (1998). New York: Puffin Books. A young girl whose father died in the Vietnam War and whose mother served as a nurse in Vietnam describes her mother's increasing difficulty in coping, its effects on the family, and some avenues for healing. Nicely told for an upper elementary-level and above audience.

Number the Stars. L. Lowry (1989). Boston: Houghton Mifflin. Two children, one Jewish, experience the Nazi occupation of Denmark. Appropriate for elementary school children.

Off to War: Voices of Soldiers' Children. D. Ellis (2008). Toronto: Groundwood. Ellis presents interviews with children whose parent or parents have served or are serving away from home. This is a nice look at how children experience frequent moves, worries for their parents' safety, and relationships with caregivers, siblings, and other family members.

One April Morning: Children Remember the Oklahoma City Bombing. N. Lamb (1996). New York: Lothrop, Lee & Shepard. Children share their thoughts and feelings about the Oklahoma City bombing, and tell what helped them cope with the tragedy. Appropriate for all grade levels.

Sadako and the Thousand Paper Cranes. E. Coerr (1977). New York: Dell. Not directly about PTSD, this is nevertheless a valuable book for children about a young girl's spirit as she is diagnosed with radiation-induced leukemia in post–World War II Japan.

Searching for Atticus. J. Marino (1997). New York: Simon & Schuster. A teenaged girl whose father returns from a tour as a surgeon in Vietnam learns to cope with and understand her father's difficulties readjusting. Appropriate for upper elementary and perhaps best suited to middle school or junior high school readers.

Soldier's Heart. G. Paulsen (1998). New York: Delacorte. A young Minnesotan recounts his participation in the Civil War, including problems he experienced returning home afterwards. Appropriate for upper elementary and older youths.

Song of the Trees. M. D. Taylor (1975). New York: Dial. A black family copes with the Depression in Mississippi. Appropriate for elementary school children.

Straight Talk about Post-Traumatic Stress Disorder: Coping with the Aftermath of Trauma. K. M. Porterfield (1996). New York: Facts on File. Porterfield does an excellent job explaining PTSD, its symptoms and how it affects the brain and mind. Straightforward and easy to understand, with multiple examples throughout.

*A **Wall of Names: The Story of the Vietnam Veterans Memorial.*** J. Donnelly (1991). New York: Random House. Suitable for young children as well as older ones, this book relates the story of the Vietnam Veterans Memorial (The Wall) with clarity and compassion.

APPENDIX F

Recommended Films

Antwone Fisher. Denzel Washington, Director (2002). United States: Fox Searchlight Pictures. With Denzel Washington, Derek Luke, Joy Bryant, and others. Based on the book *Finding Fish* by Fisher and M. E. Rivas. After an abusive childhood, Fisher joins the Navy and finally connects with a Navy psychiatrist, who helps him reorient his life.

Apocalypse Now. Francis Ford Coppola, Producer & Director (1979). United States: United Artists. With Marlon Brando, Martin Sheen, Robert Duvall, Laurence Fishburne, and Dennis Hopper. Based on Joseph Conrad's *Heart of Darkness*, burnt-out Captain Willard is sent into the jungle with orders to find and kill Colonel Kurtz, who has set up his own army within the Cambodian jungle. As he descends into the jungle, he is slowly overtaken by its mesmerizing powers and the battles and insanity which surround him.

Band of Brothers. Tom Hanks and Steven Spielberg, Producers. Various directors for different episodes, including Phil Alden Robinson and Richard Loncraine, among others (2001). United States: HBO Video. With Frank John Hughes, Ron Livingston, David Schwimmer, Donnie Wahlberg, and many others. A ten episode documentary that follows one company from training through World War II battles. Interviews with veterans reveal the effects of the war on their lives both during and after the war.

Battle for Haditha. Nick Broomfield, Director. (2007). Image Entertainment. With Matthew Knoll, Eric Mehalacopoulos, Nathan de la Cruz, Andrew McLaren, Elliot Ruiz. Based on a true story, Marines who had suffered losses from IEDs kill civilians in Haditha, Iraq. The film shows that both sides feel both compassion and remorse, and also shows a soldier suffering from flashbacks, intrusive memories, and guilt, both over killing and over the death of a buddy.

The Best Years of Our Lives. William Wyler, Director (1946). United States: MGM/UA Studios. With Frederic March, Dana Andrews, and Harold Russell as three World War II soldiers returning after the war and their efforts to readjust to civilian life.

Birdy. Alan Parker, Director (1984). United States: Columbia/Tristar Studios. With Matthew Modine and Nicolas Cage. Vietnam veteran visits old friend and fellow veteran who is institutionalized, and seeks, through friendship, to connect with Birdy and help him leave the insitution.

Born on the Fourth of July. A. Kitman Ho and Oliver Stone, Producers. Oliver Stone, Director (1989). United States: Universal Studios. With Tom Cruise and Kyra Sedgwick. The biography of Ron Kovic. As a gung-ho Marine, Kovic re-enlists for a second tour of duty in Vietnam, during which he experiences an intense firefight that causes him to question the war's morality. Returning home paralyzed, he becomes an anti-war and pro-human rights political activist after feeling betrayed by the country he fought for.

Brothers. Director Jim Sheridan, Director (2009). Lionsgate. With Jake Gyllenhaal, Natalie Portman, Tobey Maguire. This intense drama focuses on two brothers, one recently released from jail and the other a Marine being redeployed to Afghanistan. After a helicopter crash, the Marine is taken prisoner. Meanwhile, at home, his brother steps in to support the family. Upon the Marine's repatriation, tensions between the brothers arise in part due to the Marine's PTSD issues. The bonds of family are strong, and there is hope for PTSD sufferers.

China Beach. John Sacret Young, Producer. Rod Holcomb, Director (television series, 1988–1991). United States: Warner Brothers. With Dana Delany, Nan Woods, Michael Boatman, Marg Helgenberger and others. The series tells the story of an Army nurse in Vietnam, showing how the stress of constant medical emergencies results in emotional numbness, inability to feel close to others, irritability, and so on.

Coming Home. Jerome Hellman, Producer. Hal Ashby, Director (1978). United States: United Artists. With Jane Fonda, Jon Voight, and Bruce Dern. A woman whose husband is fighting in Vietnam volunteers at a VA hospital and falls in love with a vet suffering from a paralyzing combat injury. When her husband returns, he finds that she has become a vocal anti-war protester, in some ways representing changes that occurred in the U.S. itself over the course of the war.

The Deer Hunter. Michael Cimino, Producer & Director (1978). United States: Universal Pictures. With Robert DeNiro, Meryl Streep, Christopher Walken, and John Savage. An in-depth examination of the way that the Vietnam War affects the lives of people in a small industrial town in Pennsylvania.

Fearless. Paula Weinstein and Mark Rosenberg, Producers. Peter Weir, Director (1993). With Jeff Bridges, Isabella Rossellini, and Rosie Perez. United States: Warner Brothers. Bridges is a survivor of a plane crash who believes that his survival means he is now invulnerable. As he helps fellow survivor Perez cope with the loss of her child, he confronts his own convictions and need for recovery.

First Blood. Buzz Feitshans, Producer. Ted Kotcheff, Director (1982). United States: Orion Pictures. With Sylvester Stallone, Richard Crenna, and Brian Dennehy. Stallone plays John Rambo, a Green Beret Vietnam veteran, who hitchhikes to a small town to see an old army friend. The sheriff, played by Dennehy, tries to make him leave and when he refuses, arrests him for vagrancy. Rambo escapes and becomes a one-man army battling the police. This is the first of three Rambo movies.

Green Dragon. Forest Whitaker and Alison Semenza, Producers. Timothy Linh Bui, Director (2001). United States: Franchise Classics. With Patrick Swayze, Forest Whitaker, Don Duong, and Hiep Thi Le. This film takes place at a refugee camp set up at Marine base Camp Pendleton in California for the earliest Vietnamese refugees.

Heaven and Earth. Oliver Stone, Director (1993). With Haing S. Ngor, Hiep Thi Le, and Tommy Lee Jones. United States: Warner Studios. The autobiography of a Vietnamese woman during the war and her subsequent move to the United States. This engrossing film, which begins with the French Indochina War in the 1950s and ends in California, includes trauma, violence, survival, and, ultimately, acceptance and satisfaction.

Heroes. David Foster and Lawrence Turman, Producers. Jeremy Paul Kagan, Director (1977). United States: Universal Studios. With Henry Winkler, Sally Field, and Harrison Ford. Jack, a Vietnam War veteran, travels with chance-met Carol across the country with plans of starting a worm farm. They meet an old army friend along the way. The trip represents a journey into Jack's troubled postwar life.

Home for the Holidays. Alfredo de Villa, Director (2008). Anchor Bay Entertainment. With Alfred Molina, Elizabeth Pena, Freddy Rodriguez, John Leguizamo, Debra Messing, Jay Hernandez. While not the focus of the film, an Iraqi war veteran joins his Puerto Rican family in Chicago for the Christmas holiday. Other members of the family have difficulties or secrets which are revealed in the film.

Home of the Brave. Mark Robson, Director (1949). With James Edwards and Lloyd Bridges. United States: United Artists. Five American servicemen during World War II are sent to an island to survey the terrain prior to an Allied invasion. Racism, trauma, and treatment are addressed. The Army psychiatrist does a superb job of leading the traumatized soldier to understand survivor guilt.

Home of the Brave. Irwin Winkler, Director. (2007) MGM. Samuel L. Jackson, 50 Cent, Jessica Biel, Brian Presley, Christina Ricci. Follows the lives of several Iraq war veterans after their return home. Symptoms of PTSD are shown, including outburts of anger, difficulty sleeping, and survivor guilt. Also shows role of therapy in overcoming PTSD.

The Hurt Locker. Dir. Kathryn Bigelow, Director. (2009). Summit Entertainment. With Jeremy Renner, Anthony Mackie, Brian Geraghty, Ralph Fiennes. Depiction of fighting an insurgent war in Iraq; IEDs set off by cell phones, making it difficult to tell who the enemy is. Given the stress and adrenaline response of combat, it is clear that soldiers will have difficulties readjusting to civilian life.

In Country: A Story of an American Family. N. Jewison and P. Roth, producers (1989). United States: A Norman Jewison Film. With Bruce Willis and Emily Lloyd. Willis is a Vietnam War veteran who refuses to talk about the war with his niece, whose father died in the war. As she reaches adulthood, she tries to learn more about her father; other family members become part of her search for understanding. The film ends with a visit to the Vietnam Veterans Memorial (The Wall).

In the Valley of Elah. Paul Haggis, Director (2006). Warner Independent Pictures. 2006. With Tommy Lee Jones, Charlize Theron, Susan Sarandon, Jason Patric. A Vietnam era veteran is informed that his son is AWOL after combat deployment in Iraq. He teams up with a police detective to uncover what has happened to his son, and in the process, understands the trauma his son experienced.

Jacknife. Robert Schaffel and Carol Baum, Producers. David Jones, Director (1989). HBO Video/Kings Road Entertainment. With Robert DeNiro, Ed Harris, Kathy Baker. Vietnam Veteran Megs tries to help his friend and fellow veteran Dave overcome painful memories and find a reason to live. This film doesn't stereotype veterans as being out of control, and instead shows PTSD in veterans who are functioning in society, while at the same time showing their need for help and support.

Memorial Day. Jay Benson, Producer. Joseph Sargent, Director (1983). United States: Heron Communications. With Mike Farrell, Shelley Fabares, Keith Mitchell, Danny Glover, and Bonnie Bedelia. Years after the war, Vietnam veterans meet at a hotel to renew their old friendships. The diversity of postwar experiences and beliefs is played out over a Memorial Day weekend.

The Pawnbroker. Roger Lewis Langner, producer. Sidney Lumet, Director (1964). United States: Republic Pictures. With Rod Steiger and Jaime Sanchez. A Harlem pawnbroker who survived a Nazi death camp scorns the hapless characters who come into his shop. He is considerably shaken, however, when his shop assistant tries to save his life during a robbery.

Slaughterhouse Five. George Roy Hill, Director (1972). United States: Universal Studios. With Michael Sacks, Ron Leibman. Based on Kurt Vonnegut's novel about Billy Pilgrim, who becomes unstuck in time as a result of his experiences in the bombing of Dresden, Germany, during World War II.

Taking Chance. Ross Katz, Director. (2009). HBO. With Kevin Bacon. Based on a true story, Bacon's character escorts the body of a combat casualty to his family and home. Each stop and transfer shows the reactions of civilians along the way. A very personal view that also illustrates survivor guilt.

Three Seasons. Jason Kliot, Joana Vicente, and Tony Bui, Producers. Tony Bui, Director (1999). United States: October Films. With Harvey Keitel, Don Duong, Nguyen Ngoc Hiep and Nguyen Huu Duoc. In the new Vietnam of Western progress, multiple characters' paths cross in small ways, including an American in Ho Chi Minh City who looks for a daughter he fathered during the war.

The War. Jon Avnet, Director (1994). United States: Universal Studios. With Kevin Costner, Elijah Wood, and others. Children of a troubled

Vietnam veteran get into a "war" with other children over a tree house. The children's war and the father's war are juxtaposed, as the children seek strategies for winning and the father tries not to be involved.

We Were Soldiers. Randall Wallace, Director (2002). United States: Paramount Home Video. With Mel Gibson, Sam Elliot, Madeleine Stowe, Greg Kinnear, and Barry Pepper. Based on the autobiographical book by Lt. Col. Harold Moore, the film tells the story of the first major battle with the North Vietnamese Army during the Vietnam War, and also flashes back to the families of the soldiers as they wait anxiously for news of their sons, husbands and fathers.

Films Recommended for Children

Alaska. Fraser Clarke Heston, Director (1996). United States: Castle Rock. With Thora Birch, Vincent Kartheiser, and more. After the death of their mother, two children move with their father to Alaska. When the father's plane crashes and the rescue crews give up, the two children overcome great difficulties in their own efforts to save their father.

Annie. John Huston, Director (1982). United States: Columbia/Tristar Studios. With Albert Finney, Carol Burnett, Tim Curry, Aileen Quinn, and more. This musical follows the orphan Annie (Li'l Orphan Annie, a long-time newspaper cartoon character) as she seeks to create a family with the curmudgeonly Daddy Warbucks. While the rendition is lighthearted, Annie was sent to the orphanage after the death of her parents and so is seeking to overcome that trauma.

Balto. Steve Hickner, Producer. Simon Wells, Director (1995). United States: Universal Studios and Amblin Entertainment. With the voices of Kevin Bacon, Bridget Fonda, Phil Collins, Bob Hoskins. In this animated feature, Balto the dog is the survivor who is an outcast because he is part husky and part wolf. But when a diphtheria outbreak occurs, and the dogs get lost in a blizzard, Balto is able to make the trip to get medicine for the children.

Black Beauty. Robert Shapiro and Peter MacGregor-Scott, Producers. Caroline Thompson, Director (1994). United States: Warner Home Video. With Sean Bean, Andrews Knott, David Thewlis, and others. Based on the book by Anna Sewell. Black Beauty is a black horse who is taken from the country to work in the city of London. While he experiences both kind and unkind caregivers, he ultimately survives with the support of other horses and people.

Fly Away Home. John Veitch and Carol Baum, Producers. Carroll Ballard, Director (1996). United States: Columbia Pictures. With Jeff Daniels, Anna Paquin, and Dana Delany. A 13-year-old girl loses her mother in an automobile accident and goes to live with her estranged father. She learns to develop close ties with her father by adopting an orphaned flock of Canada Geese, which she and her father teach to migrate.

Oliver! Carol Reed, Director (1968). United States: Columbia/Tristar Studios. With Ron Moody, Mark Lester, and more. Based on Dickens' classic book *Oliver Twist*, this musical follows a young orphan in London who survives by becoming part of a gang of thieves. While the leader of the gang is fierce and frightening, Oliver finds that others in the gang, both adults and children, become a family.

Note: Other children's films and books may become a tool for discussing trauma with children. Classics such as *Cinderella, Beauty and the Beast, Goldilocks, Alice in Wonderland,* and *The Wizard of Oz* may all provide the opportunity for children to recognize that bad things can happen to people through no fault of their own, and also show ways that others have dealt with tragedy and overcome it.

References

Aerni, A., and R. Traber, C. Hock, B. Roozendaal, G. Schelling, A. Papassotiropoulos, R. M. Nitsch, U. Schnyder, D. J.-F. de Quervain. (2004). *American Journal of Psychiatry* 161:1488–1490.

Ahlberg, N. (2000). *"No Five Fingers Are Alike": What Exiled Kurdish Women in Therapy Told Me*. Oslo: Solum Forlag.

Armstrong, M.A., and P. Rose (1997). Group therapy for partners of combat veterans with post-traumatic stress disorder. *Perspectives in Psychiatric Care* 33 (4), 14 (5).

Assessments. National Center for PTSD. *United States Department of Veterans Affairs*. www.ptsd.va.gov. Retrieved 26 August 2010.

Basoglu, M., M. Paker, O. Paker, E. Ozmen, I. Marks, C. Incesu, D. Sahin, and N. Sarimurat (1994). Psychological effects of torture: A comparison of tortured with nontortured political activists in Turkey. *American Journal of Psychiatry* 151, 76–81.

Beck, M. (2002, February). We are all soldiers for freedom. *Oprah Magazine* (pp. 148–149, 172, 174).

Berghult, M. (2010). "Soldiers who've taken a life at greater risk for PTSD." www.wusa9.com/news/military. Retrieved 7 April 2010.

Berlin, H. (2007). "Antiepileptic drugs for the treatment of post-traumatic stress disorder." *Current Psychiatry Reports* 9:291–300.

Bockus, F. (1980). *Couple Therapy*. New York: Jason Aronson.

Bowker, J. (1970). *Problems of Suffering in Religions of the World*. Cambridge: Cambridge University Press.

Bracken, P., and C. Petty (Eds.) (1998). *Rethinking the Trauma of War*. New York: Free Association Books.

Brewin, C.R., B. Andrews, S. Rose, and M. Kirk (1999). Acute stress disorder and posttraumatic stress disorder in victims of violent crime. *American Journal of Psychiatry* 156, 360–366.

Brewin, C.R., B. Andrews, and J. D. Valentine. (2000). "Meta-analysis of risk factors for posttraumatic stress disorder in trauma-exposed adults." *Journal of Consulting and Clinical Psychology* 68 (5):748–766.

Brown, P.C. (1984, July–August). Legacies of a war: Treatment considerations with Vietnam veterans and their families. *Social Work*, 372–279.

Brunswick, M. "Repeat tours take invisible toll." *StarTribune*. Minneapolis–St. Paul. February 1, 2010. www.startribune.com/local/83305477.html?elr=KArksUUU oDEy3LGDiO7aiU. Retrieved 2 February 2010.

Canive, J.M., and D. Castillo, Ph.D. (Winter, 1997). Hispanic veterans diagnosed with PTSD: Assessment and treatment issues. *NCP Clinical Quarterly* 7, 1–9.

Cardeña, E., J. Maldonado, O. Hart, and D. Spiegel (2000). Hypnosis. In E.B. Foa, T.M. Keane, and M.J. Friedman (Eds.), *Effective Treatments for PTSD* (pp. 247–279). New York: Guilford.

Carey, B. (2009). "Mental stress training is planned for U.S. soldiers." *New York Times* www.nytimes.com/2009/08/18/health/. Retrieved 2 February 2010.

Carroll, E.M., D.B. Rueger, D.W. Foy, and C.P. Donahoe, Jr. (1985). Vietnam combat veterans with posttraumatic stress disorder: Analysis of marital and cohabiting adjustment. *Journal of Abnormal Psychology* 94 (3), 329–337.

Catherall, D.R. (1992). *Back from the Brink: A Family Guide to Overcoming Traumatic Stress.* New York: Bantam Books.

Christenson, S. (2010). "Suicide victim's wife speaks at Fort Hood." *Express-News.* www.mysanantonio.com/news/local_news/Suicide_victims_wife_speaks_at_Fort_hood.html. Retrieved 7 April 2010.

Cimino, M., B. Spikings, M. Deeley, and J. Peverall (Producers); M. Cimino (Director) (1978). *The Deer Hunter* [motion picture]. United States: Universal.

Clark, G.R. (1990). *Words of the Vietnam War.* Jefferson, N.C.: McFarland.

Cloud, H., and J. Townsend (1992). *Boundaries.* Grand Rapids, Mich.: Zondervan.

Coffey, R. (1998). *Unspeakable Truths and Happy Endings: Human Cruelty and the New Trauma Therapy.* Lutherville, Md.: Sidran.

Coleman, P. (2005). *Flashback: Posttraumatic Stress Disorder, Suicide, and the Lessons of War.* Boston: Beacon.

Coughlan, K., and C. Parkin (1987).

Women partners of Vietnam vets. *Journal of Psychosocial Nursing* 25(10), 25–27.

Craine, M.H., R. Hanks, and H. Stevens (1992). Mapping family stress: The application of family adaptation theory to post-traumatic stress disorder. *The American Journal of Family Therapy* 20 (3), 195–203.

Dao, J. (2010). "Presidential condolences and troop suicides." *New York Times.* http://atwar.blogs.nytimes.com/2010/02/01/presidential-condolences-and-troop-suicides/. Retrieved 2 February 2010.

Davey, B., S. McEveety, and R. Wallace (Producers); R. Wallace (Writer/ Director) (2002). *We Were Soldiers* [motion picture]. United States: Paramount Pictures.

De Fazio, V.J., and N.J. Pascucci (1984, Spring/Summer). Return to Ithaca: A perspective on marriage and love in posttraumatic stress disorder. *Journal of Contemporary Psychotherapy* 14 (1), 76–89.

Description of Some Essential Oils for Beginners (n.d.). Retrieved November 3, 2002, from http://www.holisticonline.com/Aromatherapy/aroma_beginners.htm.

Diagnostic and Statistical Manual of Mental Disorders (4th ed.) (DSM IV) (1994). Washington, D.C.: American Psychiatric Association.

Diagnostic and Statistical Manual of Mental Disorders (4th ed., Text Revision) (DSM IV-TR) (2000). American Psychiatric Association. Washington, D.C.

Dudley, W. (1998). (Book editor). *The Vietnam War: Opposing Viewpoints.* San Diego, Calif.: Greenhaven Press.

Dutton, M.A., and F.L. Rubinstein (1995). Working with people with PTSD: Research implications. In C.R. Figley (Ed.), *Compassion Fatigue: Coping with Secondary Traumatic Stress Disorder in Those Who Treat the Traumatized* (pp. 82–100). New York: Brunner/Mazel.

Eliot, G. (1885). *Daniel Deronda*. New York: Belford Clarke.

Elliott, D. (host). (2007). "Vietnam veterans help Iraq vets through transition." *National Public Radio* February 18, 2007.

Ellis, A. (n.d.) Rational emotive behavior therapy (REBT). Retrieved September 7, 2002, from http://www.threeminute therapy.com/rebt.html.

Emotional support crucial to helping military families deal with deployments (2009). University of North Carolina News Services. http://uncnews.unc. edu/content/view/2986/138/. Retrieved 27 January 2010.

Facts about Post-Traumatic Stress Disorder. National Institute of Mental Health. Publication No. OM-99 4157 (Revised). Printed September 1999, updated October 5, 2001. Retrieved May 1, 2002, from http://www.nimh .nih. gov/anxiety/ptsdfacts.cfm.

Faderman, L. (1998). *I Begin My Life All Over: The Hmong and the American Immigrant Experience*. Boston: Beacon.

Fadiman, A. (1997). *The Spirit Catches You and You Fall Down*. New York: Noonday.

Feldman, L.F., and F.H. Scherk (1967). *Family Social Welfare: Helping Troubled Families*. New York: Therton.

FEMA (n.d.). *Coping with Stress Caused by Natural Disasters*. Retrieved October 27, 2001, from http://www.fema.gov/ diz99/d1279n19.htm.

Figley, C.R. (1989). *Helping Traumatized Families*. San Francisco, Calif.: Jossey-Bass.

_____ (Ed.). (1995). *Compassion Fatigue: Coping with Secondary Traumatic Stress Disorder in Those Who Treat the Traumatized* (pp. 82–100). New York: Brunner/Mazel.

_____ (1995a). Compassion fatigue as secondary traumatic stress: An overview. In C.R. Figley (Ed.), *Compassion Fatigue: Coping with Secondary Traumatic Stress Disorder in Those Who Treat the Traumatized* (pp. 1–20). New York: Bruner/Mazel.

_____, and D.H. Sprenkle (1978, July 10). Delayed stress response syndrome: Family therapy indications. *Journal of Marriage & Family Counseling*, 53–60.

Foa, E.B., T.M. Keane, and M.J. Friedman (Eds.). (2000). *Effective Treatments for PTSD*. New York: The Guilford Press.

Frank, O. (1952). *Anne Frank: The Diary of a Young Girl*. Garden City: Doubleday.

Frankl, V. E.(1959). *Man's Search for Meaning*. New York: Washington Square Press.

Friedman, M.J., M.D., Ph.D. (2001). *Post Traumatic Stress Disorder: The Latest Assessment and Treatment Strategies*. Kansas City, Mo.: Compact Clinicals.

Fujishin, R. (2001). *Creating Effective Groups: The Art of Small Group Communication*. San Francisco: Acada Books.

Fullerton, C., and R. Ursano (1997). Posttraumatic responses in spouse / significant others of disaster workers. In C.S. Fullerton & R.J. Ursano (Eds.), *Posttraumatic Stress Disorder: Acute and Long-Term Responses to Trauma and Disaster* (pp. 59–75). Washington, D.C.: American Psychiatric Press.

Garland, C. (1993, July 10). The lasting trauma of the concentration camps: The children and grandchildren of survivors may be affected. *British Medical Journal* 307 (6896). From *Infotrac*, electronic collection: A14204193.

Gerson, M. (2010). "America's tenderhearted legions in Haiti." *The Washington Post* 17 February 2010: A 13.

Glasgow Coma Scale. *Traumatic Brain Injury* www.traumaticbraininjury.com. Retrieved 26 August 2010.

Glaser, J. (2001). Getting ready for winter. Retrieved October, 28, 2001, from http://www.lewrockwell.com/orig/glaser 10.html.

Goenjian, A.K., A.M. Steinberg, L.M. Najarian, L.A. Fairbanks, M. Tashjain, and R. Pynoos (2000). Prospective study of posttraumatic stress, anxiety, and depressive reactions after earthquake and political violence. *American Journal of Psychiatry* 157, 911–916.

Gerrity, E., T. M. Keane, and F. Tuma (Eds.) (2001). *The Mental Health Consequences of Torture.* New York: Kluwer Academic/Plenum.

Goldenberg, H., and I. Goldenberg (1990). *Counseling Today's Families.* Pacific Grove, Calif.: Brooks/Cole.

Gourevitch, P. (1998). *We Wish to Inform You That Tomorrow We Will Be Killed with Our Families.* New York: Picador.

Griffith, H.W., M.D. (1999). *Complete Guide to Prescription & Nonprescription Drugs, Edition 2000.* New York: Perigree.

Haley, S.A. (1984, Spring/Summer). The Vietnam veteran and his preschool child: Child rearing as a delayed stress in combat veterans. *Journal of Contemporary Psychotherapy* 14 (1), 114–121.

Halligan, S. L., and R. Yehuda. (2000). "Risk factors for PTSD." *PTSD Research Quarterly* 11 (3): 1–7.

Hamner, M., and S. E. Deitsch, P. S. Brodrick, H. G. Ulmer, J. P. Lorberbaum. (2003). "Quetiapine treatment in patients with posttraumatic stress disorder: An open trial of adjunctive therapy." *Journal of Clinical Psychopharmacology* 23 (1): 15–20.

Hefling, K. (2010). "Wife says military spouses also face suicide risk." *Associated Press.* 13 January 2010.

Hellman, J. (Producer); Ashby, H. (Director) (1978). *Coming Home* [motion picture]. United States: MGM/UA.

Hendin, A., and A. Haas (1991). Suicide and guilt as manifestations of PTSD in Vietnam combat veterans. *American Journal of Psychiatry,* 148 (5), 586–591.

Herzberger, M. (1975). *The Waltz of the Shadows.* Dubuque, Iowa: Gorsuch Grace.

Hinshaw, S. (2002). *The Years of Silence Are Past.* New York: Cambridge University Press.

Ho, A.K., and O. Stone (Producers); Stone, O. (Director) (1989). *Born on the Fourth of July* [motion picture]. United States: Universal.

Honig, R., M. Grace, J. Lindy, J. Newman, and J. Titchener (1999). Assessing long-term effects of trauma: Diagnosing symptoms of avoidance and numbing. *American Journal of Psychiatry* 156 (3), 483–485.

Index of Crime, United States, 1979–2007. www.infoplease.com/ipa/A077 8268.htm. Retrieved 20 April 2010.

Infoplease. Statistics on armed conflicts, natural disasters. Retrieved February 24, 2003, from http://www.infoplease. com.

The Iowa Persian Gulf Study Group (1997). Self-reported illness and health status among Gulf War veterans. *Journal of the American Medical Association* 277 (3), 238–245. Abstract.

Ivey, A.E., and M.B. Ivey (1999). *Intentional Interviewing and Counseling: Facilitating Development in a Multicultural Society* (4th ed.) Pacific Grove, Calif.: Brooks/Cole.

Jensen, P., and J. Shaw (1996). The effects of war and parental deployment upon children and adolescents. In R.J. Ursano and A.E. Norwood (Eds.), *Emotional Aftermath of the Persian Gulf War: Veterans, Families, Communities, and Nations* (pp. 83–109). Washington, D.C.: American Psychiatric Press.

Jewison, N., and R. Roth (Producers); Jewison, N. (Director) (1989). *In Country: A Story of an American Family* [motion picture]. United States: A Norman Jewison Film.

Johnson, C. (2000). Creative therapies. In E.B. Foa, T.M. Keane and M.J. Friedman (Eds.), *Effective Treatments for PTSD* (pp. 302–314). New York: Guilford.

Johnson, S. with M. L. Doyle. (2010). *I'm Still Standing: From Captive U.S. Soldier to Free Citizen — My Journey Home.* New York, NY: Touchstone, a division of Simon & Schuster.

Kaplan, L. (1986). *Working with Multi-Problem Families.* Lexington, Mass.: Lexington Books.

Kaplan, L., and J.L. Girard (1994). *Strengthening High Risk Families: A Handbook for Practitioners.* New York: Lexington Books.

Kim, E. (2000). *Ten Thousand Sorrows.* New York: Doubleday.

Kincaid, J. (2000). *A Small Place.* New York: Ferrar Straus & Giroux.

King, M. S. (2010). *Facing the Wall: A Mission.* U.S.A.: Xlibris Corporation. *www.Xlibris.com.*

Kinzie, J.D., J.K. Boehnlein, P.K. Leung, L.J. Moore, C. Riley, and D. Smith (1990). The prevalence of posttraumatic stress disorder and its clinical significance among Southeast Asian refugees. *American Journal of Psychiatry* 147, 913–917.

Knickerbocker, B. (2010). "Soldiers' wives: Fighting mental, emotional battles of their own." *The Christian Science Monitor.* http://www.csmonitor.com/USA/Military/2010/0123/Soldiers-wives-Fighting-mental-emotional-battles-of-their-own. Retrieved 26 January 2010.

Kormos, H.R., M.D. (1978). The nature of combat stress. In C.R. Figley (Ed.), *Stress Disorders among Vietnam Veterans* (pp. 3–22), New York: Brunner/Mazel.

Kramer, S. (Producer); M. Robson (Director) (1949). *Home of the Brave* [motion picture]. United States: Republic Studios.

Kuch, K., and B.J. Cox (1992). Symptoms of PTSD in 124 Survivors of the Holocaust. *American Journal of Psychiatry* 149, 337–340.

Kusher, H. S. (1989). *When Bad Things Happen to Good People.* New York: Schocken Books.

Laor, N., L. Wolmer, and D.J. Cohen (2001). Mothers' functioning and children's symptoms 5 years after a SCUD missile attack. *American Journal of Psychiatry*, 158:7, 1020–1026.

Lerner, H.G., Ph.D. (1989). *The Dance of Intimacy.* New York: Harper & Row.

Levine, P.A. with A. Frederick (1997). *Waking the Tiger — Healing Trauma.* Berkeley, Calif.: North Atlantic Books.

Lifton, J. (1973). *Home from the War.* New York: Simon & Shuster.

Lubin, H., M. Loris, J. Burt, and R.D. Johnson (1998). Efficacy of psychoeducational group therapy in reducing symptoms of posttraumatic stress disorder among multiply traumatized women. *American Journal of Psychiatry*, 155:9, 1172–1177.

Mahedy, W. (1986). *Out of the Night.* New York: Ballantine Books.

Marsella, A.J., Ph.D., C. Chemtob, Ph.D., and R. Hamada, Ph.D. (1990, Fall). Ethnocultural aspects of PTSD in Vietnam War veterans. *NCP Clinical Quarterly 1* (2), 9–10.

Marsella, A. J., M. J. Friedman, Spain, E. H. (1992). "A selective review of the literature on ethnocultural aspects of PTSD." *PTSD Research Quarterly* 3 (2): 1–7.

Mason, P.H.C. (1998). *Recovering from the War: A Guide for All Veterans, Family Members, Friends and Therapists.* High Springs, Fla.: Patience Press.

Mateczun, J., and E. Holmes (1996). Return, readjustment, and reintegration: The three R's of family reunion. In R.J. Ursano and A.E. Norwood (Eds.), *Emotional Aftermath of the Persian Gulf War: Veterans, Families, Communities, and Nations* (pp. 369–392). Washington, D.C.: American Psychiatric Press.

Matsakis, A. (1996). *Vietnam Wives: Facing the Challenges of Life with Veterans Suffering Post-Traumatic Stress* (2nd ed.). Lutherville, Md.: Sidran.

McCammon, S.L., and E.J. Allison, Jr. (1995). Debriefing and treating emergency workers. In C.R. Figley (Ed.), *Compassion Fatigue: Coping with Secondary Traumatic Stress Disorder in Those Who Treat the Traumatized* (pp. 115–130). New York: Brunner/Mazel.

McCarty-Gould, C. (1998). *Crisis and Chaos: Life with the Combat Veteran.* New York: Kroshka Books.

Mental Health Care for African Americans (n.d.). Retrieved February 5, 2002, from http://www.mentalhealth.org/cre/ch3_appropriateness.asp

Merridale, C. (2000). *Night of Stone.* New York: Viking Penguin.

Military suicides increase as U.S. soldiers struggle with torment of war. *New Jersey Star Ledger.* 22 November, 2009. www.nj.com/news/index.ssf/2009/11/us_military_suicide_html. Retrieved 21 January 2010.

Military suicides set record in 2009. *United Press International.* January 16 2010. www.upi.com/Top_News/US/2010/01/16/Military-suicides-set-record-in-2009/UPI-70041263674473/ Retrieved 21 January 2010.

Miller, J. (2008). Vietnam veterans help returning Iraq soldiers deal with shocks of war. *The Christian Science Monitor.* http://www.csmonitor.com/USA/Military/2008/0130/p20s01-usmi.html. Retrieved 3 February 2010.

Morgan, M. (1991). *Mutant Message Down Under.* New York: HarperCollins.

Munroe, J.F., J. Shay, L. Fisher, C. Makary, K. Rapperport, and R. Zimering (1995). Preventing compassion fatigue: A team treatment model. In C.R. Figley (Ed.), *Compassion Fatigue: Coping with*

Secondary Traumatic Stress Disorder in Those Who Treat the Traumatized (pp. 209–231). New York: Brunner/Mazel.

Naparstek, B. (Speaker) (1999). *Healing Trauma.* Akron, Ohio: Health Journeys.

Naparstek, Belleruth. *Healing Trauma (PTSD).* CD/tape. Akron, Ohio: Image Paths, Inc.

Neylan, T. C., M. Lenoci, K. W. Samuelson, T. J. Metzler, Cl. Henn-Haase, R. W. Hierholzer, S. E. Lindley, C. Otte, F. B. Schoenfeld, J. A. Yesavage, C. R. Marmar. (2006). "No improvement of posttraumatic stress disorder symptoms with guanfacine treatment." *American Journal of Psychiatry* 163: 2186–2188.

O'Leary, J. C. (1999). *Counselling Couples and Families.* London: SAGE.

Parrish, I.S. (1999). *Military Veterans PTSD Reference Manual.* Haverford, Pa.: Buy Books on the Web.com.

Pearlman, L.A., and K.W. Saakvitne (1995). Treating therapists with vicarious traumatization and secondary traumatic stress disorders. In C.R. Figley (Ed.), *Compassion Fatigue: Coping with Secondary Traumatic Stress Disorder in Those Who Treat the Traumatized* (pp. 150–177). New York: Brunner/Mazel.

Pipher, M. (2002). *The Middle of Everywhere.* New York: Harcourt.

Posttraumatic stress disorder: Proposed revision. *Diagnostic and Statistical Manual of the American Psychiatric Association.* www.dsm5.org. Retrieved 26 August 2010.

Post-traumatic stress disorder. *National Institute of Mental Health.* http://nimh.nih.gov/health/publications/. Retrieved 26 August 2010.

Post-traumatic stress disorder: Correspondence. (2002). *New England Journal of Medicine* 346 (19) 1495–1497.

Post-traumatic stress disorders risk factors. *Mayo Clinic.* www.mayoclinic.com/health/post-traumatic-stress-disorder/. Retrieved 26 August 2010.

Port, C.L., B. Engdahl, and P. Frazier (2001). A longitudinal and retrospective study of PTSD among older prisoners of war. *American Journal of Psychiatry* 158, 1474–1479.

Porterfield, K. M. (1996). *Straight Talk about Post-Traumatic Stress Disorder: Coping with the Aftermath of Trauma.* New York: NY: Facts on File.

Prepare for the challenges of multiple deployments. *Real Warriors.* www.realwarriors.net. Retrieved 25 January 2010.

Preston, J.D., Psy.D., J.H. O'Neal, M.D.,, and M.C. Talaga, R.Ph, M.A. (1999). *Consumer's Guide to Psychiatric Drugs.* Oakland, Calif.: New Harbinger Publications.

Pross, C. (2001). Every perpetrator's acquittal costs me two weeks' sleep. In S. Graessner, N. Gurris and C. Pross (Eds.*), At the Side of Torture Survivors: Treating a Terrible Assault on Human Dignity* (pp. 126–141). Baltimore: Johns Hopkins University Press.

Puttnam, D. (Producer); R. Joff (Director) (1984). *The Killing Fields* [motion picture]. Great Britain: Warner Brothers.

de Quervain, DJ, M. J. (2008). "Glucocorticoid-induced reduction of traumatic memories: implications for the treatment of PTSD." *Prog Brain Research* 167: 239–47.

de Quervain, DJ, M. J. (2008). "Glucocorticoids for the treatment of post-traumatic stress disorder and phobias: A novel therapeutic approach." *Eur J Pharmacol* 583 (2–3): 365–71.

Raskind, M. A., and E. R. Peskind, E. D. Kanter, E. C. Petrie, A. Radant, C. E. Thompson, D. J. Dobie, D. Hoff, R. J. Rein, K. Straits-Troster, R. G. Thomas, M. M. McFall. (2003). "Reduction of nightmares and other PTSD symptoms in combat veterans by prazosin: A placebo-controlled study." *American Journal of Psychiatry* 160:371–373.

Real Warriors Campaign. *Defense Centers of Excellence Psychological health and Traumatic Brain Injury.* www.realwarriors.net/aboutus. Retrieved 25 January 2010.

Refugees (2002). United Nations High Commissioner for Refugees. Volume 4, No. 129. Milan, Italy: AMILCARE PIZZI.

Refugees (2001). United Nations High Commissioner for Refugees. Volume 3, No. 124. Milan, Italy: AMILCARE PIZZI.

Report 08: At a Glance. (2008). *Amnesty International.*. http://thereport.amnesty.org/eng/report-08-at-a-glance. Retrieved 21 April 2010.

Roberts, W.R., W.E. Penk, M.L. Gearing, R. Robinovitz, M.P. Dolan, and E.T. Patterson (1982). Interpersonal problems of Vietnam combat veterans with symptoms of posttraumatic stress disorder. *Journal of Abnormal Psychology 91* (6), 444–450.

Robin, R.W., Ph.D., B. Chester, Ph.D., J.K. Rasmussen, M.S., J.M. Jaranson, M.C., M.P.H., and D. Goldman, M.D. (1997). Prevalence and characteristics of trauma and posttraumatic stress disorder in a southwestern American Indian Community. *American Journal of Psychiatry 154* (11), 1582–1588.

Rogers, E.M., and T.M. Steinfatt (1999). *Intercultural Communication.* Prospect Heights. Ill.: Waveland.

Rosenheck, R. (1986, June). Impact of posttraumatic stress disorder of World War II on the next generation. *Journal of Nervous & Mental Disease 174* (6, Serial No. 1243) 319–327.

_____, and P. Nathan (1985, May). Secondary traumatization in children of Vietnam veterans. *Hospital & Community Psychiatry* 36 (5), 538–539.

Rundell, J., and R. Ursano (1996). Psychiatric responses to war trauma. In R.J. Ursano and A.E. Norwood (Eds.),

Emotional Aftermath of the Persian Gulf War: Veterans, Families, Communities, and Nations (pp. 43–81). Washington, D.C.: American Psychiatric Press.

Sanchez, S. (2008). "Overdose kills ex-Fort Bliss soldier." *El Paso Times* July 7, 2008.

Scaturo, D.J., and P.M. Hayman (1992). The impact of combat trauma across the family life cycle: Clinical considerations. *Journal of Traumatic Stress* 5 (2), 273–288.

Schaffel, R., and C. Baum (Producers); Jones, D. (Director) (1988). *Jacknife* [motion picture]. United States: Cineplex Odeon.

Schiraldi, Glenn R., Ph.D. *The Post-Traumatic Stress Disorder Sourcebook* (2000). Lincolnwood, Ill.: Lowell House.

Schuster, M.A., B.D. Stein, L.H. Jaycox, R.L. Collins, G.N. Marshall, M.N. Elliott, A.J. Zhou, D.E. Kanouse, J.L. Morrison, and S.H. Berry (2001). A national survey of stress reactions after the September 11, 2001, terrorist attacks. *New England Journal of Medicine* 20 (345), 1507–1512.

Scott, M.J., and S.G. Stradling (1992). *Counselling for Post-Traumatic Stress Disorder.* Newbury Park, Calif.: SAGE.

Sennott, C. M. (2007). "Father-son trauma: New generation's battle rekindles earlier horrors." *The Boston Globe.* www.boston.com/news/local/massachusetts/articles. Retrieved 21 April 2010.

Sept. 11 attacks left 70,000 with stress disorder. Associated Press. http://www.msnbc.msn.com/id/26645918/ Retrieved 21 May 2010.

Shay, J. (1994). *Achilles in Vietnam.* New York: Atheneum.

_____. (2002). *Odysseus in America.* New York: Scribners.

Slater, S., and M. M. Villalba, J. Davis. (2009). "Key neurochemical markers for the prevention of suicide." *TrAC*

Trends in Analytical Chemistry 28 (9): 1037–1047.

Snow, Rev. A.L., M.A. (2002). *The Endless Tour: Vietnam, PTSD, and the Spiritual Void.* Victoria, B.C.: Trafford.

Sonnenberg, S., A. Blank, and J. Talbott (1985). *The Trauma of War: Stress and Recovery in Viet Nam Veterans.* Washington, D.C.: American Psychiatric Press.

Southwick, S.M., A. Morgan, L.M. Nagy, D. Bremner, A.L. Nicolaou, D.R. Johnson, R. Rosenheck, and D.S. Charney (1993). Trauma-related symptoms in veterans of Operation Desert Storm: A preliminary report. *American Journal of Psychiatry* 150, 1524–1528. Abstract retrieved October 2001, from http://ajp.psychiatryonline.org.

Spielberg, S., I. Bryce, M. Gordon, and G. Levinsohn (Producers); S. Spielberg (Director) (2002). *Saving Private Ryan* [motion picture]. United States: DreamWorks, Paramount Pictures & Amblin Entertainment.

Staker (2002). Personal communication.

Stanton, S.L. (1981). *Vietnam Order of Battle.* Washington, D.C.: U.S. News Books.

Styron, W. (1990). *Darkness Visible: A Memory of Madness.* New York: Random House.

Sue, W.D., and D. Sue (1999). *Counseling the Culturally Different: Theory and Practice* (3rd ed.). New York: John Wiley & Sons.

Swails, T., and C. S. Wettstone (2008). *Un-Natural Disasters: Iowa's EF5 Tornado and the Historic Floods of 2008.* Helena, MT: Sweetgrass Books.

Tanielian, T., and L. H. Jaycox (Eds). (2008). *Invisible Wounds of War: Psychological and Cognitive Injuries, their Consequences, and Services to Assist Recovery.* Santa Monica, CA: RAND Corporation.

Thompson, M. "Invisible wounds: Mental

health and the military." *Time Magazine*. 16 August 2010. www.time.com/time/mazazine/article/0,9171,2008886,00.html. Retrieved 24 August 2010.

Tovar Klinger, C. (2001). *El acto de habla y las creencias sobre el mal de ojo, el hiraguilde y el espanto en el municipio barabcoas*. Colombia: Universidad de Narino.

Traumatic brain injury. *NINDS (National Institute of Neurological Disorders and Stroke*. www.ninds.nih.gov/disorders/tbi/tbi.htm. Retrieved 7 July 2010.

Traumatic brain injury. *Mental Illness Research, Education and Clinical Center*. Department of Veterans Affairs. www1.va.gov/vhi/docs/TBIfinal_www.pdf. Retrieved 18 July 2010.

Trussoni, D. (2006). *Falling through the Earth: A Memoir*. New York: Henry Holt and Company.

Turner, E., and F. Diebschlag (2001). Resourcing the trauma client. In T. Spiers (Ed.), *Trauma: A Practitioner's Guide to Counseling* (pp. 69–96). New York: Brunner-Routledge.

Tuttle, W. (1993). *Daddy's Gone to War: The Second World War in the Lives of America's Children*. New York: Oxford University Press.

U.N.H.C.R. (2001, 2002). *Refugees*.

UNHCR Statistical Yearbook 2008. www.unhcr.org. Retrieved 20 April 2010.

Ursano, R.J., C.S. Fullerton, K. Vance, and T-C. Kao (1999). Posttraumatic stress disorder and identification in disaster workers. *American Journal of Psychiatry* 156, 353–359.

Valent, P. (1995). Survival strategies: A framework for understanding secondary traumatic stress and coping in helpers. In C.R. Figley (Ed.), *Compassion Fatigue: Coping with Secondary Traumatic Stress Disorder in Those Who Treat the Traumatized* (pp. 21–50). New York: Brunner/Mazel.

Vet charged with murder had PTSD, father says. *Orange County Local News Network*. March 1, 2010. www.ocinn.com/orange-county/2010-03-01/courts-crime/vet-charged-with-murder-had-ptsd-father-says. Retrieved 7 April 2010.

Vietnam Veterans Memorial Fund (2001). http://www.vvmf.org.

Vu, T.T. (1988). *Lost Years: My 1,632 Days in Vietnamese Reeducation Camps*. Berkeley, Calif.: University of California Press.

Wang, X., L. Gao, N. Shinfuku, H. Zhang, C. Zhao, and Y. Shen (2000). Longitudinal study of earthquake-related PTSD in a randomly selected community sample in North China. *American Journal of Psychiatry* 157, 1260–1266.

Webb, N. B. (2004). "The impact of traumatic stress and loss" in N. B. Webb (Ed). *Mass Trauma and Violence: Helping Families and Children Cope* (pp. 3–22). New York, NY: Guilford Press.

Weil, A. (1995). *Spontaneous Healing*. New York: Alfred A. Knopf.

Weine, S.M. (1999). *When History Is a Nightmare*. New Brunswick, N.J.: Rutgers University Press.

Weine, S.M., D.F. Becker, T.H. McGlashan, D. Laub, S. Lazrove, D. Vojvoda, and L. Hyman (1995). Psychiatric consequences of "ethnic cleansing": Clinical assessments and trauma testimonies of newly resettled Bosnian refugees. *American Journal of Psychiatry* 152, 536–542.

Weinstein, P., and M. Rosenberg (Producers); Weir, P. (Director) (1999). *Fearless* [motion picture]. Burbank, Calif.: Warner Home Video.

Wilson, E. (2010). "Morphine may reduce PTSD risk, study shows." *American Forces Press Service*. http://www.defense.gov/news/newsarticle.aspx?id=58288. Retrieved 9 September 2009.

Wolfe, J., T.M. Keane, and B.L. Young

(1996). From soldier to civilian: Acute adjustment patterns of returned Persian Gulf veterans. In R.J. Ursano and A. E. Norwood (Eds.), *Emotional Aftermath of the Persian Gulf War: Veterans, Families, Communities, and Nations* (pp. 477–499). Washington, D.C.: American Psychiatric Press.

Woodcock, J. (2001). Trauma and spirituality. In T. Spiers (Ed.), Trauma: A practitioner's guide to counseling (pp. 164–188). New York: Brunner-Routledge.

Working in a war zone: Post traumatic stress disorder in civilians returning from Iraq. Hearing before the Subcommittee on the Middle East and South Asia, House of Representatives. Serial No. 110–71. June 19, 2007. Retrieved 15 January 2010 www.foreignaffairs.house.gov/

Wyler, W. (Director) (1946). *The Best Years of Our Lives* [motion picture]. United States: MGM/UA.

Yalom, I.D. (1995). *The Theory and Practice of Group Psychotherapy* (4th ed.). New York: Basic Books.

Yassen, J. (1995). Preventing secondary traumatic stress disorder. In C.R. Figley (Ed.), *Compassion Fatigue: Coping with Secondary Traumatic Stress Disorder in Those Who Treat the Traumatized* (pp. 178–208). New York: Brunner/Mazel.

Young, A. (1995). *The Harmony of Illusions: Inventing Post-Traumatic Stress Disorder*. Princeton: Princeton University Press.

Young, M.B. (1991). *The Vietnam Wars: 1945–1990*. New York: Harper Perennial.

Zatrick, D.F., C.R. Marmar, D.S. Weiss, W.S. Browner, T.J. Metzler, J.M. Golding, A. Stewart, W.E. Schlenger, and K.B. Wells (1997, December). Posttraumatic stress disorder and functioning and quality of life outcomes in a nationally representative sample of male Vietnam veterans. *American Journal of Psychiatry* 154 (12), 1690–1695.

Index